enCycleopedia

… to alternatives in cycling

● *There is little on this earth more special or enjoyable than combining the wonderful potential of our bodies with our most perfect machine. Cycling is many things: a sport, a fashion, a form of transport: but we need to bring it into the very fabric of our lives, if it is to help bring about real change.*

Only if it is constantly refreshed by new ways of thinking can cycling remain vibrant. enCycleopedia is a book of

enCycleopedia

First published in Great Britain 1997. Reprinted 1997.
enCycleopedia was first published in Great Britain in October 1993
by Open Road Ltd, The Raylor Centre, James Street, York YO1 3DW, UK.
Tel +44 1904 412200 Fax +44 1904 411155
email peter@bcqedit.demon.co.uk
Website http://bikeculture.com/home/

First published in the United States in 1998 by
The Overlook Press,
Peter Mayer Publishers, Inc.
Lewis Hollow Road, Woodstock, New York 12498

Copyright © 1997 Alan Davidson and Jim McGurn

A CIP Cataloging-in-Publication Data for this book is available from
The Library of Congress.

ISBN: 0-87951-854-5

246897531

Address for worldwide (including UK) subscriptions/ordering enquiries,
except from countries mentioned separately below:
Open Road Ltd
P.O. Box 141, Stockport, SK2 7BX, United Kingdom
Tel +44 1904 412200 Fax +44 1904 411155
email sales@bikecult.demon.co.uk

North America and Canada
To order additional copies of this book, contact
The Overlook Press, 2568 Route 212, Woodstock, N.Y. 12498, U.S.A.
Tel: (914) 679-6838 Fax: (914) 679-8571

For back issues and other merchandise, contact
Dylan MacDonald, Open Road USA, PO Box 291010, Los Angeles,
Tel 213 468 1080 Fax 213 462 4359
email dylan@bikeculture.com

Germany, Austria, Switzerland
Kalle Kalkhoff, KGB, Donnerschweerstr. 45, 26123 Oldenburg
Tel 0441 8850389 Fax 0441 8850388

Australia
Ian Sims, Greenspeed, 69 Mountain Gate Drive, Ferntree Gully, VIC 3156
Tel (03) 9758 5541 Fax (03) 9752 4115
email greenshp@ozemail.com.au

New Zealand
Cycle Works, PO Box 33051, Christchurch.
Tel (03) 338 6803 Fax (03) 338 6231
email bikes@tpnet.co.nz

Netherlands
Subscriptions: Fietsersbond enfb, Postbus 2828, 3500 GV Utrecht.
Tel 0348 417 058 Fax 0348 423 119
Shops supplier, single issues, merchandise and back numbers:
Luud Steenbergen, Trapperkracht, Soerabayastr. 4, 3531 EB, Utrecht.
Tel/Fax 030 296 1015

Denmark
Carl-Georg Rasmussen, Leitra APS, Box 64, DK-2570 Ballerup, Denmark.
Tel/Fax 0421 83377

*Conceived, compiled, edited and produced by
Alan Davidson and Jim McGurn*

Editor in Chief: Jim McGurn
Managing Editor: Peter Eland
Editorial team: Jim McGurn, Peter Eland, Edgar Newton,
Dylan MacDonald, David Perry, Peter McGrath
Commercial Direction: Alan Davidson
Design and Art Direction: Brian Holt
Assistant Designer: Nicole Hall
Subscription Manager: Amy Davidson
Representatives: Germany: Kalle Kalkhoff. USA: Dylan MacDonald.
Australia: Ian Sims. Netherlands: Luud Steenbergen.
Denmark: Carl-Georg Rasmussen
Product care and assembly: Mike West
Studio Photographers: Paul Batty, 6 Derwent Park, Wheldrake, York,
YO4 6AT, UK. Tel/Fax +44 1904 448 663. Chris Mason, The Old School House,
Cherry Tree Ave, Newton on Ouse, York, UK Tel +44 1347 848787.
Additional photography by Sue Darlow, Via Bellentoni 36,
Modena 41100, Italy. Tel/Fax +39 59303 436.

Video:
Camera Work: Trevor Craddy, Roger Morly, Dervin Sherriff & Amy Davidson
Production and Editing: Trevor Craddy & Amy Davidson
Consultants: MVR Corporate Television, Unit 3 Buslingthorpe Green,
Leeds LS7 2HG, England. Tel +44 113 2621136 Fax +44 113 2374008

Printed in England by The Digital Page Printing Company Ltd.

In the UK ISBN 1 898457 03 4 enCycleopedia 4:
The International Buyers' Guide to Alternatives in Cycling

RRP in the UK: £12.00

*Open Road Ltd, publishers of enCycleopedia
and Bike Culture Quarterly is a small company
based in York, England. It is partly financed by a
sociable club of over 200 supporter-shareholders:
cyclists from several countries. Bike Culture Club
membership costs £10 per year, and is open only to
shareholders. For all details, including membership
benefits, contact: Open Road Ltd, The Raylor Centre,
James Street, York, YO1 3DW UK.
Tel +44 1904 412200 Fax +44 1904 411155.*

How to use enCycleopedia
Read this first!

Welcome to enCycleopedia

This is a rather unusual book, so please take a few moments to read this page before going any further. We hope it'll put the book in context, and give you some idea about why we went to all this trouble.

What's it all about?

enCycleopedia is a platform for imaginative inventors, designers and engineers who are trying to change the world for the better by offering real practical transport alternatives. By bringing them all together in one book we provide them and their ideas with credibility and status. We also hope it's a fascinating read for everyone out there who cares, and who might one day need one of these marvellous products in their own lives.

Behind it all is our conviction that pedal-power has an enormous contribution to make in bringing this planet back from the brink towards a more human-scale, sustainable future. Cycling harms no-one and benefits everyone. Human-powered transport is more than getting from A to B: it's a way of life and a state of mind.

Who's behind EnCycleopedia?

We're a bunch of bike fans based in York, England, although our agents and correspondents are scattered around the world. We're supported by a broad base of reader-shareholders, and have no commercial interest in any of the products we present in enCycleopedia.

Do manufacturers pay for space in enCycleopedia?

Yes, although neither we nor they see it as advertising. They take part by invitation only. We write the text for each entry, in consultation with the manufacturer, and we design the pages. The fee (which we keep deliberately low to give smaller manufacturers the chance to take part) just covers our costs: as well as the editorial work there is photography, video filming, translation, and coordinating the manufacturers' sales information to hundreds of enCycleopedia-affiliated cycle shops around the world.

Getting hold of the products

Your first port of call should be one of the affiliated bike shops listed towards the end of this enCycleopedia. We believe strongly that a good network of specialised, local bike shops is vitally important for the future of cycling. Please do support your local shop, even if it does sometimes cost a little bit more than mail-order.

You may strike it lucky and find that they have the product you're looking for in stock, but it's more likely that the dealer will have to source it for you. We provide all of our affiliated shops with ordering information about each of the products in enCycleopedia. It may be, though, that for a variety of reasons they're unable or unwilling to get hold of the product without a firm order.

In some cases you should approach the manufacturer directly. In some cases the manufacturer only ever sells direct. We explain things on the page itself and give you, where relevant, the details of the company. If they have agents or distributors in other countries, we've indicated that as well – and contact addresses for these countries are listed on page 144. Incidentally, some of the more specialised shops may run hire services, so that you can try out some of the bikes before you decide to buy. Ask the shops directly.

What will the products cost?

It's very difficult to give an idea of the price of a product beyond its country of origin. Not only is it expensive to send bicycles around the world, but insurance, import duties, local taxes and the overheads involved all mean that you can expect to pay significantly more outside the country of origin – often twice as much if the product comes from another continent.

For this reason, we've given the price of products in the country of origin, in the currency of that country (with some rare exceptions). enCycleopedia is read in so many countries that no other approach makes sense.

enCycleopedia in German

enCycleopedia is also published in a full German-language edition.

The enCycleopedia Internet Website

The Open Road Website *http://bikeculture.com/home/* is viewed by thousands of people each month. It includes extracts from enCycleopedia and Bike Culture Quarterly. We feel that while the technology is not yet ready to support full, paperless editions of our products, it does provide a valuable communications tool, and has the potential to allow considerable reductions in the consumption and transport of raw materials and paper around the world.

We are aware, though, that very many readers have no access to the Internet, nor would they necessarily want it. We retain our commitment to full paper editions, and believe strongly that there is something special about a well-produced book. We hope enCycleopedia qualifies.

Bike Culture Quarterly

If you enjoy enCycleopedia, you'll also enjoy Bike Culture Quarterly, the magazine for the open-minded cyclist. It's a colourful, ads-free celebration of the diversity of cycling, and amongst other things, it's a 'breeding ground' for products which could appear in future enCycleopedias, but which are not yet commercially available or are just prototypes. There's much more too – history, art, campaigning, and, as with enCycleopedia, there's a German edition too. Many people take out a combined subscription to both enCycleopedia and Bike Culture: details are on page 138.

Taking Control

All over the world they've tried to repress the bicycle, but it's always been too good to keep down. Be it a speed machine on a banked racing track or a heavy black roadster on the streets of Calcutta, the bicycle is poetry with pedals on. However, cycle design became rather narrow in its vision, with little interest in new thinking. Bubbling through now is a revival of interest in alternatives, a refreshing new imaginativeness in the design and manufacture of cycles and accessories.

Sometimes this new thinking results in an existing bicycle design being taken to an exciting level of refinement, and we present some good examples in this book. Other times the whole concept represents new thinking. Some of these machines seem unusual because they are designed to achieve more than the standard bicycle can. That achievement may be in a specialised area – such as going faster than a conventional bike, or carrying huge loads, or carrying children efficiently. These are totally practical aims, and have little to do with wanting to be different. They extend what pedal power can do, so that we are more able to take control of our own transport decisions.

The standard diamond-framed bike remains a superb machine, and we feature several in this book. It's silly to talk in terms of conflicting ideologies. Hundreds of millions ride standard cycles, with great pleasure. There is a new culture of cycling which appreciates all forms of cycling: from high-spec touring bikes to new ideas in folding town bikes, from fast, low, track-racing recumbents to large carrier trikes. Whatever their role, each machine in this book shows a balance between craftsmanship and mass-production. For example, many top-end cycles, hand-built with loving care, are fitted with mass-produced Shimano or Sachs componentry.

Almost every cyclist has room for at least one more specialist cycle in his or her life. Like most things involving physical effort, using the right tools can help turn what were once chores, or at least marginally pleasant activities, into truly enjoyable experiences. It would be nothing short of utopian to expect each household to own a stable of specialised bikes, each for a different purpose. Yet the market for specialised bikes will grow, as pedal-power reaches into parts of our lives where it has not gone before – at least not in recent history.

We've been here before. In the 1880s it was not entirely clear which way cycle design would go, especially after the invention of the now familiar safety bike. Would the high-wheeler fall from grace or would it see off the squat little newcomer? Would the tricycle be the only alternative for the weak and the wobbly? Would the delivery trike triumph over the horse and cart? Victorian inventiveness was in full flood, and pedal technology was clearly there for the advancement of civilisation, and trial and error were part of the inventive process. We have learned a lot since then, about what works and what doesn't. But one thing hasn't changed. The development of new ideas is still largely in the hands of individuals rather than big business, and the world of small-scale designers and manufacturers is gloriously dynamic.

The diamond frame won through. It worked fine for most people's practical purposes, and its victory was consolidated in the 1930s when the International Cyclists' Union banned from international cycle sport any machine deviating from very restrictive 'diamond' frame design parameters.

However, there are now, in many countries, cycle retailers who promote more than the usual range of conventional bikes. This has allowed many new concepts onto the market, and contributes to a culture of cycling which does not challenge other kinds of cycling, but deepens and enriches the entirety of vehicles which are human-powered. With this in mind we hope you enjoy the ideas and products in the pages which follow.

Contents

portables

The folding bike has long been a challenge for bike designers, driven by the technical challenge and by the real demand for this type of product. Flat-dwellers, boat-owners and train commuters faced with awkward guards: all need a good folder.

The earliest efforts were mediocre – the main vices were weight, sluggishness, poor brakes, and the infamous greasy hinge and kingpin. Later designs, such as the Bickerton, used aluminium to bring the weight down, but even this innovative design could hardly be regarded as a compact object when folded.

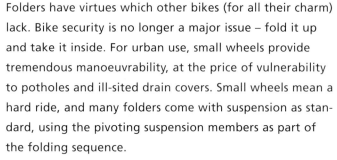

The Bickerton was the starting point for the Brompton – a small-wheeled bike which folded into a neat package and behaved as a bike should. The Brompton's qualities were recognised in 1996, when the German national cycle organisation, the ADFC, proclaimed it 'Bike of the Year'.

The boom in the design and building of folders is driven by the engineer's urge to tackle a problem, and the demand for transport in an increasingly congested, frenetic urban world. There is a pleasant ironic appeal to taking a modest folding bike off a train, and pedalling it past a slowly-crawling traffic jam of cars, worth millions of pounds, all that horse-power going to waste.

The 1990s saw the folder come of age – it was an idea that was right for the time, and considerable engineering talent has been applied to the genre.

They are no longer slow, unreliable, graceless objects, as anyone who has ridden a Bike Friday or Birdy will tell you. Folders are low-tech no longer – look at the titanium-framed FASTnet. Design requirements often leave the bike with an odd appearance, but good engineering, in whatever shape, has its own functional beauty. A recent FASTnet demonstration in London left one Encyclopedia writer open-mouthed at its performance.

Folders have virtues which other bikes (for all their charm) lack. Bike security is no longer a major issue – fold it up and take it inside. For urban use, small wheels provide tremendous manoeuvrability, at the price of vulnerability to potholes and ill-sited drain covers. Small wheels mean a hard ride, and many folders come with suspension as standard, using the pivoting suspension members as part of the folding sequence.

There is a folder available for most of your cycling reasons: the full-sized Worksong folding ATB, the D.O.G. (Demountable Orthodox Geometry) for fast road riding (both are featured in previous Encyclopedias), numerous models ideal for commuting and yes, there are folding recumbent bicycles and tricycles.

For most, the folder will be an everyday commuting bike – able to fold quickly with no special tools. More specialist folders and portables such as the Bike Friday and Moulton AM need a few easily-pocketed Allen keys to do the job. Folding bike owners often become passionate about their mounts, and the British-based but internationally-popular Folding Society is evangelical about the virtues of folders. It publishes *A to B* magazine to keep members abreast of developments in this compact world. *A to B* has devotees throughout Europe, and devotion to the world of folding bikes is growing. Just as well that there are still talented engineers coming up with radical, practical, enjoyable designs.

The Folding Society, 19 West Park, Castle Cary, Somerset BA7 7DB, England. Tel +44 1963 351 649 E-mail folder@dome.demon.co.uk

birdy

Markus Riese and Heiko Müller

"Hit the potholes, not the traffic" – that's how one owner summed up the Birdy ride. The suspension frees you from worry about damaging your wheels and backside: you can take advantage of the light-weight and stiff frame to accelerate into gaps in traffic regardless of the state of the tarmac beneath your 18" wheels.

The riding position is identical to a conventional 700c touring bike, and the Birdy is hands-off stable. It's a tribute to painstaking development work that the geometry has been refined to this degree, on a bike which also folds in less than 20 seconds to a 76 x 58 x 28cm bundle. It's the equal and more of many of its non-folding relatives.

Birdies come in four flavours: Red (Shimano Alivio and Gripshift), Blue (Shimano STX and Gripshift), Elox (Shimano XT and Gripshift) or Green (GLAD belt drive and Shimano Nexus 4-speed hub gear). All feature the same frame and suspension, and have a vast range of accessories available – from rack, lights and mudguards to a carrier bag which converts into a rucksack. The elastomer suspension elements can be changed in seconds to tailor the ride to the rider's weight and preference. A 'comfort' stem is also available for those who prefer a more upright riding position.

Weight ranges from 10.2kg for the Elox to 11kg for the Nexus equipped Birdy Green, and for a special edition of just ten Birdy Black bikes, the weight was brought down to a remarkable 8.7kg. Be quick if you want one – before they fly the nest.

Riese & Müller

Birdys can fly, and that's official. A paragliding fanatic in Germany uses the Birdy to cycle up to the top of mountains, then jumps off with the bike folded up on his back. Then there's the one equipped with disk brakes front and rear, another which completed a 186km race through the Italian Dolomite mountains, and the two owned by Birdy 'test-pilots' and designers Markus Riese and Heiko Müller, are used for mountain-bike races, triathlons and road-races at every opportunity. With over 1000 now on the road, there must be more stories out there...

Riese & müller, Erbacher Str. 123, D-64287 Darmstadt, Germany.
Tel +49 6151 424034
Fax +49 6151 424036

In Germany, prices range from DM 1790 (red) to DM 2990 (elox) and will vary greatly worldwide.

brompton

I t could be a quiz question. What is small enough to fit into a suitcase, can carry ten times its own weight, and can transport you without a motor for 60-70 miles a day? The answer, of course, is the Brompton, the classic British folder with enough worldwide appeal to to win its makers a prestigious award for export. Brompton owners tend to be devotees, happy to demonstrate the beauty of the 20-second fold, which leaves a compact package with the oily bits on the inside. The Brompton is increasingly being used for longer-distance touring, especially since it can be carried hassle-free on all forms of long-haul public transport.

The bike has 16" alloy rims, hub gears, and a rubber suspension unit just behind the seatpost to iron out the bumps. The folded dimensions are 565mm high, 545mm long, and 250mm deep.

The basic models are the three-speed L3 and five-speed L5, while the T3 and T5 come with racks and dynamo lighting. These extras do not affect foldability, but add 10% to the weight, bringing it to 12.2kg: about the weight of a mid-range touring bike.

There is an optional quick-release front bag with two external pockets and an internal documents pocket. This has virtually no effect on handling, being attached to the frame, not the steering assembly. A quick-release foldable basket is also available. The seatpin can be lowered through the frame to suit smaller riders, and taller riders can order extra-long ones to fit. It's a true case of 'one bike fits all'.

Andrew Ritchie

Once a chap has established a thriving business after 20 years of hard work, he can allow himself some fun. Andrew Ritchie certainly enjoys trying out the prototype single-speed 'Brompton Companion'. "I've been riding around on the machine and I absolutely love it. It's jaunty, light and fun." Without mudguards, rear rollers or lights, it should weigh just 10.2 kg. Meanwhile, Brompton continues to grow. Distributors in Holland, Germany and the USA report that 'Brompton mania' is international, and exports are booming. In every case, it is the bikes and their satisfied owners who are responsible for most of the 'advertising'.

Brompton Bicycle Ltd, 2 Bollo Lane, Chiswick Park, London, W4 5LE, UK.
Tel +44 181 742 8521
Fax +44 181 742 8353
Holland, Germany and USA:
see page 145

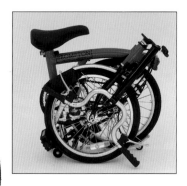

In the UK prices range from £378 to over £600, and vary greatly worldwide

In the UK, the Fold-It costs £349 (three-speed) or £439 (seven-speed), and the Micro costs £279. Prices will vary greatly worldwide

fold-it & micro

U K

The Fold-It is an 'everything bike': it's a capable runabout, stable at speed and on the rough, yet it's also a folder. It's a low-maintenance, all-weather workhorse. With a carrier on the back, this would make a good bike for anyone limited to one machine.

The Fold-It is also excellent value. The fold may not be as compact as some, but it is extremely quick and easy: simply fold the bike in half, swivel the handlebars and it's done. The folded package measures 86 x 86 x 30cm, and the bike weighs about 14kg.

Hub gears from Sturmey-Archer give three or seven speeds, and drum brakes, front and rear, stop equally well whatever the weather. Options include a rear pannier rack, folding pedals, dynamo lighting and a Carradice carrier bag.

Both the Fold-It and the other Cresswell folder – the Micro – were originally designed by Peter Radnell, a Birmingham cycle component manufacturer with an interest in sailing. In 1978 he designed the Micro as a small, simple and affordable folder to keep aboard his yacht. It has a simple hinge, just like the Fold-It, but the use of 16" wheels and a folding handlebar makes it considerably more compact (70 x 55 x 29cm folded) and lighter (around 10.8kg). A three-speed hub gear is provided as standard, but five-speed (Micro Sprint) or single-speed (Micro Lite – 9.1kg) versions are also available. They all fold in about 12 seconds, and fit in the optional Carradice carrier bag, which rolls up and attaches to the handlebar when not in use.

By reviving and updating these two designs for the 1990s, Cresswell Cycles seem to have hit the nail on the head. The Fold-It and Micro bridge the gap between the conventional cheap and heavy 'shopper' bikes and the more elaborate and expensive compact folders. As the 'Folder' magazine put it, "It's a snip!"

Richard Cresswell

After 15 years running his own general engineering business, Richard Cresswell decided in 1995 to set up as a specialist bike builder. His Rapide folding recumbent appeared in the 1994/5 Encycleopedia, and since then he has developed new products at a bewildering pace, identifying gaps in the market and serving them with well-engineered machines at affordable prices. His family cycling products are a particular strength: he produces a fine tandem as well as a range of innovative trailers. One of these, the U+2, appears in last year's Encycleopedia. The 'Two's Company' tandem and several other trailers are described in Encycleopedia '96.

Cresswell Engineering, 342 Cherrywood Road, Bordesley Green, Birmingham, B9 4UU, UK.
Tel +44 121 772 2512
Fax +44 121 773 9548

Richard Cresswell

In the UK, prices range from £899, and will vary greatly worldwide

Pashley Cycles

Pashley have never been afraid to operate outside the fashionable mainstream, with robust, practical vehicles to answer needs which conventional bike-makers often ignore. From their base in Shakespeare's own Stratford-upon-Avon, they sell thousands of machines each year, and their customers include many large manufacturing concerns who use the vehicles for transport around their factories. Individual customers are not forgotten: child and adult tricycles, unicycles and quality work and town bikes for all tastes are now joined by the APB. The Moulton design is in safe hands.

Pashley Cycles, Masons Road, Stratford-upon-Avon, Warwickshire, CV37 9NL, UK.
Tel +44 1789 292 263
Fax +44 1789 414 201

Land Rover APB

UK

Practicality, distinction and elegance are three virtues rarely combined in a bicycle, but the Land Rover APB achieves them all. It is the latest in the range of 'All Purpose Bicycles' built under licence from Dr.Alex Moulton by the long-established British firm Pashley Cycles.

The APB design combines portability and the comfort of a suspended ride with the classic elegance of the unisex Moulton thin-tubed space-frame. The Land Rover APB is distinguished from the other bikes in the range by a 21-speed Sachs gearset with twist-grip changers. This combines a three-speed hub with a seven-speed derailleur block and 20" wheels to give a gear range from 24" to 102" with a single chain wheel.

The famous Moulton suspension system uses leading-link front suspension, easily tuned for both ride-height and damping, combined with rubber-cone rear suspension. The bike can sail down rough tracks or over drain covers. The familiar Moulton front and rear racks and bags can be added to take a full touring load or to bring home the family shopping. It is available in British Racing Green or Golden Yellow.

The bike divides easily into two pieces using a single 6mm Allen key. The two halves are then easily stored, or are ready to be transported in the optional carrier bags. Other options include mudguards and lights.

Nigel Sadler, editor of the 'Moultoneer' magazine, has owned an earlier version of the APB for over four years, and uses it as a versatile general-purpose bicycle for his desktop publishing business. He also has no hesitation using it for 50-60 mile weekend rides.

Damian Fellowes

FASTnet

UK

Damian Fellowes

Titanium, special steels and aircraft alloys – these are the ingredients for a very fine folder indeed. The FASTnet is 13.5kg (29.7lb) of fully-equipped portable performance, built around a particularly sturdy and stiff frame. It folds or unfolds in 12 seconds, and once on its wheels, the FASTnet lives up to its name and specification with blistering acceleration and crisp handling. The Shimano seven-speed Nexus hub with roller-brake provides smooth shifting and strong all-weather braking. With 'Bob Florin' differential wheel-size geometry, the minimum footprint makes for manoeuverability in traffic, while the larger rear wheel gives no-compromise 'stride'. Respectable distances can be ridden in comfort, thanks to elastomer suspension tuned to a titanium seat post: a smooth ride is achieved without bouncing or power loss, while stem suspension prevents jarred wrists. The FASTnet is available in two versions to suit most sizes of rider: 18" front with 24" rear, or 20" front with 26" rear. A carry-bag and other accessories are available.

Bigger wheels roll more freely, especially over the bumps, and they bring that elusive momentum to your ride. Calling this principle 'Big-Wheel Dynamics', the designers of the FASTnet have introduced the Springbok, a fast tourer with 30" rear wheel and 700c front. The supply of high-performance tyres in this size is assured by Continental for many years to come. Shorter Springbok enthusiasts can order a version with 700c rear and 24" front wheels, while the largest riders might require 30" front and rear. The titanium and cromoly Springbok weighs 12.25kg (27lb), uses stem suspension, and is a machine for serious distances.

Fast New Pedal Power

Damian Fellowes discovered his affinity for the Njinga (bicycle) over the dusty distances of the central African savanna. That experience was to result in his Springbok super-tourer. Wide open spaces were a thing of the past when he moved to London, where the clogged streets and hostile cycling climate convinced him that a light, high-quality, well-specified folding bike was essential for efficient transport and survival on the roads.
The FASTnet and Springbok were developed in partnership with Arthur Needham, a well-respected frame-builder and engineer based in Bristol. The build quality of both machines is a tribute to his expertise.

Damian Fellowes, FNP Ltd, 24 Old Mill Road, Portishead, Bristol BS20 9BX, UK. Tel +44 1934 820308 Fax +44 1275 818 288

In the UK, prices range from £1250 for the FASTnet and £1100–£1450 for the Springbok, depending on the specification. Prices will vary worldwide.

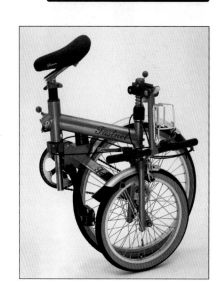

bernds

'Bernds – mobility to suit our times'. This is how the makers of this fine folding bicycle define themselves. It's a powerful concept, adressing the need for today's transport to be small, versatile and ecologically-friendly. It also points up the need for flexibility and open-mindedness: the Bernds can fit easily on most forms of public transport.

Central to the concept is a bike with enough performance to make riding a pleasure. The Bernds zips along, thanks to the stiff cruciform frame and 20" wheels, with rear suspension to take out any sting. An adjustable stem allows fine-tuning of the riding position. The pleasure is not spoiled by grease marks on your trousers: a belt drive and hub gears (four-speed Shimano, with back-pedal or roller-brake) ensure clean and maintenance-free transmission. On the front, a quality calliper brake does some effective stopping. A variety of luggage-carrying devices are available, including the 'Klick-Fix' handlebar bag carrier shown here. Depending on the equipment chosen, the Bernds weighs between 11.5 and 12.8kg.

The folding action of the Bernds has been considerably refined for 1997. A unique 'pull out and fold' action on the seatpost means that, on reassembly, the saddle is automatically adjusted straight, and at the correct height. The rear assembly flips under, pedals fold, and the handlebar pulls out, secured by an elastic shockcord. Like the seatpost, the handlebar assembly is aligned automatically when re-assembled. Finally, the front wheel is flipped around and secured neatly with the spring-loaded propstand. Folded, the Bernds stands securely, measures 90 x 75 x 15cm, and can be carried comfortably by a fork blade, through a carefully-positioned pocket in the carrier-bag.

Thomas Bernds

Thomas Bernds

In the early years it was a hard slog for Thomas Bernds to persuade bike shop owners to give him a hearing, near impossible to convince them to buy an innovative folding bike. Perseverance paid off, and Bernds is now an established and respected name in the German cycle trade. As often as not, the shops now come to Thomas.

Alongside the folder, an elegant Bernds 'scooter' has proved popular, especially in Germany, where they can be used legally in pedestrianised town centres. Both products benefit the local economy: Thomas Bernds insists that the frames be made in Germany, believing that customers will support this policy.

Bernds zeitgemäße Mobilität, Wittekind Str. 16, 32758 Detmold, Germany.
Tel +49 5231 17777
Fax +49 5231 17778

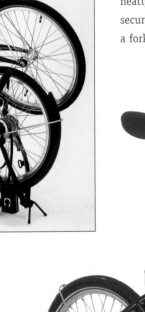

In Germany, prices range from DM 1699, and will vary worldwide

In the US, prices range from $695, and vary greatly worldwide.

Design Mobility Inc.

The Swift Folder was created in a cross-country collaboration between Peter Reich of Design Mobility in Long Eddy, New York, and Jan VanderTuin of Human Powered Machines in Eugene, Oregon (see Bike Culture Quarterly Eight, and elsewhere in this Encycleopedia).
Peter has also developed mobility aids for quadriplegics, and runs a 'Bed & Breakfast' on the Delaware River with his wife and three small children. Jan is an experienced designer and builder of utility bikes and a dedicated advocate of decentralised manufacturing. Though Jan has fabricated all Swift frames to date, he and Peter each build up frames to order.

Design Mobility Inc., PO Box 33, Long Eddy, NY 12760, USA
Tel +1 800 884 5541 or +1 718 875 3080 or email Human Powered Machines at cat@efn.org

Peter Reich

swift folder

USA

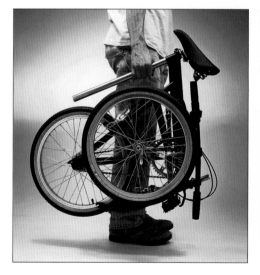

Experts in the field maintain that the ideal folder collapses to a stable package, with the drive-train protected, and rivals a conventional bike in weight and handling. These were the goals of the Swift's designers, who have given their 12kg (26.5lb) portable a durable fold-and-lock facility using a simple transverse pivot, with the seatpost serving as the structural kingpin.

Frame and forks are made of 4130 chromoly tubing, TIG welded and powder coated. The standard frame fits people 1.58 to 1.808m tall (5'2" to 6'2"), and custom modifications can be made to the frame, seatpost and stem assembly to fit almost any rider or riding style. Components include the Sachs seven-speed hub gear with twist-grip shifter, calliper brakes and 20" (47-406) hybrid tyres.

The Swift folds to a compact 54x80x25cm. All joints are equipped with Allen bolts or quick-releases. First, remove the seatpost by releasing two levers. Then, lift the main tube, allowing the hinged rear triangle to swing underneath the bike. The fold can then be locked by reinserting the seatpost all the way. To make it even smaller, the front wheel and handlebar stem can be quick-released and strapped to the package. No tools are necessary unless the pedals are to be removed, which trims ten more centimetres (2") from the depth.

Most rear carrier racks can be custom fit to the frame. A travel bag, and front and rear carrier bags, will soon be available.

Family

Cycling with children is a pleasure
and a responsibility – a balance of
risks and rewards.

When you cycle as a
family, you give up
the crumple-zone,
but gain the great
outdoors, sharing
the healthy pleasure of
cycling with your children
and those you meet. Contrast
this with an impersonal, joyless
journey in a motor-car, children
bored and confined, out of touch with
their environment. The 'safety' of the motor-car means
isolation from the world outside, and passive, dependent
travel: yet with sensible choice of route, equipment and
techniques, most journeys can safely be made by bike.
The mental and physical stimulation that cycling
gives for growing minds and bodies encourages self-
confidence and awareness, and is a great demonstration
to children of a happy, harmless and fun way of getting
around in life.

To help you do it safely and easily, there's a host of
products and techniques available. The nuts and bolts of
cycling as a family could fill a book, and many books
about cycling cover the topic to some extent. Not many,
though, can claim to cover the whole range of what is
available: from baby slings for the very small to bikes of
their own for the larger child. Encycleopedia can't hope
to cover everything either: but we can introduce some
less-well-known, high-quality products which make
family cycling a practical pleasure.

voyager childback tandem

When a child is too old to sit passively in a trailer, and too young to ride independently, one of the best ways to keep the family together and pedalling is a childback tandem. It's an excellent way for the child to feel part of the team, and simply by raising the saddle and adjusting the stoker bars for reach, many years of growth can be accommodated.

The Voyager range from St John Street Cycles, which includes this childback tandem, has been carefully designed to bring the price of tandeming down, without affecting safety or riding pleasure. It uses low-cost components where this is appropriate: the transmission, and top-quality parts where safety is involved: brakes, rims and headset. The frame is butted cro-moly steel. The Voyager range is available from stock in three sizes for adults, as well as two childback sizes. There is also a higher-specification 'Enduro' version, with drop bars, carriers, mudguards and lighter rims.

Outgrow the Voyager, and SJSC will part-exchange it for a Discovery, their top-of-the range touring tandem. Several are known to have circumcycled the world, and an even lighter, stiffer and more resilient version is available in Reynolds 853 tubing.

All of SJSC's tandems can be supplied with the S and S Bicycle Torque Coupling, featured elsewhere in this Encycleopedia. Using this system, a tandem frame can be split and fitted into a 66 x 66 x 25cm (26 x 26 x 10") suitcase, making regular use of public transport a practical proposition, and taking your tandem away from the not-so-tender care of baggage handlers. SJSC have also commissioned hub specialists Gold Tec to produce a tandem cassette hub, with four double-width pawls, a titanium nitride bearing for the cassette body and two sealed bearings each side. The hub will be threaded for an Arai drum brake, and available in 140 or 160mm widths. A direct-drive tandem chainset has also been commissioned, and will be available in crank lengths of 160, 165, 170 or 175mm front or rear.

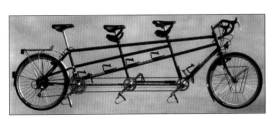

St John Street Cycles

St John Street Cycles has been trading for 14 years, specialising in Audax bikes, touring bikes and tandems. Under the leadership of Robin Thorn, the business has grown steadily, and now employs 28 keen cyclists. According to their internet website, their 'no-bullshit' approach to advising customers can sometimes offend, but is more often appreciated by customers as a refreshing change. They also operate a no-quibble 'refund service' of particular interest to customers ordering at a distance.
St John Street Cycles have particular expertise in small, diamond-framed ladies cycles, and also build a wide range of solo bikes for touring.

91-93 St. John Street, Bridgwater, Somerset, TA6 5HX, UK.
Tel +44 1278 441 502
Fax +44 1278 431107
Email sjscycles@dial.pipex.com
Website http://www.sjscycles.com

In the UK, Voyager prices range from £699, and will vary worldwide.

dolphin and donkey

The Dolphin is a fine family trailer, with plenty of room (60 litres) for extra luggage – and plenty of legroom for the passengers. The 75cm track gives good stability, and the children are well protected from most directions. The Danish manufacturers, Winther, are particularly proud of the aerodynamic shape – not only does it make pulling easier, but it ensures a quiet ride for the passengers, helped also by the elastomer suspension. The waterproof hood and the insect net fit closely to the aluminium frame, and there is plenty of ventilation. The Dolphin carries one or two children up to about six years old, and the recommended maximum load is 60kg.

The trailer is supplied with a push-bar and front wheel, letting you turn it into a versatile child-buggy for walks, or even for jogging. A parking brake is standard. When it's not in use, it folds down (without tools) to a 101 x 78 x 39cm package. It weighs 13kg, and is built from rust-free aluminium and plastic. The 20" wheels reflect the Dolphin's no-compromise quality – they have alloy rims, stainless spokes, and sealed-bearing alloy hubs.

The Donkey is altogether simpler, but no less functional. Its 65 litre box swallows all sorts of loads with ease, of up to 50kg in weight. It attaches to a special tow-bar, which leaves the rear carrier free for other uses – such as panniers or a child seat. The narrow design passes easily through most doorways, up stairs, into shops, or onto buses or trains. A jockey-wheel lets you park the trailer upright. The box is made from wipe-clean, frost-resistant moulded plastic, the frame is powder-coated steel (guaranteed for five years) and the 16" wheels have proper ball bearings. The Donkey weighs 11.9kg, complete with coupling.

A. Winther A/S

In Denmark, using your bicycle to transport children or goods is just a natural part of life. This feeds a demand for long-lasting, well-designed cycling gear, and Winther have been supplying just that for many years. Their range extends beyond trailers to a fine range of children's bikes and trikes, as well as adult cycles.

A. Winther A/S, Rygesmindevej 2, DK 8653 Them, Denmark.
Tel +45 8684 7288
Fax +45 8684 8528
Germany: see page 145

In Denmark, prices range from 1500 kr for the Donkey, and from 5500 kr for the Dolphin, and will vary worldwide.

In the US, prices range
from $390 for the Piccolo,
and from $380 for the
d'Lite, and vary greatly
worldwide.

Burley Design Cooperative

When customers call Burley
asking for the owner, the
short reply is: "Speaking".
That's because Burley Design
Cooperative is operated and
equally owned by Burley's 95
workers, with each employee
paid the same hourly rate no
matter what his or her position. Located in America's
Pacific Northwest, Burley is
frequently cited as the lead-
ing example of a successful
cooperatively-owned and
managed business in the
United States. Since 1975,
the company's two aims have
been to create high-quality
bicycle products for active
families and to contribute to
the local economy by not
exporting jobs overseas for
the sake of short-term
profits.

Burley Design Cooperative, 4020
Stewart Road, Eugene, Oregon
97402, USA.
Tel: +1 541 687 1644
Fax: +1 541 687 0436
email: Burleybike@aol.com
Website: http://www.Burley.com

See page 145 for national
agent details

burley piccolo

USA

Burley's meticulous designers spent five years to research
and develop the Piccolo: they've redesigned the standard
trailercycle for foolproof operation, easy handling and classic
good looks.

With its striking 'S' shape and bold red colour-scheme,
Burley's 8.6kg (19lb) Piccolo features some clever design
solutions. The trailercycle hitches to Burley's 'Moose Rack'
(supplied with the bike): a rigid, cro-moly platform with a
clever coupling device for quick and secure engagement.
According to Burley, the Piccolo's perpendicular attachment
has the advantage that both bikes lean at the same angle in
turns. The coupling's location directly over the rear axle of
the lead bike provides snug, in-line handling around bends, eliminating potentially

dangerous 'curb clipping' on corners. Furthermore, Burley have
designed the screw-down attachment with a backup safety lock –
reducing the possibility of accidental detachment.

The Piccolo is designed for children between the ages of four and
ten. It comes with alloy handlebars, a 20" wheel and a six-speed,
freewheeling rear cluster so the child can help the pilot pedal along
or simply coast when tired. The Moose Rack accepts panniers even
when the Piccolo is mounted, and both rack and Piccolo come with a
lifetime warranty.

Burley's other family product is the tried and tested d'Lite trailer: a
stable two-wheeler in lightweight aluminium, which folds down in
seconds. It's ideal for transporting children too young for the Piccolo,
or for bringing home the weekly shopping.

kool-stop original trailer and kool stride

USA

Cycle child trailers make natural pushchairs. It's because they need so many of the same properties. They must be smooth-rolling and lightweight, yet strong and stable enough to be safe. They must support their cargo of children comfortably, over a wide range of weights, heights and ages, and they must both be designed with the thoughtful details which are so important where children are concerned. The child must be strapped securely within the vehicle, with limbs well clear of moving parts. There should also be space for essential childcare items, and, last but not least, the whole machine must be visually appealing and attractive, not only for the child, but also for the proud parent.

Kool-Stop's Original trailer satisfies on all counts. Launched just too late for a picture to be included in this Encycleopedia, the latest model has a new centre-pull attachment, full suspension and is now made with a complete alloy chassis, still foldable in minutes to a compact package. The design has been proven over many years – it is now more comfortable, lightweight and manoeuvrable than ever before.

An idler wheel converts the Original into a buggy, but Kool-Stop also make a purpose-designed next-generation pushchair: the Kool-Stride. Top of the range is the Paramount, equipped with two parking brakes, a five-point harness for the passenger, and wheels with stainless-steel spokes and sealed-bearing alloy hubs. This 16.5lb (7.5kg) stroller is suitable for infants and toddlers up to 85lb (39kg) – usually up to around 6 years old. The chassis is powder-coated aluminium tubing, and the fabric seat can be adjusted for an upright or reclining position. A mesh bag is provided for storage, and an optional canopy is available for wind and rain protection. Travel and storage bags are also available.

Kool-Stop International Inc.

The Kool-Stop Original trailer has been refined by Kool-Stop International over many years. Based in La Habra, California, Kool-Stop also produce the Kool Mule luggage trailer (see the 'load-carrying' section), and a range of innovative accessories. This includes the brake blocks with which they made their name in cycling (see the 'Accessories' section, where Kool-Stop Tire Chains and Tire Cleats are also featured – these are snow-chains for cyclists). Previous Encycleopedias have featured their valve adaptors, the minimalist Repair Kit, and the Tire-Gard and Rim-Gard puncture protection products.

Kool-Stop products are available through cycle shops throughout the world. See Shops, page 142.

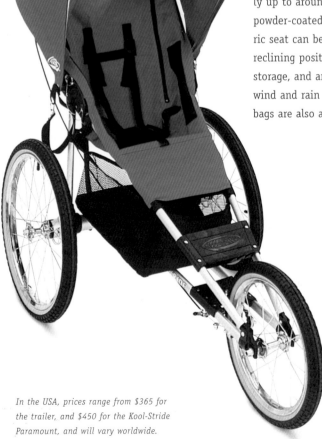

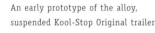

In the USA, prices range from $365 for the trailer, and $450 for the Kool-Stride Paramount, and will vary worldwide.

An early prototype of the alloy, suspended Kool-Stop Original trailer

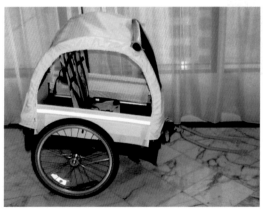

In the USA, prices range from $750 for the Siderider to $1250 for the Siderunner, and vary greatly worldwide. SideKids offer a 60-day money back guarantee.

Terry Ellard

For as long as he can remember, Terry Ellard has been making things. After informal training in high school workshop classes, he earned his Journeyman's License in metal pattern-making from the Ford Motor Company. Terry lives with his wife and daughter in Seattle, designing and fabricating precision medical equipment. His business partner, Peter Titcomb, has a Masters degree in business administration, and handles the day-to-day business details of running the company. He also has a daughter who loves to ride by his side.

SideKids, 6717 Palatine Ave. No., Seattle, WA 98103, USA.
Tel +1 206 784 1190
Fax +1 206 789 3202

sidekids

USA

Terry Ellard of SideKids has a child-centred design philosophy. He feels that kids want to be near their parents, to talk to them and to see the same things they see when they are cycling. They'll be happier on longer rides if they can interact with the parents. Kids, he says, don't want to feel like they're just tagging along.

Ellard believes his 11.4kg sidecar solves these problems and has performance advantages as well. The sidecar's high-pressure 16" single wheel is centred underneath the sidecar, allowing the cyclist to ride tight to the curb and away from speeding traffic. The aircraft-grade aluminium skeleton is hardened and welded, and provides full roll-cage protection. Finally, the patented parallelogram

attachment means that the sidecar leans in synch with the bike, so centrifugal force works with you as you turn.

There are two models of SideKids sidecars: both versions (Siderider and Siderunner) come equipped with weather-proof nylon canopy with zippered window, as well as a carrier rack that attaches to the rear of the bike. The entire device attaches and detaches in minutes without tools. The Siderunner has the additional advantage that it converts to a state-of-the-art running stroller. Full suspension on this version also makes light off-roading possible – and makes any journey a smoother experience.

Terry is currently perfecting a new version of the sidecar with pedals and a drivetrain so that his 10-year-old daughter can help in getting up the really big hills.

u+2

Two children to transport and just one parent available? No problem with the U+2. With tricycle-like stability provided by two wheels (20") at the back, youngsters can just climb aboard, and the handling of the bike is pretty much unaffected if they wriggle as they ride. A universal joint on the coupling ensures that the trailer finds its own level on the road, and it remains stable even if the towing bike falls over.

An optional luggage-rack fits between the two rear wheels, and incorporates mudguards. Another option is a bracket to convert a saddle to a childseat, so that children too young to pedal themselves, can 'grow into' the bike.

The U+2 can be quickly dismantled for storage or transport. It comes with six-speed indexed gearing, and it's surprising what two children can contribute to the pedalling. Just make sure you can keep up at your end of the machine!

Cresswell Engineering, 342 Cherrywood Road, Bordesley Green, Birmingham, B9 4UU, UK. Tel +44 121 772 2512 Fax +44 121 773 9548

In the UK, prices range from £485, and will vary greatly worldwide

add+bike

In Germany, the Add+Bike costs DM 648. Prices may vary worldwide.

Family fights over the breakfast table may seem an unlikely consequence of buying an Add+Bike, but that's what happened to one reviewer for a German cycle magazine. His six and nine-year-old daughters were so keen to travel to school under their own power, rather than in the car, that rides on the Add+Bike became a valuable parental treat, a reward for good behaviour.

The Add+Bike has no brakes, so the adult has complete control. The child is free to pedal (through a three-speed Sachs hub gear) or freewheel, and the mudguard keeps everything clean. It attaches via a custom luggage rack, and space is left behind the saddle for a conventional child seat or panniers. The rack weighs 0.8kg, and the bike itself about 8.5kg.

Robert Hoening Spezialfahrzeuge GmbH, Ulmer Str. 16/2, D-71229 Leonberg, Germany.
Tel +49 7152 797490
Fax +49 7152 979499
For national agent details around the world, see page 145

Mobility

Why do the disabled want to or need to cycle? For the same reasons as the able-bodied, and then some! First, recreation – cycling can be a pleasure for the exercise it provides, and for the chance to travel through beautiful scenery and enjoy the great outdoors. For the able-bodied there are other activities that can give the same or similar pleasures – rambling, running, hill walking or climbing. But for the locomotor-disabled only the wheeled variety of recreation may be available.

The second reason is health. The benefits of exercise are subject to the law of diminishing returns. Thus a disabled person who gets less exercise from his or her daily living routine will derive more health benefit from a cycle ride than an able bodied person. Like recreation, the forms of exercise available to a disabled person are severely limited, often to swimming and 'wheeling' only.

Most disabled people do not die of their disability. They still die prematurely. They die of the degenerative diseases associated with lack of exercise such as cardiovascular disease. They often die of an inactive disabled lifestyle.

It doesn't have to be like that! There are now a wonderful range of vehicles on the market which will allow almost any person, whatever their disability, to appreciate the joys of cycling. They range from tandems to highly-specialised equipment which is often custom-made. Recumbent tricycles (see the Recumbents section), sometimes with a hand-crank adaption, may also be suitable.

trio and t-bikes

Three points of contact make for stability, and three wheels make the Trio an excellent platform for anyone who finds a two-wheeled bike uncomfortably wobbly. Elderly, infirm or partly-disabled riders in particular appreciate a vehicle which will steer perfectly straight even at the lowest speeds, yet which has the performance and braking to take full advantage whatever amount of power the rider puts in.

The relaxed seating position and rear suspension ensure comfort, even on longer journeys, and both handlebar and seat have a wide range of adjustment. A version is available for those with the use of only one hand. The Trio can be fitted with a range of special adaptations to suit other particular needs.

Standard equipment includes 21-speed Sachs gearing, full lighting, mudguards and a large carrier between the 26" rear wheels. Braking is by Magura rim brakes on the front 20" wheel, and two hydraulic discs at the rear. A parking brake makes mounting and dismounting steady and secure, and the handling is safe and predictable. The standard Trio weighs about 25kg, and a motor-assisted version is also available.

Another option for those wishing to resume their cycling on three wheels is a T-Bike, Well-known and widely respected for many years in the Netherlands, these tricycles are now being distributed worldwide (outside the Netherlands) by Robert Hoening. With two wheels at the front, obstacles can be negotiated with the widest part of the bike fully visible – and there are major benefits for stability, especially when braking. There are five sizes for all ages, and a host of possible modifications, including a motor-assisted version. The space between the front wheels can be filled with a capacious luggage basket.

Robert Hoening Spezialfahrzeuge GmbH

The power of the pedal never ceases to amaze Robert Hoening. He feels that his is one of the best jobs in cycling – providing pedal-powered solutions to the mobility needs of thousands who might otherwise never know the pleasure of inde-pendent, self-propelled travel. His product range has been extending over many years – some machines originated elsewhere, but all are fully tested and further developed in the Hoening factory.

These products offer real therapeutic benefits for the rider, and the cost is often covered by health insurance or social security schemes. Robert Hoening is pleased to offer advice to those apply-ing for such schemes.

Robert Hoening Spezialfahrzeuge GmbH, Ulmer Str. 16/2, D-71229 Leonberg, Germany.
Tel +49 7152 979490
Fax +49 7152 979499

For national agent details around the world, see page 145

In Germany, the Trio costs from DM5750, and the T-Bikes cost between DM1890 and DM3480. Prices will vary worldwide.

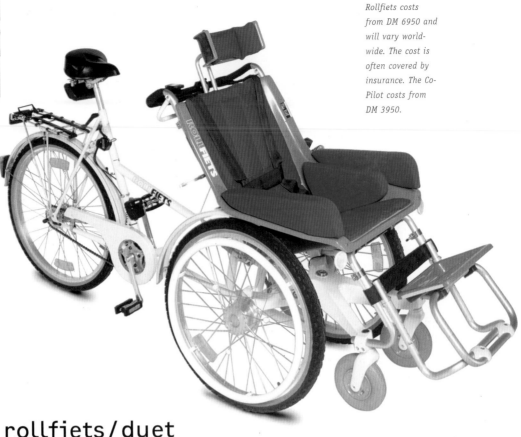

In Germany, the Rollfiets costs from DM 6950 and will vary world-wide. The cost is often covered by insurance. The Co-Pilot costs from DM 3950.

Robert Hoening Spezialfahrzeuge GmbH

The Rollfiets, Trio and Add+bike (which appear elsewhere in this Encycleopedia) are made under the auspices of Robert Hoening, who ensures that they are distributed worldwide through agencies in individual countries, since he believes that special needs are best understood and fulfilled at a local level.

Robert Hoening also distributes the delightful Co-Pilot: a tandem which allows a disabled or partly-active child to take part in the steering process, giving them the therapeutically important sensation of being in control. The adult rider has wider handlebars, and so can override any mistakes or wilfulness on the part of the youngster.

Robert Hoening Spezialfahrzeuge GmbH, Ulmer Str. 16/2, D-71229 Leonberg, Germany.
Tel +49 7152 979490
Fax +49 7152 979499

For national agent details, see page 145

rollfiets/duet

G E R M A N Y

The dynamics of moving at cycling speed through the countryside and through society, mixing it with the world on the streets, can be enjoyed not only by the fit and healthy cyclist, but also by a disabled passenger on a Rollfiets (known as the 'Duet' in English-speaking countries). Having the wind in your hair is not just a pleasure in itself, it's also an experience with real therapeutic value, stimulating the senses, exciting the mind, and promoting communication between passenger and 'pilot', and also with those you meet on the way. It's a concept that thousands have embraced with delight across the world.

The Rollfiets makes all this possible with a refined design of the highest quality – it passed with flying colours the rigorous testing of the German safety standards institute (TÜV), and has won numerous design awards. The wheelchair is based on an aluminium chassis, and is a fully-functional vehicle in its own right. Headrests, arm supports and other specialised adaptations are available to suit almost any need. Two custom-made drum brakes ensure powerful stopping, and a parking brake is fitted. The 26" wheels make for easy rolling.

The 'bicycle' rear half attaches in seconds, and is normally equipped with a seven-speed Sachs hub gear. There are other options – a 'Mountain-Drive' two-speed bottom-bracket gearbox (see the 'Accessories' section) and five-speed hub, or power-assisted versions with small electric motors. The standard combination weighs 37kg, of which 26kg is the wheelchair unit.

The cost of a Rollfiets is covered in many countries by various health insurance or social security provisions. Support for applicants to such schemes, is offered by the 'Rollfiets Club' – an active association of thousands of enthusiastic users worldwide.

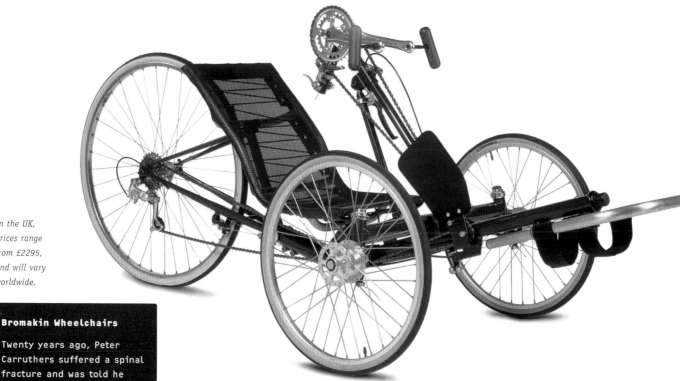

In the UK, prices range from £2295, and will vary worldwide.

Bromakin Wheelchairs

Twenty years ago, Peter Carruthers suffered a spinal fracture and was told he would never walk again. He refused to believe the doctors' verdict. Two decades later, he admits they might have a point, but he's not the kind of person to let extensive paralysis get in the way of life. With Sheila, his wife and business partner, they opened Bromakin Wheelchairs, working from home to produce competition-standard wheelchairs. Riding one of his own models, Peter went on to win a gold medal at the 1988 Seoul Paralympics. Visitors are welcome at the Bromakin factory.

Bromakin Wheelchairs, 12 Prince William Road, Belton Park, Loughborough, Leicestershire, LE11 5GU, UK.
Tel +44 1509 217569
Fax +44 1509 233954
Email peter@bromakin.co.uk

Peter Carruthers

trice conversion

UK

A broken neck would mean immobility and despair for some, but not for Peter Carruthers. For him, adversity was the mother of invention. He builds wheelchairs. Not just ordinary wheelchairs, but the sort that pirouette around basketball and tennis courts, tackle rugby pitches and win medals. Bromakins have become fiercely competitive wheelchairs, the choice of top-level athletes worldwide. At the 1996 Paralympics in Atlanta, David Holding set a new world record for Britain, winning the 100m in a time of 14.45 seconds (see picture, right). He was in a Bromakin, and so was the man who came second.

All this started in a garage, welding together bits of bicycle tubing and moulding fibre-glass seats. If that sounds like the way many recumbents got started, it's no coincidence. Peter Carruthers soon turned his mind to recumbent trikes, and started with the proven Crystal Engineering Trice. The task of converting it to hand-drive was not easy: the modified crankset must transmit the power of possibly Olympic-strength arms, and let the rider steer, change gear, and brake. The adaption unit is fitted with ankle-loops and bumpers to protect the protruding lower legs. Since the photograph was taken, the three chainrings and front changer have been replaced by a single ring and the Sachs 3x7 hub gear system, and detail changes have been made to the braking and gear systems. Handling and braking are still excellent.

Peter's attitude is that when he cycles, he leaves the world of disability behind and becomes a cyclist, albeit (he says) slightly on the lunatic fringe. We agree with the first half of that sentiment, and vehemently disagree with the second.

bicone

Prof. Pieter Tauber

Eight to eighty and older, suggests architect Professor Pieter Tauber, is the age range of cyclists who will enjoy the Bicone. The design of conventional cycles is, he says, best suited to the young and fit: the upright position places the saddle more or less directly above the pedals, which means that Mother Earth is always more than a leg-length away (otherwise the pedals would hit the ground!) When you stop, you have to stretch out and balance on tip-toe, and when you're riding, the neck is usually kinked uncomfortably upwards.

By moving to a semi-recumbent position, and making the whole bike as low as possible, Prof. Tauber has done away with these problems. The saddle is now at seat level, and mounting and alighting become relaxed and easy. When you stop, the feet can be placed flat on the road. With the upper body upright, the neck is straight and free. The wide-cushioned saddle ensures comfort, and the small backrest allows you to put on the power without shooting off the back. And in the event of a crash, there's no top-tube to catch your legs.

With stem folded and saddle lowered, the bike becomes long and thin, which is a very practical arrangement for transport or storage. Widely available 20" wheels and a full set of equipment and accessories make this a comfortable and safe machine in all weathers.

The Bicone's smaller sibling is the Biconette: a short-wheelbase semi-recumbent. Steering is by a combination of body-weight shifts and handlebar movement – giving a fine feeling of 'oneness' with the machine. It's of simple construction, easily takes a rear carrier, and Prof. Tauber reports that it can be used just like a 'normal' bike – only with more comfort!

Professor Tauber

When Pieter Tauber began his architectural practice in 1955, he couldn't have known that by 1996, he'd be a Professor, heading a successful architecture bureau employing 45 people. His commissions have included the Dutch Embassy in Washington and seven town halls. Entering a 'Safe Bike' design competition in 1984, his winning design was developed by Van Raam cycles, who now manufacture around 200 of the 'Tavara' each year. The Bicone and Biconette are made by a Van Raam engineer, Wim Hoefman, in his private workshop, where he works with Prof. Tauber on a variety of projects, including a recumbent.

Prof. Tauber, Beatrixlaan 2, 1815 JN Alkmaar, Netherlands.
Tel +31 7251 12495
Fax +31 7251 50246

In the Netherlands, prices range from f 1900, and will vary greatly worldwide.

Planning for cyclists

Look around any city or town, and you see a landscape
formed around the demands of motor transport: it's not just
the totality of cars and lorries which have hit critical mass:
it's also the structures needed to convey and regulate them. Now it's the turn of the
bicycle. It's time that
pedal-power made a
physical impact on the urban landscape. It's time cyclists and non-cyclists alike were
reminded daily of the idea and potential of cycling, in the form of cycle paths, cycle
signposts, cycle crossings, cycle parking, cycle security systems, cycle shops, cycle
courier businesses, and so on. Every city should shout cycling. Cycling should be part
of the very fabric of life, and constantly evident, even when there happen to be no
cyclists around.

Useful infrastructures for cycling are already to be found on certain well-cycled
tourist routes in Germany and Austria. Along the Tauber Valley cycle route, and the
Danube cycle path, there are repair stations, cycle security stands, cyclists' information boards, and cafes and restaurants which actively seek cyclists' trade. In the
urban context there are extensive multi-function 'cycle centres' in certain large cities
in Northern Europe. These centres offer, amongst other things, secure parking, cycle
repair, and a cycling information service. Of course, this is nothing new to cyclists in
China, where large numbers of cycle repairers sit by the roadside ready to give
immediate assistance to any of the thousands of cyclists passing by.

But cycling will not really come home in the industrialised world until it has left its
mark in every street, at every parade of shops and in every business. It is immaterial
whether cycling provision is undertaken by the state or by business. Showers at
work are no more or less a cycling facility than a cycle path or a cyclist's advanced
stop line at traffic lights. An interest-free loan scheme for employees to buy bicycles
is no more or less a cycling facility than the free bikes of Copenhagen, provided
largely by public money.

We find acres of print in glossy magazines telling us about the merit of this or that
bicycle: it's now time to study and evaluate the various facilities being developed for
cyclists: the stands, the lockers, the indoor storage ideas, the cleaning facilities, and
public provision generally.

There is no easy way in which local authorities around the world can find out about
the best commercial ideas in cycle provision. It is very often caring and persistent
cyclists, operating alone, or as part of a cycle campaign group, who are in a position
to bring new ideas and products to their local traffic engineers and cycle planners.
To encourage this, we hope to include an extensive cycle facilities section in the next
Encycleopedia, and to find a way of centralising all such information for the professionals who need it. We therefore welcome product information for that purpose.
To get things started, we feature in this section two products which break new
ground, and which deserve to be taken up worldwide.

bicycle-lift

Big hill ahead. The words strike terror into the heart of many cyclists. Who knows how many have been put off cycling by a not-so-gentle gradient? The solution comes from Norway, in the shape of the patented Bicycle Lift. The first Lift to be installed is in Trondheim, and has now (by the end of 1996) carried over 100,000 cyclists up the 130 metre-long, 1 in 5 (20%) Brubakken hill, with no injuries.

To use the lift, riders put a foot down onto a footplate, briefly insert a plastic card, and press the start button. The lift gradually builds up speed to about jogging pace, and the rider is propelled up the hill on an outstretched leg.

Capacity is around 300 cyclists per hour, and Bicycle Lifts can be several hundred meters long. It can be a very cost-effective pro-cycling facility. A typical 200m-long Bicycle Lift costs in Norway around 2,000,000 Norwegian Kroner ($312,000, £187,000) with running costs of around 90,000 Kroner ($14,000, £8,400) per year. Enquiries are welcome from hilly cities worldwide.

Mr. Jarle Wanvik, Design Management AS, Teknostallen (Trondheim Innovation Centre), Prof. Brochs gt. 6, N-7030 Trondheim, Norway.
Tel +47 7354 0266
Fax +47 7394 3861

In the USA, prices range from around $600 each, and will vary worldwide.

bike lid

The Bike Lid combines the ease-of-use of a simple bike stand with the security of a locker – without the complication, cost and installation problems that lockers can often involve. The spring-assisted swing-down recycled polyethylene shell is vandal-resistant and tough, is available in just about any colour, and provides an excellent platform for advertising. Two bikes will normally fit in each Lid, and can be locked to the metal frame, and the Lid is then locked either by a key lock, a coin-operated lock, or by the user's own cycle lock. The gap below is small enough to prevent access, yet allows security personnel to monitor the contents.

Plastron Products, manufacturers of the Bike Lid, have patents pending in 52 countries. They're also expanding their dealer network in other countries – contact them for details, or try their Internet website.

Bike Lid, Plastron Products, 10434 NE 17th St, Bellevue, WA 98004, USA. Tel +1 206 455 9014 Fax +1 206 455 1750 Email wrw1958@worldnet.att.com Website www.bikelid.com
International agents: see page 145

Carry a big load on a bike and in most of the 'developed world' you'll provoke surprise and delight.

Load-carrying

Why this should be is a bit of a mystery for the inhabitants of some more enlightened cities, such as Amsterdam and Copenhagen, where load-carrying bicycles are a daily fact of life. And of course the bicycle is the load-carrying mainstay of industry and commerce in many less affluent countries.

Carrying a load by bike is a very sensible alternative in today's cities: quiet, pollution-free and relatively slow-moving, it is friendly towards pedestrians as well as the environment. Mixing with motorised traffic is no problem: the road presence of these machines means that drivers keep their distance and show respect.

Bikes, trikes and quadricycles are now available for almost any load-carrying situation: and possibilities are also opened up by trailers and tandems. Even if your carrying need isn't covered directly, very often the stable load platforms that these machines provide are perfect for custom modifications.

There is a limit to what can be carried: manufacturers will specify a maximum load, and this should be respected. Another limit is the power in your legs: a lot of these machines will have very low gears, but do be realistic about hills when full-loaded. Check the brakes before you set off, and take a few moments somewhere safe to get used to the 'feel' of the loaded vehicle. Riding with big loads is a great experience and superb fun, especially if you take it seriously.

transporter & long john

DENMARK

In Denmark, transport cycling is just part of life. Two delivery-bike classics – the Transporter and Long John – have been around since the twenties, and in their modern form, remain just as relevant today. They are used in some numbers for practical transport of goods around modern Danish shipyards and large industrial sites.

The 29kg Transporter (known as the 'Truck' in Denmark and the 'Bäckerrad' in Germany) has a 60kg-capacity load-carrying platform over the reinforced front fork. The specification is chosen for reliability and low maintenance. Seatpost and stem are stainless steel, and the 20" x 2" front wheel is equipped with a Sachs drum brake. The 23" x 2" rear wheel can be fitted with either a single-speed freewheel or a three-speed Sachs hub gear. Both wheels are built with sturdy black-painted steel rims and galvanised DT spokes. Also included are a cartridge bottom-bracket and dynamo lighting.

The splendid Long John represents probably the limit of what can safely be carried on two wheels. The carrying capacity is 100kg, with a rear rack as well as the 58.5 x 65cm loading area. The equipment is to the same robust standard as on the Transporter, with three speeds as standard. The front hub brake is actuated hydraulically, ensuring that the long cable run to the rod-steered front wheel does not result in any loss of braking power. The Long John weighs around 39kg, and the total length is 247cm.

Both products are painted in a distinguished black, and the solid construction will withstand a lifetime of hard use. Large metal panels are built into the frames for advertising purposes, and are a powerful disincentive to theft. The obvious quality and 'classic' styling has a strong 'period' appeal, and can only enhance the image of any company associating itself with such an environmentally and socially beneficial form of transport.

Everton Smith A/S

Everton Smith A/S was founded in 1995, when two of the oldest names in Danish cycling merged. Smith & Co was set up in 1894, at the dawn of the cycling boom, and has made the Long John and Transporter since around 1925, selling the bicycles under the name S.C.O. The other company, Everton, was founded in 1936. The thirties were a 'golden age' for load-carrying bikes in Denmark: every grocery store had a boy to pedal around making door-to-door deliveries. Such a system of local employment and pollution-free shopping is something modern-day society would do well to recreate.

Everton Smith A/S, Gl. Grandvej 4, DK-5580 Nr. Åby, Denmark.
Tel +45 64 28 11 22
Fax +45 64 28 1144
Germany: see page 145

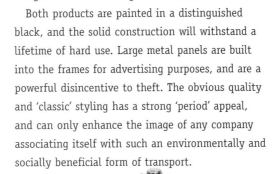

In Denmark, prices range from 4995 Kroner (Transporter) or from 7995 Kroner (Long John)

lightweight long haul

Impressed by traditional long front-carrier transporter bikes made in England (the Pashley Long Emma) and Denmark (the SCO Long John), Jan VanderTuin set about adapting and developing these designs for the American market, to produce a high-performance cargo bike which is both comfortable and efficient. That was ten years ago. Today, the Long Haul is the vehicle of choice among a growing number of cargo bike courier companies across America. The Long Haul has been ridden to victory in the Cycle Messenger World Championships cargo race for three consecutive years: this year the bike carried a payload in the final heat that included the winner's girlfriend, proving that the bike is as versatile as it is rugged.

The Long Haul frame is cro-moly steel, and can handle a load of up to 90kg (200lb). With the aluminium cargo rack, the bike weighs 21.5kg (48lb). When equipped instead with a weatherproof and lockable fibreglass container, the bike tops out at 32.5kg (72lb). The Long Haul has a 1.85m (73") wheelbase with a drum brake on the 20" front wheel, cantilevers on the 26" rear (although the bike pictured has the optional rear drum brake), and is equipped with a Sachs 3x7 rear hub, which allows shifting at stops: a much-appreciated feature for transporter bikes.

Tucked beneath the load bearing section is a spring-activated, double-leg kickstand for stable parking when loading and unloading. Both the rack and container are the same width as the handlebars, narrow enough to pass through traffic just like any other bike.

Jan is an accomplished designer and fabricator, and he's named the Long Haul for its lasting qualities. Human-Powered Machines offer a line of nine bikes, trikes, trucks, and trailers – valued for combining cargo-carrying capacity with true lightweight performance.

In the USA the Long Haul with aluminum rack costs $1395, with weatherproof container $1795. Other models cost from $350 for a 135kg (300lb)-capacity trailer, to $2,200 for a 360kg (800lb)-capacity flatbed trike.

Human Powered Machines

As founder and Executive Director of Eugene's Center for Appropriate Transport (CAT), Jan VanderTuin divides his energy between fabrication and education. His company, Human-Powered Machines, builds fine utility bikes, employing young people locally and teaching them fabrication skills. The CAT also serves as a home base for a cycling community, with design, manufacturing, publishing, bike advocacy, retail and repair, education programs, a cycle courier company, a valet bike parking service and the Human-Powered Parade headquarters – all under one roof.

Human-Powered Machines, 455 West 1st Avenue, Eugene, Oregon 97401 USA.
Tel +1 541 343 5568 (or from the USA 800 343 5568)
Fax +1 541 686 1015
Email: cat@efn.org
Website: http://www.efn.org/~cat

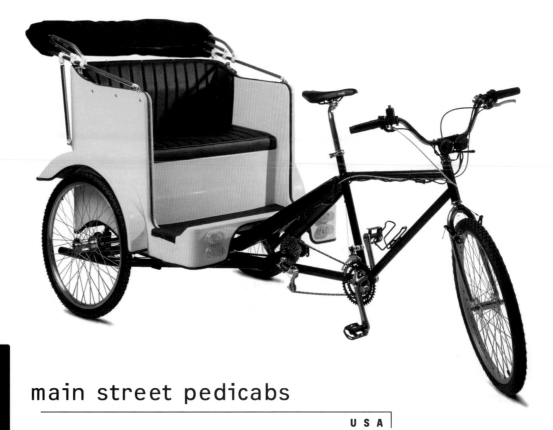

In the USA, you can expect to pay $3600 for the standard Main Street Pedicab. Conversion units cost $400 for the Pedal Express and $500 for the Pedal Pick-Up. The basic Pedal Pick-Up starts at $2800.

Main Street Pedicabs Inc

An interest in traffic-calmed communities led Steve Meyer to develop and produce his modular pedal taxi system. Originally trained as an economist, Steve began the project in 1992, gathering technical support for his designs from the local university, and learning fleet operation and management skills from Denver's business community.
Having refined their design over many years, Main Street Pedicabs welcomes enquiries from companies outside the US who might wish to produce the vehicle under licence.

Main Street Pedicabs, Inc.,
3003 Arapahoe Street, Suite 222,
Denver, Colorado 80205 USA.
Tel: +1 303 604 2330
Fax: +1 303 604 2404
Email: pedicabs@usa.net
Website: http://www.pedicab.com

Steve Meyer

main street pedicabs

USA

In Washington DC, Main Street pedicabs are the only vehicles allowed on the auto-free avenue in front of the White House. In Denver, Colorado, fifteen pedicabs work the streets. And in over a dozen cities across the USA, Main Street's zero-emission pedicabs and pedal trucks are transporting people and goods pollution-free, challenging unthinking motorisation and enhancing the urban environment for all.

The sheer number of pedicabs on the road, combined with Main Street's own pedicab and package delivery services, allow the company to test designs in the field and to experiment freely with new ideas, giving them a fine appreciation of what's important in a pedicab.

For ease of maintenance, most of the components and parts are available off-the-shelf. Rear lights and automatic brake lights, turn indicators, dual beam halogen headlamps, 21-speed 'Gripshift' gears

and, of course, a bell, are all standard equipment. The powder coated cro-moly frame is cut and coped by laser according to a digital blueprint originally programmed at the University of Colorado. The pedicabs have a rear differential for safe, scrub-free, fast cornering, and 'floating' hydraulic disk brakes give powerful all-weather stopping. The fibreglass passenger compartment has a steel frame and is fully suspended. There is also a front fork suspension option.

The pedicab weighs 72kg (160 lb), and is 2.58m (101") long by 1.27m (50") wide. Its wiring harness has a male/female plug, so that the body can quickly be swapped with other modules, including the 'Pedal Express™' cargo container and the 225kg (500lb) capacity 'Pedal Pick-Up™' flat-bed unit.

Kool-Stop products are available through cycle shops throughout the world. See Shops, page 142.

Kool stop International Inc.

The Kool Mule was originally developed by designer Roelof Kammenga from Eindhoven in Holland. He was introduced to Kool-Stop by their European agent, Third Wave Carriers in Amsterdam, who spotted the potential of the trailer and took it to the 1996 IFMA cycle show in Cologne, Germany. Such was the level of interest shown at the event that Kool-Stop decided to take the product to full production, and it now joins their product lineup, which includes the Kool-Stop Original child trailer, brake blocks and other accessories. Several of their products are featured elsewhere in this Encycleopedia.

Kool-Stop products are available through cycle shops throughout the world. See Shops, page 142.

kule mule

USA

Take a bike touring, and you generally have to bedeck it with carriers front and rear. The weight and complication of these accessories remain with your bike even when it's unloaded. You also need a bike with the braze-ons and heel clearance to fit the carriers in the first place – and even then you can't usually fit more than four panniers. Panniers to fit on front carriers are generally smaller to boot.

With the Kool Mule, you get round all of these restrictions. It is a trailer which hooks onto the rear seat stays of any bicycle, using a unique ball and socket hitch clamp. Stripped-down racers, folders, small frames, or any bike for which attaching standard carriers front or rear is a problem can all have add-on *randonneur* capacity to the tune of six full-size pannier bags. Carrying capacity is 38.5kg, and the trailer itself weighs 7kg.

Aside from the extra capacity, there are other advantages to this arrangement. First, because the bags are close together and in a narrow package, there is an aerodynamic advantage. Further, the problem of 'unweighted' front wheels and twitchy steering due to heavy luggage in rear carriers behind the back axle is much reduced, as the Kool Mule attaches directly to the rear of the bike.

Finally, loading a standard tourer can be difficult unless there is something to lean it against. The Kool Mule comes with a two-legged stand, which supports both trailer and bike.

One of the greatest pleasures when you're on tour is to leave your luggage behind one day, and to go off unencumbered for a fast day ride. The Kool Mule makes this flexibility possible, and represents an important innovation in towing cycling.

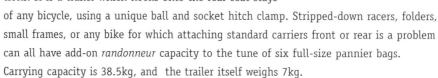

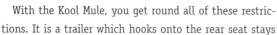

citytramp

Robert Lehle

A few tens of kilos is enough of a load to make many people reach for their car-keys – and even those who reach for their bicycle may have difficulties loading up, and then travelling steadily (and legally!) at low speed through pedestrian areas. Or, they can't travel fast enough to integrate with the traffic flow on the roads. The Citytramp tackles all of these issues and more, opening up a whole new genre in the area of short-haul load-carrying.

It is a 'foot-powered vehicle', with an impressive carrying capacity of 160kg, and highly-adaptable loading surfaces. The centre of gravity is low, the turning circle is small, and the wide tyres (with sealed ball-bearing hubs) roll smoothly over even rough surfaces. It's designed to fit into a standard escalator, onto trams or trains, and can even be loaded up directly inside a supermarket. A wide, biped stand makes loading stable and safe. Two simple yet effective brakes act directly on the tyres. The whole construction is light, strong and recycleable: weight is around 13kg. For extra-bulky or heavy loads (to 250kg), the 16kg 'Transporter' version with extended front platform and caster supports can be used, and a 'featherweight' version is also available, weighing just 11kg, with a load capacity of 130kg and a folding handlebar – which brings the folded dimensions to 113 x 25 x 67cm.

The Citytramp is best suited to level ground. It's intended as an instantly-available, no-maintenance means of transport, convenient for town-centre shopping, even if the town's a train-ride away. It's also well-suited for indoor use in hospitals, exhibition centres or factories. The load-carrying platforms can, of course, be equipped with special-purpose containers to suit every application. Other options include a steering lock, a built-in chain lock with a 'credit-card' key, indoor tyres which leave no marks on the floor, and ergonomic 'Biogrips' for the handlebars.

In Germany, costs range from DM 800, and will vary worldwide

Citytramp TransportRoller GmbH

Robert Lehle has had a long and successful career in the industrial automation and packaging industries, and, as he approached the end of his working life he realised that it was time for him to work on something for people rather than machines. Forced during a holiday to carry his food shopping home by hand, and inspired by a design project carried out by one of his sons, Robert Lehle decided to use his industrial skills to bring the Citytramp idea to production. He sees it as the simplest, effective solution to extending human speed and carrying capacity, and an appropriate response to the waste and inefficiency of using a 1300kg car to transport relatively small payloads.

Citytramp TransportRoller GmbH, Teckstr. 37, D-71116 Gärtringen, Germany.
Tel +49 7034 22100
Fax +49 7034 26661
Email: 0203664323-0001@t-online.de
Website: http://www.citytramp.com

pickup

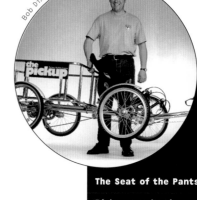

Bob Dixon

I f pedal-power is to be taken seriously as a transport solution, it must offer a range of vehicles as diverse as the petrol-burning competition. There are plenty of excellent speed machines and practical run-abouts, but the bicycling equivalents become that little bit rarer when it comes to pedal-powered replacements for small trucks and vans.

The Pickup has the potential to put a lot of these petrol-powered anachronisms off the road for good. With a payload of 180kg, plus the weight of the rider, it is a cheap, simple and people-friendly alternative.

Pickups are used in a myriad of ways: from family transport to local transport of goods for business. Others have been sold to municipal parks and ground maintenance companies. Enterprising people-carrying operations are investigating the Pickup as a modern, high-performance replacement for the traditional rickshaw.

The Pickup is now equipped with an articulating chassis, keeping all four wheels on the ground as it crosses uneven terrain. The design, developed in partnership with Mike Burrows and a local university, uses the Pickup load-bed as a structural element, linking the two halves of the machine.

The chassis is steel, and braking is provided by Sturmey-Archer drums. The transmission is usually via a three , five or seven-speed hub gear, although derailleur-geared versions are still available. At 28kg, it is still remarkably light for such a useful machine.

Clever, practical design is a hallmark of the Pickup: for example, the export model packs down into its own load bed. The use of standard components throughout – a design priority – is particularly important overseas. In fact, every wearing part, even those used in the ingenious differential system for the two-wheel drive, is available off the shelf worldwide.

In the UK, prices range from £1600, and vary greatly worldwide

The Seat of the Pants Company

Pickup production now keeps six people busy in the Seat of the Pants Company factory near Manchester, England. The Pickup is made entirely in-house. Proprietor Bob Dixon maintains an 'open door' policy, and customers are welcome to observe Pickups, Windcheetahs and the new Windcheetah Carbon Monocoque racer under construction. He also maintains regular contact with designer Mike Burrows, whose close involvement with the Pickup project shows his considerable versatility – he is also the inventor of two fast and hedonistic machines: the Windcheetah recumbent and the Carbon Monocoque, both of which are featured in this Encycleopedia.

The Seat of the Pants Company, Unit LKR4, L&M Business Park, Norman Road, Altrincham, Cheshire WA14 4ES, UK.
Tel: +44 161 928 5575
Fax: +44 161 928 5585

Germany: see page 145

In Germany, prices are around DM1200 for the TransSport 'Fun', and around DM1300 for the 'Fun Plus'. Prices will vary worldwide.

Schulz & Weber

Markus Schulz and Wolfgang Weber, friends for fifteen years, were out touring together when they hit upon the idea for the TransSport. With Markus' bike shop and framebuilding experience, and Wolfgang's technical expertise, they were well-equipped for the two years it would take to develop and test the design. They now have plans for a sportier 'Bike' version with 24 gears, and for a three-speed version aimed at heavier industrial use.
The TransSport is made in Germany by the respected manufacturers Bernhard Fischer GmbH, and sales within Germany are handled by distributors BICO. All international enquiries should be directed to Schulz & Weber.

Schulz + Weber, Postfach 102931, 66029 Saarbrücken, Germany. Fax +49 681 48489 Fax +49 681 48496. Email schulz_weber@t-online.de From Mid-March 1997: Tel +44 681 985 0902 Fax +49 681 985 0903

TransSport

GERMANY

Skidding around on gravel, pulling wheelies and bunny-hopping is not typical utility bike behaviour. On the TransSport from Schulz & Weber, however, it's easy to slip into such exuberence. The designers, Markus Schulz and Wolfgang Weber, are happy to demonstrate their bike's agility, performing BMX-style stunts with abandon. Showmanship is fine, but does not distract from the TransSport's very practical load-carrying character.

The TransSport is designed, say Schulz and Weber, as an all-purpose family bike. The cro-moly frame has an easy step-through design, and fits riders from 1.5 to 1.9m (4'11" to 6'3") tall. Quick-release adjustments on stem and seatpost allow different riders to use the bike with a minimum of fuss – and a patented security catch on the stem adjustment provides additional safety. Full braze-ons are provided, and various rear carriers can be fitted.

The most striking feature of the bike is the aluminium front carrier,

which is fixed to the frame. Up to 25kg of shopping or deliveries can be accommodated – but the designers stress that this platform is unsuitable for carrying children. Instead, a child-seat can be mounted behind the rider. Decent, no-fuss, carrying capacity on the front of a bike becomes all the more important when you have a child on the rear. There is also room for a neat quick-release D-lock mounting behind the front carrier.

The standard 'Fun' version (around 13.9kg) is equipped with a seven-speed Shimano or Sachs hub gear with back-pedal brake, and Shimano V-brakes front and back. These provide effective braking with little hand effort – so even riders with smaller or weaker hands have stopping power in plenty. The 'Fun Plus' (around 15.3kg) has, in addition, full mudguards and dynamo lighting.

Markus Schulz and Wolfgang Weber

high box transporter

It often surprises people that a solid, industrial product like a transporter tricycle finds so many friends beyond the industrial setting. The High Box Transporter from Christiania Bikes is a case in point.

Families appreciate the closeness and security of carrying their children in full view, safely surrounded by the sturdy box of 9mm marine plywood. You can stop to load up shopping – even with children on board, there's plenty of room, and the parking brake keeps everything steady. Also available are a bench seat, safety belts and a waterproof hood complete with windows. A child in a wheel-chair can be accommodated in a specially adapted version.

For load-carrying, the trike is a functional all-weather workhorse, carrying up to 100kg. Three different box heights are available, as are waterproof containers or modifications for special loads such as ice-cream vending equipment. Extended versions up to 30cm longer than standard are possible, and the solid steel chassis can be fitted with single-speed transmission, hub gears (three, five or seven-speed) or 24-speed derailleur transmission. Unloaded, the trike weighs around 40kg (89lb).

Christiania Bikes also manufacture a heavy-duty trailer, with the same solid construction as their trikes. Load-carrying capacity is also 100kg, and it can be detached from the bike and used as a hand-cart. As for the trike, various rain-covers, hoods and alternative boxes can be fitted.

The High Box Transporter has recently been finding many more friends among the Danish Postal Service, who have used it for many years. They now have to deliver packages up to 5kg in weight, and have more than 40 trikes in service.

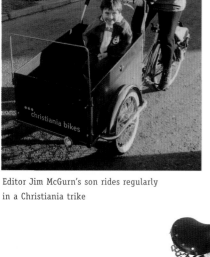

Editor Jim McGurn's son rides regularly in a Christiania trike

Christiania Bikes

Lars Engstrøm's urge to move heavy loads by pedal power came from living in Christiania, a car-free suburb of Copenhagen. Denmark's progressive transport policy means that 10% of trips are made by cycle, and Lars saw that a pedal-powered lorry is a necessary part of a cycling environment. He works closely with his Dutch partner and importer Freddy Hoogland, who makes a fibreglass box version for the trikes. Cykelfabrikken trikes are available direct, through their agents in the Netherlands and Germany, or through many bike shops in these countries.

Christiania Bikes, Christiania Smedie, Dammegårdsvej 22, DK-3782 Klemensker, Denmark.
Tel +45 5696 6700
Fax +45 5696 6708
Germany and the Netherlands:
see page 145

In Denmark, prices range from 7470 kroner. Prices will vary worldwide.

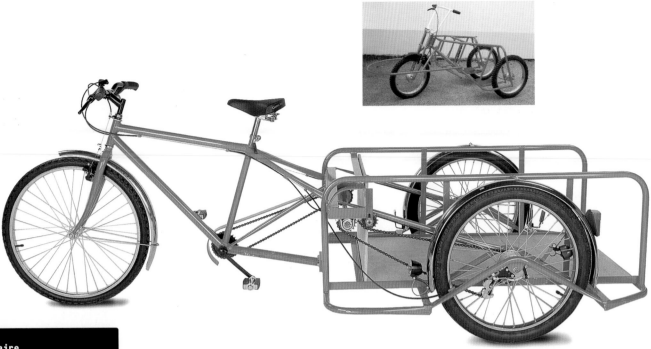

Valdenaire

Shortly after the Second World War, there were around 250 independent cycle manufacturers in France. Today, you can count them on the fingers of two hands – the others either closed or were taken over by foreign conglomerates.

Valdenaire, based on the banks of the Moselle river where it passes through the Vosges mountains, are one of the survivors. Founded by René Valdenaire almost 80 years ago, the company is now run by his grandson Pierre Valdenaire. Their 65 employees produce 15,000 cycles a year.

Valdenaire, BP 103-88204 Remiremont, Cedex, France. Tel +33 329 23 23 46 Fax +33 329 62 12 33. From outside France, contact Eurocycles: Tel +31 316 265 511. See page 145 for full details.

Pierre Valdenaire

traffic & mercurius

FRANCE

In France, prices range from FF6025 (Mercurius) or from FF 7880 (Traffic), and will vary worldwide

Valdenaire express their fascination for the potential of pollution-free pedal power with an incredible range of specialised cycles, including railbikes, roadsters, circus machines, mountain-bikes and a trike to be pulled by husky dogs. These are all produced alongside the 'Blaker's' range of fine racers and mountain bikes which make up the bulk of Valdenaire's business. They also make two exceptional load-carrying tricycles, developed in partnership with Henk Schuys of Eurocycles in the Netherlands, who has long experience in the utility bikes business.

The Mercurius carries the load between the two front wheels, and the Traffic has the two wheels at the back. Both have very low loading heights, so that even taller loads can be carried with good stability.

The Mercurius is particularly suitable for the vending of ice-cream, hot snacks or drinks, and Eurocycles can advise on suitable equipment to fit the 66 x 102cm loading area (which can be lengthened to 150cm). Loading capacity is 250kg plus the rider, and the machine itself weighs 45kg. Single, three or five-speed hub gear transmission can be specified. Full dynamo lighting, with a bumper to protect the rear light against knocks, stainless steel mudguards, rear carrier and bell are all standard. Sunscreen or roof, wheel disks and a price board can also be fitted.

The Traffic turns the Mercurius back-to-front, and shares many of its features. Carrying capacity and loading dimensions are the same, although the gearing must use either single-speed or a three-speed derailleur transmission, because of the need to 'divert' the drive to the side of the load-carrying platform. Empty weight is 50kg. The Traffic is intended for general local transport tasks, use by municipal parks or gardens, or for transport within car-free holiday villages or resorts. It also finds application with hospitals and anyone dealing with disabled people: the loading platform can easily and safely accommodate a wheelchair and occupant.

In the UK, prices range from £480 (Courier), £580 (Delibike), £865 (Loadstar). Prices will vary worldwide.

courier

U K

In towns up and down Britain, at the crack of dawn, a mass of cyclists emerge from the gates of the local Post Office to deliver the day's letters and parcels. They're riding one of Pashley's wide range of delivery cycles. The 'backbone' of the range is the Pashley Courier has a similar layout to the Post Office bikes, and is used extensively in factories, industrial sites and for general delivery duties everywhere.

It's a tried-and-tested design for heavy-duty use. The front container can carry 25kg, and can be either traditional wicker or moulded plastic. Three-speed gearing and hub brakes are standard, and the 26" wheels have full metal mudguards supported by heavy-duty stays.

Both the Courier and the 'Delibike' – with smaller 20" front wheel, and larger basket – have a large nameplate for promotional purposes. The Delibike is particularly popular for delivery businesses: parked outside a shop securely supported by the large, two-leg front stand, it makes people stop and stare, and on the road it's the best moving advert for your business, communicating your commitment to green transport.

The Loadstar is Pashley's heavy-duty tricycle: with 200kg carrying capacity and a 76 x 71cm loading area. An electric-assist option is also available.

Specially-designed for vending ice-cream, soft drinks or hot foods, the 'No. 33' is Pashley's traditional tricycle work horse. It can carry up to 200kg of refrigerator, grill or any front box measuring 66cm wide, 72 cm high, and 83cm long (or larger to special order).

Each of these workbikes is equipped with a comfortable sprung leather saddle, and the frames are made in heavy-duty steel. Pashley can often undertake modifications to the standard designs if special loads are to be accommodated, and with large orders bikes can be delivered in the livery of your choice.

yak trailer

When mountain-bike magazines start taking trailers seriously, you know something special is on offer. The BOB Yak is no ordinary trailer. The revolutionary single-wheel design presents a narrow profile for tight squeezes on off-road single-track, or in city traffic, and its low centre of gravity minimises the effect on the lead bike's manoeuvrability. The versatile Yak can haul up to 32kg (70lb) of camping equipment, groceries or delivery packages (as many bike messengers can attest). The water-resistant 'Yak Sak' duffel bag keeps up to 94 litres (5700 cu. in) of cargo dry and clean while the high-pressure 16" x 1.75" tyre combines durability with low rolling resistance. The Yak attaches to almost any bike's rear hub via a specially-modified quick-release skewer (extras are available for your second bike). Special 'BOB NUTZ' are available for solid-axle hubs.

In the USA, prices range from $259 (including the Yak Sak and QR), and vary greatly worldwide.

B.O.B. Trailers, 3641 Sacramento Dr. #3, San Luis Obispo, CA 93401, USA.
Tel +1 805 541 2554 Fax: +1 805 543 8464
Email bobinc@callamer.com
Website http://www.callamer.com/bobinc

bike-hod

'You don't know it's there' is a common reaction among first-time Bike-Hod users. Other road users are much more aware of the Hod, and give towing cyclists a wide berth. It is also lightweight, nimble, follows faithfully, and is narrow enough to pass through any standard doorway. The tow-arm swivels for compact storage or for carriage on public transport. A range of purpose-made bags and baskets is available. With a carrying capacity of 50kg, the Hod can haul sacks of sand, gas cylinders, crates of beer, and cumbersome items like golf bags, fishing tackle, another bike, or musical instruments. Detach the Hod from your bike by pulling the pin from the patented rubber hose-hitch, and it's a versatile, manoeuvrable hand-cart.

Bike-Hod All Terrain Trailers, PO Box 2607, Lewes, Sussex BN7 1DH, UK.
Tel/Fax +44 1273 480 479

In the UK, prices range from £150 for the trailers, and from £22 for the bags. Prices will vary worldwide.

City

City cycling will be the unlikely spiritual
and physical saviour of civilisation.

The Tour de France and the thriving mountain-bike race scene are a far cry from most people's cycling needs. The bulk of the population lives in towns, where journeys are short, the roads are often in poor condition and the need is for predictable handling, protection from the elements, conspicuity and load-carrying.

Countries with an an established bike culture, such as Denmark, Germany, Switzerland and the Netherlands, have a cycle industry geared to producing bikes for every day use. You can leave a bike-shop with a bike, and be ready to commute to work, ride to the shops or take an evening trip to friends knowing that the bike comes with rack, mudguards, skirt guard, bell, dynamo lights, low-maintenance running gear and a seating position suitable for perching above the mêlée of urban traffic. The city bike is the vehicle for a small planet.

1996 saw a growth in the range of city bikes, with volume manufacturers bringing out ranges of hybrid bikes which draw their design inspiration from both mountain-bikes and tourers. They're equally at home weaving through city traffic, or cruising on a country lane. City bikes hark back to the roadsters of the '50s and before, with the emphasis on reliable, low-maintenance bikes to withstand the rigours of daily use in town.

The renaissance in city bikes was kick-started by the market muscle of the Japanese giant Shimano, with the introduction of its Nexus groupset. Nexus provides a four or seven-speed hub gear, complemented by hub roller brakes: both gear-shifting and braking are enclosed and low-maintenance. Hub brakes mean that wet-weather braking is as effective as dry. Suddenly, with the Shimano marketing machine behind Nexus, manufacturers became aware of a volume demand for a city bike with dependable, ergonomic components – the long-established and functional Sachs groupsets had never achieved the same 'clout'. Designs are being produced to make the best of this opportunity, with even the conservative British cycle industry finally beginning to specify cycles with lights, racks, mudguards and chain-guards.

Western civilisation has just come to the jarring conclusion that cars are proving to be the ruination of society, although it is being only whispered in some circles. Even Detroit, home of General Motors, is looking at mass-transit systems to replace the ubiquitous car. The British government has realised that its former 'Roads to Prosperity' program is actually a road to ruin, and it has endorsed a national cycling strategy, aiming for 8% of all trips in Britain to be by bicycle, by the year 2012. This would bring levels of cycle use close to those now achieved in Germany.

This all argues a great future for the city bike and the city cyclist. The city bike is only part of the equation – the bike needs panniers, the rider needs waterproofs, insurance, somewhere safe to lock the bike at work or the shops, and needs to be able to use the roads – or cycle paths – with safety and confidence.

A city bike is a very quiet tremor, presaging the earthquake which may revolutionise how we live, move and order our societies. More people riding these modest but significant bicycles means fewer deaths on the road, a decline in heart-attack fatalities, and every cyclist means one less car making a short, wasteful, polluting journey. The growth in the market for city bikes puts cheap, practical, door-to-door, green, healthy and enjoyable transport at everyone's disposal. As the visionary H.G.Wells said: "When I see a man on a bicycle, it gives me hope for the human race." The human race is an increasingly urban animal, the city bicycle its salvation.

sine

The long-wheelbase roadster of Dutch tradition is a threatened species. Utopia have reached this conclusion because the Dutch chaincases which they once used are no longer available. Rear triangles today are becoming shorter – perhaps a good idea when you need to climb hills offroad, not so great when you just want to make comfortable journeys in town. Utopia do not follow such illogical fashions, and hold true to the long-wheelbase, upright designs which have so much to offer in terms of comfort. If that means a search for the best matching components, so be it.

Utopia also know that many people favour a bike with a low step-over height, so you don't need to be a gymnast to get in the saddle. Lowering the step-over height without losing the stiffness of the frame is not easy, but with the triangulation of the gracefully-curving tubes from which it gets its name, the Utopia Sine maintains considerable solidity and strength. It has a wheelbase of 114cm (44"), a step-over height of 38.5cm (15"), and the frame is made from cromoly tubing, painted in red or black. As with other bikes in the range, Utopia's customers can choose from a vast range of equipment and components to complete their machines.

The Sine joins Utopia's range of ten models, among which most cyclists will find a machine to suit their needs. It includes a model particularly suitable for taller riders (the 'London'), and lightweight touring bikes (the 'Silver Seagull'). All can naturally be fitted with a child seat, but their Kranich is particularly suitable – it's another strong and stable machine with low step-through. Utopia can also supply Winther trailers (also featured in this Encyclopedia) to complement any of their bikes.

Utopia

Utopia strike a fine balance: they provide the benefits of large-scale production without losing the individual choice and service so important in such a personal purchase as a bicycle. A skilled team of craftsmen build the bikes by hand, with machines being used only where appropriate. The 'RadRadgeber' – a German-language catalogue in which all of the options are clearly set out and discussed – is a vital component in the package, allowing the customer to make an informed choice to fit their particular needs. Utopia bikes are then normally supplied through a good local bike dealer, who can give on-the-spot customer care.

Utopia Fahrradmanufaktur, Eschberger Weg 1, 66121 Saarbrücken, Germany.
Tel +49 681 816506
Fax +49 681 815098
Email utopia@saarmail.de

In Germany, prices range from DM1589 (Sachs Super-7) to DM2063 (Sachs Quarz 3x7), and will vary worldwide

la luna

Hans Schauff

'Park and Bike' schemes are all about the pragmatic search for cleaner cities: in today's world of suburbs and commuting, the best way to make a short-term difference to the gridlock and pollution of car-clogged city centres is to persuade people to leave their cars on the outskirts of urban areas, then to complete the journey by bike. Cities across Europe have been embracing the concept: some provide bikes or secure cycle storage at the parking site, others rely on commuters bringing their cycles from home.

Most people like to ride their own bike to work – and to have it available for use at home – and that is where La Luna comes in. It is designed to be an attractive, practical and reliable town runabout, yet travels on cars for longer, out-of-town journeys, with an absolute minimum of fuss. The bike rack fits the back of most cars, and can be delivered with La Luna as part of the package. Loading up is simplicity itself: the prongs of the rack simply slide through two holes in La Luna's crescent main tube. Pull tight a few straps, and off you go.

On the road in its own right, La Luna rolls easily on the specially-developed 20" tyres, and the specification also includes Nexus four-speed hub gearing, cantilever front brake and mudguards, stand, halogen lighting (with rear 'standlight') and rear rack. An optional front basket is available.

The step-over height is a remarkable 26cm (10"), and the finishing touch is a motorcycle-standard headset lock as a theft deterrent. The key code is printed in the 'Bike ID' documents which accompany each machine.

Schauff have plans for a tricycle version, and an electric-assisted La Luna is also under development.

Fahrradfabrik Schauff

Schauff is one of Germany's largest cycle manufacturers, yet it remains very much a family business. Hans (above) and Ute Schauff, who run the company today, took over in 1968 from the founder Hans Schauff, who set up the original Schauff cycle shop and framebuilding workshop in 1932.

Their son Axel Schauff specialises in computer-aided design, and his work on La Luna has won several design prizes. The 'Wall Street Duo' tandem – another of his award-winning designs – is featured elsewhere in this Encycleopedia.

Schauff products are available at cycle shops throughout Europe. In case of difficulty, contact Fahrradfabrik Schauff, Postfach 1669, Industriegebiet, D-53406 Remagen-on-Rhein, Germany.
Tel +49 2642 93640
Fax +49 2642 3358
Email schauff@aol.com

In Germany, prices range from DM1099 (without car rack) or DM1199 (with car rack), and will vary worldwide

*In Germany, prices range
from DM 2501 (without
Exclusive-Stem), or from
DM 3476 (with the stem).
The stem costs DM 1000.*

Firma Egon Rahe

Egon Rahe has a long background in the cycle business.
As well as producing the
Eleganz and Exclusive-Stem,
he runs a cycle distribution
company. It was early in 1996
when he decided to create
the Eleganz, bringing together the most beautiful and
aesthetically-satisfying
accessories from around
Germany. He reports that his
customers feel a sense of
responsibility when they own
one of these machines. The
stately riding position
encourages dignified
progress, and regular careful use can only enhance the
pleasure of ownership.

Firma Egon Rahe, Adenauerstr. 8,
33428 Marienfeld, Germany.
Tel/Fax +49 5247 800 44

Egon Rahe

eleganz

GERMANY

Each of us has an individual sense of 'right' design, an
appreciation for the well-conceived and proportioned, and an
instinctive respect for fine workmanship. There are nevertheless
certain objects which are generally perceived as beautiful and
covetable, perhaps because of their inherent value, perhaps
because of their provenance. A beautiful object is appreciated
even more if a third vital ingredient is added: rarity. Into this
category comes the Eleganz, created by Egon Rahe of Marienfeld,
Germany – first for himself, and now for all those who will
appreciate its quality.

The Eleganz is manufactured by hand, with every component
chosen for intrinsic quality, matched by colour and material, and assembled into a
harmonious whole. The frame is hand-brazed in custom-crafted lugs. The finely-pol-
ished wooden mudguards, chainguard and
headlamp are complemented by cork grips. A Sachs Super-7 hub
gear system is usually fitted, although – as with any aspect of the
specification – the choice of gearing can be tailored to the
customer's wishes.

The saddle chassis is brass-coated, giving an elegant colour
counterpoint to the 'Exclusive-Stem', which is also available separately. Carefully cast in solid brass and hand-polished to a mirror-
finish, the stem is a collector's item in its own right.

The finishing touch on the frame is a gold-plated headbadge,
again hand-finished. This gives the final stamp of quality on a
bike which can carry itself with dignity in the most aristocratic
company: it is a prince among cycles.

In the Netherlands, prices range from f 950, and will vary worldwide

Sparta

In an age of corporate pre-dation, Sparta is proud of its position as an independent bicycle and motor-assisted bike manufacturer. Sparta have been building bicycles since 1917, and their 160 employees now produce 90,000 cycles a year. They also produce traditional Dutch roadsters and Marathon bikes, capable of lengthy, strenuous tours. Sparta bikes leave the bike shop equipped with lights, lock and carrier and, if you want, a small two-stroke engine from Sachs to take the sting out of hills and headwinds.
Sparta bicycles are available in bicycle shops throughout the Netherlands and beyond.

Sparta Rijwielen- en Motorenfabriek B.V., P.O. Box 5, NL-7300 AA Apeldoorn, Netherlands.
Tel +31 55 355 0922
Fax +31 55 355 9244

See also shops listing, page 142

silver bullet

NETHERLANDS

Inspired by 1950's America and stylish as West Coast cool jazz, the Sparta Silver Bullet is in a class of its own. The flowing curves of the light, rigid, polished aluminium frame are as easy on the eye as the rolling surf.

It's also easy on the legs. Most cruisers have one gear (if you're lucky). The Silver Bullet uses the Shimano Nexus groupset and hub gears – Sparta say that it won't break any speed records, but if your cruising pleasure has to take in a hill or a headwind, the seven gears will have the range to cope. And if your eye catches a particularly chic bistro, the cantilever front brake and rear roller-brake will have you stopped before you can say 'Cappucino'.

It might be built by Sparta, but it's anything but spartan. The luxurious equipment includes sprung-suspension saddle, burnished mudguards and chainguard and a wooden rear carrier. The swept-up, turned-back handlebars give a relaxed, upright riding position, and with the 'Revoshifter', changing gear calls for no more than a flick of the wrist. Cruising is smooth on 50mm Vredestein Street Razor 26" (559) tyres.

Producing a cruiser with a lightweight frame and Shimano Nexus equipment is a bold move by Sparta, reflecting a new demand for bikes which are bought and used for sheer pleasure. The Silver Bullet is an evocation of easy living: close your eyes and imagine it languidly resting outside a California jazz cafe at dusk, with a Miles Davis trumpet solo floating out of the open door. Cool solo, cool bike.

Zero-G

USA

Randy Schlitter

Aglance at their aircraft catalogue shows that RANS are fond of taking design orthodoxy – and throwing it out of the nearest window. RANS' main business is light aircraft kits, but their passion for speed and offbeat design also keeps two wheels on the ground, with their radical recumbent bikes and the new Zero-G, a cruiser for the modernist.

With its air/oil rear wheel suspension, laid-back riding position and Girvin Flexstem front handlebars, the Zero-G can outcool any surf-punk's beach cruiser on the sidewalk or in the dunes. Add the seven-speed Gripshift transmission, well-tried Shimano cantilever brakes and robust 26" wheels, and the Zero-G becomes a stylish package that is a practical bike for the cycling hedonist. It's a cruiser that can really cruise.

Find a willing partner and you can try another unique RANS design – the Screamer. RANS like the idea of tandems because as with aircraft, they've got pilots. The Screamer is a recumbent tandem with the thoughtful design hallmarks you'd expect from aircraft manufacturers – an emphasis on lightness, safety and ergonomics. The wheelbase is reduced by tucking the stoker's legs underneath the pilot's seat, and the seat and handlebars have enough adjustment to accommodate all builds of rider.

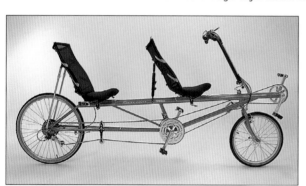

The name suggests the Screamer's emphasis – fast fun, so don't expect sober additions like mudguards and a rack, except to special order. The Screamer has the accessories that really matter on a tandem – powerful hydraulic brakes for stopping and a drag-brake for scrubbing off speed when you're screaming just a bit too much.

RANS Recumbents

Randy and John Schlitter have been avid cyclists for years, never believing that design was a given. 1973 saw a pedal-assisted recumbent sail trike leave the drawing-board and take to the Kansas freeways. It weighed more than 33kg, and a large sail area caused occasional handling problems! By 1980 they had refined it to a two-wheel recumbent that 'flew' just like their other products – a range of lightweight, affordable aeroplanes. Their recumbent names reflect RANS' aviation background – Nimbus, Stratus and Tailwind are long wheelbase products. V-Rex (full name, Velocitas Rex) is a predatory short-wheelbase speedster.

RANS Recumbents, 4600 Highway 183 Alternate, Hays, Kansas 67601, USA. Tel +1 913 625 6346 Fax +1 913 625 2795.

In the USA, prices range from around $1000 for the Zero-G, and from around $4000 for the Screamer. Prices will vary worldwide.

roadster

When coloured or white-wall tyres were all the rage, and black rubber was 'unsporty and heavy', Utopia refused to bow to fashion. Their reason? The unnecessary production of titanium oxide and solvents used in these products, and also the increased sensitivity to ozone and sunshine which made coloured tyres age and fail prematurely.

This example illustrates Utopia's two priorities: environmentally sensitive production and customer satisfaction. The first means that their products should not only be made in an environmentally-benign fashion, but should be long-lasting and wherever possible, recycleable. Hence their frames are of steel, and components are chosen for longevity as much as for light weight. To reduce transport pollution, 90% of Utopia's equipment is sourced from Europe. Their painting process requires no solvents.

Customer satisfaction means for Utopia that they will not, simply on grounds of cost, supply components whose performance is unsatisfactory. Thus, they use single-butted Sapim spokes on every rear wheel, and insist that unsuspended saddles have no place in their range, because they cannot deliver the comfort needed for the upright riding position. This style of cycling is, they believe, the most suitable for the everyday or touring cyclist for whom speed is not everything – the benefits include good visibility, an unstrained neck and lightly-loaded wrists.

The Roadster is Utopia's latest model, an elegant light touring bike. They have equipped it with the best of European components, including a Brooks leather saddle, Magura Race-line components, and the 'Schmidts Original' hub dynamo, driving Busch & Müller lighting. Both front and rear lights have a 'standlight' facility – they stay on for a few minutes even after you've stopped moving. The 'Robot' stem is adjustable for angle, and the 'Arrow' handlebars offer a multitude of hand positions. Weight is from around 17kg, complete with ESGE carrier, mudguards and stand, and depends on the customer's own choice of specification.

Utopia Fahrradmanufaktur

When Inge Wiebe and Ralf Klagges set up Utopia in 1982, they were mocked by some as hopeless idealists, whose strong environmental principles and enthusiastic attitude to comfort and quality in cycling would not match up to harsh commercial reality. Luckily, the sceptics have been proved wrong, and Utopia are flourishing, even publishing the German-language 'RadRadgeber' (Cycle Guide): a wonderful and educational compendium all about their philosophy, about the bikes, and about the choice of components to complement these designs. The seventh edition is available from Utopia or their dealers for a small charge. Utopia are looking for overseas distributors – please contact them for details.

Utopia Fahrradmanufaktur, Eschberger Weg 1, 66121 Saarbrücken, Germany. Tel +49 681 816506 Fax +49 681 815098

In Germany, prices range from DM2896 (Sachs Super-7) to DM3345 (Sachs Quarz 3x7), and will vary worldwide

In the Netherlands, prices range from f 1995, and will vary worldwide.

Koga-Miyata

Koga-Miyata is a partnership between the Dutch company Koga and the Japanese company Miyata, who manufacture frames to Koga's specification and send them to Holland for assembly. Koga have a 20-year history of developing and producing bikes, and they pride themselves on their 'quality philosophy'. Director C. Rijcken points to their 'Bike-Pass' scheme: as each bike is completed, the assembler's name goes onto the name-tag which accompanies the bike through quality control, and then to the carefully-chosen dealer network. Finally, the Bike-Pass becomes the customer's guarantee certificate.

Koga B.V., Postbus 167, 8440 AD Heerenveen, Netherlands. Tel +31 513 630 111 Fax +31 513 633 289 Email info@koga.com Website www.koga.com

C. Rijcken

emotion

Dirt, oil and the squeak of a rusty chain are all happily banished from the cycling experience when belt-drive takes over – and for the utility cyclist looking for cleanliness, reliability and efficiency, it's an unmitigated blessing. Belt technology has advanced to the point where durability rivals that of conventional drives, and Koga's self-tensioning system cures the old problem of belt slippage – and it also provides a smooth take-up of pedalling force. A clean and well-lubricated chain may be a few percent more efficient, but requires regular, unpleasantly grimy maintenance to retain the advantage.

Koga Miyata say that the belt drive was a logical part of the Emotion design. It is aimed primarily at the female cyclist, and the priorities were reliable performance, comfort and style. Low step-over on the oversized aluminium frame, and a wide range of seat height adjustment means that more than one member of the family can take it for a spin.

Nexus four-speed hub gearing, with an integrated roller-brake, is operated by a simple and reliable 'Revoshift' changer. At the front, cantilever brakes are regulated by Koga's own-design of anti-lock braking system – it controls the braking force, so that under normal weather conditions, a 'panic braking' manoeuvre should not result in a skid.

The Emotion is equipped with the Shimano Nexus hub dynamo: halogen lighting is available at the touch of a handlebar-mounted button.

Wheels are 26" front and rear, built with stainless steel spokes. The Emotion is equipped with a full complement of accessories - including frame lock, bell and clothing guard. The total weight is around 19.1 kg (43lb). Carrying capacity - essential for a town bike - is available in the form of specially-designed racks for the front (with basket) and at the back. It comes in metallic black, yellow or pearl white.

In the UK, prices range from £399 for both Tube Rider or Paramount, and will vary worldwide.

W.R.Pashley Ltd

Pashley are an eclectic bunch. They produce work-bikes for the British post office, and the Tube Rider for California-style cruising. They make tricycles to carry 200kg loads, and 'mountain' unicycles ('Muni's). From their factory in Stratford-upon-Avon come quality bikes and trikes for children alongside the lightweight spaceframe of the fully-suspended Moulton APB, featured elsewhere in this Encycleopedia. Pashley's diversity in specialised bikes is unrivalled in Britain, and they plan to extend it further by launching a short-wheelbase recumbent in early 1997. Pashley are looking for distributors to take their range further afield.

Pashley Cycles, Masons Road, Stratford-upon-Avon, Warwickshire, CV37 9NL, UK. Tel +44 1789 292 263 Fax +44 1789 414 201

tube rider

UK

The Paramount

You are what you wear – strangely, this makes perfect sense when it applies to what bicycles wear. When the same frame is clothed with two completely different sets of equipment, you can have two bikes so utterly unlike that while one draws admiring glances from aficionados of classic, dignified cycling, the other is rated as 'cool' by the beach-groupie whose other love is surfing.

This versatile frame is a gracefully-curved item from Pashley, and the two bikes into which it so elegantly transforms are the Paramount and the Tube Rider. It's not hard to guess which is which.

The Tube Rider is blue to match the waves, and the wide, sweeping bars give a fine upright riding position. With Sturmey-Archer hub brakes front and rear, and a 5-speed hub gear to boot, there are no salt-sensitive bits left open to the spray. A neat bracket reinforces the frame where the reaction-arm from the rear hub brake is attached. The wide, suspended Brooks leather saddle helps you cruise in comfort, and the 26" (559) wheels are fitted with wide, smooth balloon tyres.

The Paramount, meanwhile, is a town bike with practical equipment for daily use, giving it a style of its own. It is fitted with full wide-section mudguards and an alloy carrier-rack, Brooks saddle, and cantilever brakes. Gearing can be seven-speed derailleur, seven-speed Nexus hub gears, or the Sachs 3x7 system. The frame is satin black.

Both bikes are fitted with alloy chainsets, sealed bottom-bracket and sealed headset bearings. They also have extra-long seatposts so that the single frame size can accommodate most riders.

octos

USA

People of many cities have crewed the Octos, and it has a powerful and universal social effect. It induces laughter and lowers inhibitions, and after just a few minutes riding, total strangers will often defy the paranoia of today's crazy world and exchange phone numbers. This marvellous machine can work miracles for the humanity of our towns and cities, if applied with real imagination.

Inventor Eric Staller suggests a multitude of uses for the Octos. Instead of being carried along cocooned in a closed, armoured van, trainee policemen could interact with their local community, projecting an open, friendly image and enhancing the urban environment, as they bond into an effective team through shared physical activity. A board of corporate directors could enjoy a stress-relieving ride in the country or a city park, the 'face-to-face' seating arrangement giving them the most unusual board meeting imagineable. Schools and community groups will also find the Octos a stimulating location for 'round-table' meetings. The Octos can also be hired for major cycling festivals and other cultural events.

The Octos contains some serious engineering to cope with the weight and power of eight riders (and an optional child seat can also be fitted). The main tube is of hydraulically-rolled aluminium, and other parts are CNC-machined alloy. The drive system uses both chains and gears to power a patent-pending infinitely-variable traction transmission. The 510lb (227kg) vehicle is fully-suspended, and has rack-and-pinion steering and hydraulic disk brakes. Motorcycle components are used to cope with the stress – and

the total weight when ridden by eight adults can approach 2000lb (790kg). The Octos is guaranteed for one year, and the designers have been careful to make maintenance as easy as possible. Options include solar-charged lighting, an electric-assist system, a tow bar and a cover.

*Prices range from $50 000
(at the factory in New York, USA),
and will vary greatly worldwide.*

Eric Staller

The creator of the Octos, Eric Staller, is an American artist and inventor living in Amsterdam. His witty and humanistic public works have been acclaimed across the world. You can read more about his life and art on page 126 of this Encycleopedia. He believes that the bicycle is a perfect vehicle for his type of artistic expression: "Art should uplift the spirit and expand the imagination. It should invite participation and enrich community life. It should not be for an elite few – it should proclaim to all people the joy of being alive".
Enquiries about the Octos should be directed to Eric Staller.

Eric Staller, Herengracht 100, 1015 BS Amsterdam, Netherlands.
Tel/Fax +31 20 624 9198
Email urbanufo@euronet.com

sögreni of Copenhagen

DENMARK

The bicycle is a wonderful mode of expression for an artist – a timeless statement of minimalist functionality, simple, affordable and familiar enough for everyone to identify with, and yet adaptable enough to express any amount of what Søren Sögreni calls 'crazy notions'.

Søren Sögreni is a designer, and the line, form, and eye-catching aesthetics of his bicycles have found him many friends, especially in the design community: Swedish furniture designer Sven Lundh and his design company Källemo A/S have commissioned a Sögreni special in Columbus tubing. Sögreni often work in Columbus or other quality tubing, and made-to-measure frames are a speciality. Their elegant machines have also been recognised by the Danish Design Council, who have one on semi-permanent display.

All of the bikes have personal names: 'Old Shatterhand' is a town bike, and 'Dirty

Harry' is Sögreni's mountain-bike, with a sand-blasted aluminium frame. Sandblasting (often using glass beads instead of sand for a finer finish) is frequently used on 'silver' parts, giving a fine matt finish. A vast and unusually diverse range of surface treatments is used on the bikes, such as transparent powder-coating, copper-plating and acid dipping. The latter gives the bikes a 'pre-rusted' look: but the frames are still expected to last for many years. Equipment is to customer's choice, but if no strong views are expressed Sögreni usually fit Sturmey-Archer gears and other European equipment.

Søren Sögreni

Søren Sögreni began making bicycles in the early '70s, and since then he's been constantly experimenting, keeping up with technology and ahead of the public's imagination. His recent developments have included components such as leather grips, mudguards in multifarious colourings, bells in stainless steel or aluminium, handlebar end plugs in polished wood, and he's even modified the humble cable lock to give a dash of style and contrast, by replacing the crimped aluminium sleeve with copper.

Sögreni of Copenhagen Aps, Sankt Peders Straede 30A, 1453 København K, Denmark.
Tel +45 33 93 98 99
Fax +45 33 12 72 71

In Denmark, prices range from around 4000 Kroner, and will vary worldwide

touring

You can't say you've really visited a country until you've cycled through it. What other kind of holiday lets you travel at 'look at that' speeds, gives you the flexibility to see a road, track or a destination you fancy, then lets you just turn off and explore? A cycle tourist is the world's most innocent traveller. You're open to the elements, you've put some effort into your trip, and you are travelling your host country rather than rushing through it looking through a smoked glass window. Cycle tourists never cease to be amazed at the hospitality they receive.

Cycle touring can be something of a sub-culture. The bikes are special, and a good touring cycle is one of the best all-round bikes you can buy. Many find that recumbent bikes and trikes make wonderful tourers. Owners develop a passionate, protective relationship with the bike which has carried them along thousands of miles of roads, over hills and mountains, at home and around the world.

Some tourists travel light, with just one change of clothes, a fast bike and a credit card. Others go for the half-luxury of carrying clothes but eating in cafés and restaurants, and sleeping in hostels and hotels.

Most take great delight in carrying everything they need with them; tent, stove, sleeping bag, clothes, tools, spares, maps, books, eating irons; all are swallowed into carefully allocated spaces in panniers. The cyclist is the ultimate green tourist; the fuel is completely biodegradable, there's no room for ostentatious consumption and, once a cyclist leaves, there's just a patch of slightly flattened, soon-recovered grass to indicate there was ever anyone there.

Touring on a tandem is a further pleasure: twice the power and only slightly more weight and air resistance than a solo bicycle helps eat up the miles. Tandems are also the machines of choice for those wishing to ride with children, blind or disabled friends, or for those incurable romantics who can't bear to be more than a top-tube apart.

One way or another, most tourers will experience the phenomenon that defies description. You're into the second or third day of the holiday, spinning along the road when 'it' happens. Without perceptible effort, the pedalling gets easier, the road slips by quicker, the climbs are less of a challenge, the descents that much more exhilarating, the bike feels part of you, and if your smile gets any bigger, your head will fall in half. Some days, 'it' never happens, but sometimes day after day your cycling breaks the bounds of ordinary enjoyment into the kind of pleasure sinful man was never meant to know.

If you think this is purple prose, you've never toured properly, and you've probably never drowsed in a hammock slung between trees in a Provence orchard, munching French bread and fresh goat's cheese (which the farmer's just given you), sipping wine (the vineyard owner almost got violent when you insisted on trying to pay him), watching the fireflies and listening to the nearby river after 80 miles (130km) of 'it'.

Sure, you have your awkward days. It rains, you break a spoke and your wheel won't go round, goats raid your food pannier while your back is turned, leaving just crumbs. But such days are rare.

Some tourists deserve the title of explorer, leaving home and heading for the horizon, not resting until the world has been circumcycled. But an equally worthwhile tour is two days in autumn, maybe straying only tens of miles from your home town, the trees ablaze with dying leaves. Read on. There are some beautiful bikes waiting to be pedalled, and your County, *Département, Land*, Region or State is waiting to be explored, as well as everyone else's. And there's 'it' to be experienced. Cycle touring? There's nothing quite like it.

mesicek high bicycle

CZECH REPUBLIC

There is an element of daring in the high-wheeler's attraction: get it wrong and there's a long way to fall. Nevertheless, many devotees contend that a well-ridden high wheeler perfectly expresses the delicate equilibrium of man, machine and motion. In the late 1890s, as the high bicycle was gradually replaced by the 'Safety', traditional high cyclists derided the newcomers as graceless 'pygmy bikes', unworthy of a true cyclist.

Few high-bike owners would go that far today, but the extinction promised by peeved 'pygmy-bike' riders hasn't happened either. There is a thriving fellowship of modern-day 'wheelmen', and a growing number of them ride Mesicek High Bicycles.

The Mesicek does not pretend to replicate the 19th century originals. Modern materials are used without apology, with seamless Mannesmann tubing for the backbone, durable rubber for the tyre, and high-performance bearings for the wheels. The frame colour can be chosen from a palette of 89 shades while the tyres and pedal rubbers can be black or red. The saddle is of cowhide, pre-stretched for several weeks before installation.

Wheel sizes go from 28" to 56": the bigger the wheel, the further you go with each revolution of the pedals. The limit is the length of the rider's leg. Even the largest bike, fully equipped, weighs no more than 14kg.

Accessories include a battery-operated replica of an oil lamp, a bell, a horn, a handlebar-mounted luggage holder and a tool-bag.

An on-going project for the Mesiceks is a re-creation of an 1880s high-wheeled tricycle. We'd hoped to present it to you in this Encycleopedia, but production pressures have been such that the development process has been slow. They have, however, put together a prototype.

Mesicek

Mesicek High Bicycles are built with meticulous care by Josef Mesicek and his son Zdenek. With only six of these machines being produced each month, nothing is rushed. According to Josef, a high bicycle is not only a bike, but a philosophy – and their philosophy is not simply to produce a copy of an original High-Wheeler, but to surpass that original with the best that hard work, love and sound engineering can offer. They often make a point of delivering personally to their customers, seeing the world as they carry out this pleasant duty.

Mesicek High Bicycles are distributed through Kalle Kalkhoff, KGB, Donnerschweerstr. 45, 26123 Oldenburg, Germany.
Tel +49 441 885 0389
Fax +49 441 885 0388

In Germany, prices range from DM 5,400, and vary greatly worldwide.

In the UK, prices range from £2600 to £8000 for a Swallow custom tandem, depending on specification. There is a one-year waiting list.

Swallow Tandems

For Pete and Lorraine Bird, tandeming is a way of life, and they pursue every part of their business in tandem. Pete caught the tandem bug at 15, and after completing a goldsmith apprenticeship began making frames full-time, soon teaming up with Lorraine, whose wholesome vegetarian food and marketing skills have brought Swallow and Tandemania to the nation's attention. Lorraine also knows all about sizing and positioning for women tandemists, and Swallow are well-known for paying at least as much attention to stokers as to captains – after all, it takes two to tandem.

Swallow Tandems, The Old Bakery, LLanrhaeadr Ym Mothnant, Oswestry, Shropshire SY10 0JP.
Tel +44 1691 780050
Fax +44 1691 780110
E-mail info@swallow-tandems.co.uk
Website www.swallow-tandems.co.uk

Pete and Lorraine Bird

tandemania (swallow tandems)

Tandems are one of the best-kept secrets in cycling, but Peter and Lorraine Bird of Swallow Tandems are working like fury to get the news out. These tandem evangelists are based in the Welsh borders, and they don't just sell tandems, they sell the idea of tandeming, and they run the only tandem-specific shop and showroom in Britain.

Swallow aren't just retailers – prospective owners can take a two-day 'Try A Tandem Break', where they can be gently eased into the infectious world of tandem riding on the peaceful lanes around the Swallow Tandem shop. Most people who visit end up buying one of the 50 or so models available – and some of the most exquisite tandems on offer are the Swallow Custom Tandems. You could even build your own tandem on one of their framebuilding courses.

Built by tandem lovers, for tandem lovers: end of story, start of love affair. Love affair, or mania? Find out by attending Tandemania, a four-day international event aimed at spreading the tandem gospel still further. Tandemania takes place in July and does more than just show people what a tearing good time can be had on a bicycle made for two. On-road and off-road rides allow novices to try out an unrivalled selection of tandems, and tandem enthusiasts flock to Tandemania for the company, the shared love of tandems and – it has to be said – the tandem mania. The rides are complemented by talks, workshops, demonstrations and heady evening entertainments involving beer and dancing. This is true service in a world where even supermarkets sell bikes, and results in many pairs of happy customers.

Koga Miyata

Talk to people at Koga Miyata, and one thing strikes you. Everyone, from marketing managers to the newest recruit, loves bicycles. Ask about a design feature, maybe their anti-lock brake system, and they will tell you why it was done, about the tests which prove that it works, and they'll probably draw your attention to at least one other nuance of technology which you'd otherwise never have noticed. It's a refreshingly enthusiastic approach from one of the big players in the Dutch cycle industry.

Koga Miyata also produce the Emotion, an innovative town bike featured elsewhere in this Encycleopedia.

Koga B.V., Postbus 167, 8440 AD Heerenveen, Netherlands.
Tel +31 513 630 111
Fax +31 513 633 289 Email info@koga.com Website www.koga.com

globetraveller

NETHERLANDS

Take a good look at this bike. If you think the GlobeTraveller is just another expedition touring bike, then take a closer look and enjoy the surprise.

The most obvious innovations are the suspension seat-post and suspended stem. They provide full shock isolation with a minimum of moving parts and complication, leaving reliability uncompromised. The stem is supported by a needle-bearing headset.

Then note the neatly-positioned bell before moving on to the front V-brakes – and that strange black gadget on the cable. It's a fully-tested, well-proven and very simple anti-lock braking control, which limits the force which the rider can apply. Stopping distance is apparently reduced and the danger of skidding removed, even for experienced users practised in modulating their braking.

Look down to the wheels, and you see Mavic ceramic rims, 40 spokes at the rear and 36 at the front. Hubs – and the rest of the running gear – are drawn from the Shimano XT groupset.

Then there are the accessories. Alongside pump, frame lock, ESGE mudguards and carriers, even the water-bottles are out of the ordinary – they are insulated.

The lighting shows even more innovation. The 'All-In' headlamp brings the benefits of rechargeable lights to tourers without regular access to the mains: the dynamo can be used not only to run the light directly, but also to charge the battery. A lever operates the dynamo as you ride – so switching it on for charging as you crest a hill does not interrupt the flow of your ride.

With a double-butted aluminium frame, complete with full braze-ons, the GlobeTraveller weighs around 16.9kg, and is available in frame sizes from 50 to 63cm (19.6" to 24.8").

santana

Santana are proud to call themselves the largest manufacturer of tandems in the world. This means that they don't have to accept solo components or tubing for their machines – and road-tests across the world have confirmed the benefits. So have the customers: over 25,000 tandems have ridden out of Santana's factory to date.

Specialisation in tandems also means that Santana can make every sort of tandem you might desire: from tourers like the 'Vision' in the main picture, to the 'Red Track', a machine for indoor track-racing. They also make triplets, quads, or longer...and they work in steel, aluminium or titanium. If your tandem is used to transport an infant, Santana will fit a child stoker kit.

Any of Santana's steel or titanium tandems can be fitted with the 'S and S Bicycle Torque Coupling' system to turn them into travel tandems par excellence. It's not possible to fit this system on the aluminium versions. There is a production 'Stowaway' model with the coupling system as standard.

Need to fit a tandem in a suitcase? Santana have done it, with the help of S and S Bicycle Torque Couplings. These simple inventions allow a frame builder to produce a high performance bike which dismantles into a suitcase as large as its wheels. The Couplings are stainless steel lugs, silver brazed into the frame tubes. The tapered teeth lock together, and a threaded sleeve screws over the joint, securing play-free against both torsion and bending. Only available fitted by quality frame-builders, these devices are a wonderful way to make any bike portable.

S and S Machine, 9334 Viking Place, Roseville, CA 95747, USA.
Tel +1 916 771 0235
Fax +1 916 771 0397
Email steve@sandsmachine.com
Website http://www.sandsmachine.com

Santana Cycles Inc.

When two slower friends on a tandem outpaced aspiring racer Bill McCready, an obsession was born. As editor of Bicycle magazine in 1975, he'd run the world's first comparative tandem tests, and found every bike then on the market heavy, unwieldy and unreliable. Fired by these disappointing results, he opened Santana in 1976. Within four years, Santana was the world's biggest tandem producer. McCready holds that most manufacturers will use choice materials and components on their solos, but often compromise or specify lower quality for tandems – although stresses on frame and running gear are higher. Such thinking has no place at Santana.

Santana Cycles Inc., Box 206 La Verne, CA 91750, USA. Tel +1 909 596 7570 Fax +1 909 596 5853
National agents: see page 145

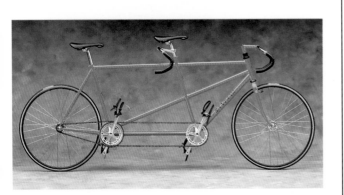

In Europe, prices range from DM5750 to over DM17500. The Stowaway costs DM9100. The S and S system adds DM1950 to steel tandems, DM4990 for titanium. Prices will vary worldwide.

pedersen of copenhagen

DENMARK

Jesper Sølling

One late and mellow evening Jesper Sølling, maker of Copenhagen Pedersens, was deep in discussion with his world agent Kalle Kalkhoff. It was the sort of going-nowhere argument old friends can allow themselves: how would you build a Pedersen frame of wood? Jesper Sølling went for tradition: the very first Pedersen bicycles were made of hickory. Kalle Kalkhoff, who used to live in Hong Kong, was convinced that bamboo was the answer. They didn't settle the argument, but the 'bamboo' Pedersen was born: standard steel Pedersen tubing finely airbrushed to give a most convincing bamboo effect.

Twenty-five tubes and a lot of love go into producing these tandems, which are supplied as framesets only. The characteristic 'bridge-like' structure of the Pedersen is very evident, each force balanced by another, the whole a glorious harmony of equilibrium, for which the riders' weight is an indispensable element. The hammock saddles are not only comfortable but durable: a replacement was recently sold to a customer who had taken the original over 60,000km. The 'feel' is certainly different to that of a conventional saddle, and several back pain sufferers have found that the seat and dignified upright riding position of a Pedersen make riding a pleasure.

The Pedersen structure has intrinsic strength, without any harshness in the ride. Kalle and his wife Gaby recently took their tandem almost 1000 miles from Oldenburg in

Germany over to Italy, fully loaded for touring. They had no problems, even though they went "down the Alps hitting the hydraulic brakes for 20 miles".

The Pedersen is, of course, also available as a solo bicycle, in a vast array of sizes and options. A triplet frameset is also available for togetherness at speed. Not for nothing were Pedersens a force to be reckoned with on the racetracks at the turn of the century.

In Germany, prices range from DM 1790,- for a solo frame, triple that for a tandem, and four times as much for a triplet. Prices will vary greatly worldwide.

Jesper Sølling Cykelproduktion

Mikael Pedersen, a Dane living in Dursley, England, was the inventor of this remarkable bike. Coming onto the racing scene in the late 1890s, Pedersens established their credentials with a string of wins and speed records, and were produced in their thousands, luxuriously finished for discerning cyclists. In the end, the expense was too much, and Pedersen sold up in 1905. Pedersens continued to be made, on and off, to the present day. Jesper Sølling Cykelproduktion in Ebeltoft, Denmark, is the world's largest Pedersen manufacturer, with distribution worldwide through Kalle Kalkhoff at KGB, and agents in many countries.

Pedersen of Copenhagen, c/o Kalle Kalkhoff, KGB, Donnerschweerstr. 45, 26123 Oldenburg, Germany.
Tel +49 441 885 0389
Fax +49 441 885 0388

UK and USA: see page 145

Jesper Sølling

*In Germany, the Pittsburgh
Alu Shox costs around DM5000.
Prices will vary worldwide.*

Schauff

Axel Schauff, head of Schauff's composites department, was following a tradition of building record-breaking tandems in developing the Wall Street Duo. In 1981, an unofficial record was set as a Schauff tandem reached 187km/h (117mph) behind a pacing vehicle.
Axel Schauff is also behind the development of more prosaic bicycles – the 'La Luna' city bike is featured elsewhere in this Encyclopedia. He believes that Schauff, still a family-run business, must keep ahead of technology to continue its success.

Schauff products are available at cycle shops throughout Europe. In case of difficulty, contact Fahrradfabrik Schauff, Postfach 1669, Industriegebiet, D-53406 Remagen-on-Rhein, Germany.
Tel +49 2642 93640
Fax +49 2642 3358
Email schauff@aol.com

Axel Schauff

wall street duo

GERMANY

This tandem weighs less than most solo bikes, and at just 14.2kg, we're not going to argue with the manufacturer's claim that it is the lightest, fully street-ready production tandem in the world. Details to note include the cable runs – with teflon tubes moulded into the composite monocoque – and the carbon-fibre disk brake. It's testimony to the expertise of Schauff's composites department, and could be yours for just £15,000 ($24000). Luckily, it's not the only tandem which they make.

Schauff have made a name for themselves as tandem specialists, with more than 22 years of tandem production – from affordable 'family' machines all the way through to the Wall Street Duo. Many people have first experienced the pleasures of tandeming on a Schauff. One of the largest bike-makers in Germany, they benefit from a huge dealer network to sell and service their machines.

If the Wall Street Duo is the ultimate in road tandems, the Pittsburgh Alu Shox represents Schauff's bid for off-road supremacy. The frame is polished aluminium, and Tioga suspension forks cushion bumpy single-track or broken potholes. Magura hydraulic brakes and special tandem rims cope with the extra loads which tandems must carry.

Off-roading on a tandem is quite possible – some of the wilder air-borne manoevres are out, but the extra momentum and stability of a tandem, especially with front suspension, can often make rough descents both faster and more comfortable than they would be on a solo. Should your tastes change and a weekend road tour be on the agenda, the Pittsburgh Alu Shox will just take it all in its stride.

*In Germany,
prices range from
around DM2400,
and will vary
greatly worldwide.*

Fahrrad-Manufaktur

Fahrrad-Manufaktur was set up by the VSF, a grouping of forward-thinking German bike shops, to build the bikes their customers wanted. The 35 employees work to environmental principles: their bikes are equipped for long life, and every bolt they use is of stainless steel. Powdercoating does away with the need for the unpleasant solvents and heavy metals involved in painting. Links with the VSF bicycle shops mean that with each Fahrrad-Manufaktur bike comes a free first service, and a voucher scheme for regular maintenance after that. A ten year guarantee on frame and forks is also included.

Fahrrad-Manufaktur, Zum Panrepel 24, 28307 Bremen, Germany.
Tel +49 421 438 570
Fax +49 421 438 5799
See shops, page 142

c-140 tourer

GERMANY

The heart of a bike, so they say, is the frame. It gives life to your ride. A tourer's frame can set the heart racing on a downhill, or support the pulsing rhythm of the pedals as you travel. It does this with tens of kilos of luggage stacked front and rear, never breaking into a heart-stopping shimmy or feeling slack and heavy. Stiffness is the key, and the designers of the C-140 understood that very well. Learning from the generations of touring bike framebuilders before them, they have avoided gimmicks and simply built a fine modern interpretation of the classic tourer.

The frame is constructed of cromoly steel, with traditional tourer geometry. It is equipped with full touring braze-ons, including fixings for low-rider racks on the fork. Both front and rear racks can be supplied, in aluminium or from the top-class 'Tubus' range, made from thin-walled steel tubing. The Lumotec dynamo lighting has a 'Standlight': the rear light stays on for a few minutes after you have come to a stop. SKS mudguards (with a neat arrangement of the stays at the front) are fitted. Wheels are built with Mavic rims and DT stainless spokes.

The C-140 can be fitted with either Shimano LX or Sachs Quarz components, and the precise specification can be chosen to suit individual customers. Traditionalists might choose to replace the combined brake/gear levers with bar-end shifters, or use the Gripshift system. Any traditionalist would be proud of the Brooks leather saddle – after the required wearing-in period, most people find that the saddle moulds itself to the rider's shape.

Total weight including racks is around 14.8kg, reflecting the very full specification. That is for a 60cm (23.6") frame - the C-140 is available in sizes from 50 to 63cm (19.7" to 25"). The powdercoating comes in unobtrusive green, vivid yellow or black.

guylaine WL

Silver solder is not used much for bicycles. The reason is cost, but the benefits are considerable. Although careful workmanship can minimise the problem, brazing with brass solder (with a melting-point around 900°C) inevitably heats the frame tubes beyond 700-750°C. At these temperatures, changes to the structure of the metal occur and weaken the tube – precisely where the stresses are highest, at the joint. This holds true for practically every steel tubing except Reynolds 853.

So when Guylaine tourers are built from steel (they also work in aluminium and titanium), they're brazed with silver solder, which melts below 650°C. Not just any silver solder: commercial grades (low in silver) contain environmentally-harmful and toxic cadmium. Schubert & Schefzyk go for a solder which contains 56% silver and is cadmium-free: not cheap, but the best.

Although there is a standard Guylaine tourer, customers can choose from an enormous range of equipment, drawn from the best on the market. The options are detailed in considerable technical depth in the Gulaine catalogue – and the makers of these bikes are always willing to discuss customer's needs personally. Framesets are also available.

One particularly innovative 'extra' is the rechargeable lighting system. Batteries are concealed in the seatpost, and a small box under the saddle allows the batteries to be

charged by the dynamo whenever convenient. Equally, the light can be used without the dynamo running – invaluable for map-reading and repairs. A lever mounted on the downtube can switch the dynamo on or off as you ride along.

Guylaine use Columbus SPX tubing as standard (that's the one with internal spiral reinforcements). Their frames are equipped with full braze-ons. With the standard equipment, Guylaine steel tourers weigh from around 13kg (29lb), including mudguards, rear carrier and dynamo lighting. Titanium models weigh around 1kg (2.2lb) less.

Fahrradmanufaktur Schubert & Schefzyk KG

Ask Detlef Schubert and Rainer Schefzyk why, since its founding in 1983, their German company has sold bikes under the French name 'Guylaine', and they'll just say "It was the name of a girl..." No such mystery surrounds why they make bikes. They wanted to go on tour and found that they simply couldn't buy their ideal bike. It was such an effort to assemble a good touring bike from scratch that they decided to give their customers a 'one-stop-shop' for all their touring needs. At first they assembled bought-in frames, then in 1986 started building their own. They have special expertise in small frames, and are 'just thinking' about developing suspension systems for their bikes.

Fahrradmanufaktur Schubert & Schefzyk KG, Magdeburger Str. 12, D-64372 Ober-Ramstadt, Germany. Tel +49 6154 52466 Fax +49 6154 52467

In Germany, prices range from DM1150 (frameset) or from DM2200 (complete), and will vary worldwide.

racing

Ever since the first bicycle hit the road, people have held bicycle races. Technology has come on somewhat since then, and the last decades have seen exciting innovations. Bjarne Riis won the 1996 Tour de France on a bike equipped with components invented for racing, and refined by the millions of kilometres which pass under the wheels of the racing fraternity. Combined brake and gear levers kept his bike under full control whether he was in an aero-crouch, charging an Alpine col or scrapping his way to the front of the peloton. Shoes were locked into clipless pedals, and in time-trial stages, his bikes would be fitted with aero bars and tri-spoke or disk wheels.

Racing is big business – only companies with deep pockets can afford to run a professional racing team. It's also a big pleasure, with thousands of road clubs worldwide running time-trails and races. Many cyclists have a cherished fast road bike, kept in the warm and taken out only on dry days for a fast, exhilarating blast along the road, and for a bit of fantasising about taking a *maillot jaune* – the Tour leader's celebrated yellow jersey.

Racing bikes are light, strong, high-quality machines designed to accelerate well and roll with minimum effort. They handle as though they're on rails and brake strongly. Shimano and Campagnolo have spent years battling for supremacy in the racing-component market, and even their mid-priced groupsets are fine pieces of equipment. Campag Super Record and Shimano Ultegra are a joy to look at before you even put them on your bike.

All our bikes feel the trickle-down effects of race-tried componentry. Those effects have given us components which are precise but brittle, light but short-lived, sealed-for-life and so unmaintainable – a situation which may be regrettable to those who feel that cycling should not be a consumer activity.

Cycle racing is probably one of the most testing of human endeavours. Finishing a single Tour de France stage with the peloton needs the kind of physical fitness, stamina and psychological resilience, to which most mere mortals can only aspire. And after 200 or more gruelling kilometres, they've got to do it all again the next day.

Cycle racing is a popular sport in many European countries. The World Championships, Giro d'Italia and six-day events are hugely popular and command large audiences. And at the 1996 Atlanta Olympics, America's long tradition of cycle racing threw itself into the event with Superbikes and enthusiasm. From Olympic track events to a muggy club-run in the rain, the world of racing contributes enormously to the world of cycling.

condor cycles

Grant and Monty Young

The Tour de France and the Olympics are part of Condor's racing pedigree, which stretches over almost half a century. They are no less proud of the world tourists, the dedicated commuters and the mountain-bikers who have learned that riding a bike which 'fits' in every sense - visual, biomechanical and functional - gives a truly life-enhancing sense of aesthetic satisfaction.

Condor's customers have ranged from pro pursuit champion Hugh Porter to rock idols the Rolling Stones. Condor are based just around the corner from London's Fleet Street, for many years the home of British journalism, so it's no surprise that they are often called on to provide bikes for media and showbiz personalities. Condor try to play this down, preferring to point instead at the racing successes which they feel are a truer measure of their worth.

They have long experience in the design of frames for every type of cyclist, yet the demands of their professional racing customers mean that their bikes must be bang up to date with the latest technology. Reynolds 853 tubing, frames to fit the latest riding position or mountain-bike geometry: in all of these areas, Condor can give you chapter and verse, then build you a frame to suit. For the tourist, this year's 'Heritage' is the latest incarnation of a model which has been part of the Condor range for over 45 years. They were happy to build one recently in Reynolds 753 rather than the traditional 531ST, and another was welcomed home after a tour of five continents.

The most popular frames are often available off-the-shelf, ready to be fitted with wheels built personally by Condor founder Monty Young. A variety of framebuilding techniques are used - usually lugged and brazed for road bikes, fillet-brazed for ATBs, and welded for some track bikes The lugs are specially-made in Italy to Condor's specification. For connoisseurs of fine lugwork, the 'Crown Jewels' range use traditional hand-crafted ornate designs from the company's early years, carefully feathered and shaped for maximum strength and rigidity.

Condor Cycles

Monty Young founded Condor almost 50 years ago, in the post-war austerity years. He was a mechanic in international races worldwide, and a Condor-Makeson team rode the Tour De France in the early '60s. He is now framebuilder to the stars, and has been joined in the business by his son Grant. Condor are not just about racing, and are proud of their versatility: they often make very small or large frames, once constructed a quintuplet, and enjoy the challenge of an out-of-the ordinary request from a customer. Enquiries from overseas are very welcome, and Condor would also like to hear from anyone who might like to act as their representative abroad.

Condor Cycles, 144-148 Gray's Inn Road, London WC1X 8AX, UK.
Tel +44 171 837 7641
Fax +44 171 837 5560

In the UK, prices range from £300 (frames), or from £600 (complete bikes), and will vary worldwide

paris-roubaix

USA

The 'Hell of the North' – the race over the cobbles from Paris to Roubaix in Northern France – is a traditional testing ground for suspension on road bikes. Yet, at first glance, you might take the Boulder Bikes Paris-Roubaix for a typical, rigid road frame. That's exactly the point. Designer Rich Williams learned early on that the then-radical idea of full suspension would only be accepted among the relatively conservative mountain bike purchasers if it were incorporated in a traditional-looking diamond frame. After designing the world's first full-suspension mountain bike, Rich pioneered the logical migration of suspension technology from the mountain to the road.

The titanium Paris-Roubaix frame pictured here weighs 2.00kg (4.4lb), while the aluminium and steel versions weigh 2.04kg and 2.40kg (4.5lb or 5.3lb), respectively. They all incorporate Boulder's patented top tube shock absorber system, with 32mm (1.25") of rear wheel travel. Coupled with a front suspension fork with 30mm (1.18") of travel – the one shown here is from RockShox – the Paris-Roubaix has ample suspension to smooth the ride on most roads. In fact, Rich believes that his bikes are faster than standard rigid frames because they can soak up bumps at speed, allowing riders to race through terrain that rigid frames must carefully navigate.

Though the Paris-Roubaix is ideally suited to anyone who wants a performance advantage, typical customers are cyclists who are 'old enough to know better', seeking to reduce bodily wear and tear. The bike's suspension, sloping top tube and triple chainring will probably not appeal to some, to whom Rich refers as "super-purist, Italian steel roadies." Open-minded cyclists, however, will appreciate the performance, comfort and quality of this handbuilt frame. A complete aluminium bike weighs approximately 9.97kg (22lb), little more than a conventional rigid bike. Price and weight vary depending on the size and tubing material, and on the component groupset, all of which can be chosen to suit the individual customer.

Boulder Bikes

In the late 1980s, Rich Williams began cycling to get into shape for his first love: offroad motorcycle racing. Dissatisfied with his mountain bike's performance, he redesigned it to incorporate the suspension technology that had so radically transformed motorcycling a decade earlier. Two years later, his first production bike put Boulder at the forefront of the suspension revolution that soon swept the industry. Today, Boulder Bikes produces 300-400 mountain, road and tandem bikes a year. Plans for the future include a line of components as well as a full-suspension recumbent.

Boulder Bikes, P O Box 1400, Lyons, CO 80540, USA.
Tel +1 303 823 5021
Fax +1 303 823 5025
Email rkd_llc@indra.com
Website http://cyclery.com/boulder_bikes/

In the USA, frame prices range from $1499 for steel, $1799 for aluminium and $2999 for titanium, and will vary worldwide

In the UK, prices range from about £4000, and vary greatly worldwide

Mike Burrows

windcheetah carbon monocoque

U K

So remarkable and revolutionary was the bike which British cyclist Chris Boardman rode to victory in the 4K pursuit at the 1992 Olympics, that it almost eclipsed the achievement of its rider. Although branded the 'Lotus' bike, design and early development work came from British designer Mike Burrows, and it has now been reborn for production as the Windcheetah Carbon Monocoque. According to Burrows, it is still the most advanced bicycle in the world to conform to the regulations of the international racing authority, the UCI.

The frame is a hollow monocoque construction of carbon fibre and epoxy resin, manufactured by the specialist company HQ Fibre

Products. Cranks are made exclusively for this bike by respected component specialists Middleburn, and are designed by Mike Burrows to work in harmony with the aerodynamics of the rest of the bike. Chain and saddle are about the only standard components on the machine.

This is a machine for the serious competition rider, who will use it to full advantage. Such a machine must be for the lucky few, but it's by going to the cutting edge of technology that the breed evolves. The Windcheetah Carbon Monocoque is produced by The Seat of the Pants Company, who expect to produce about 40 a year, fitted to individual customers. Priority will, they say, be given to riders seriously intending to race on the machines. The rest of us can enjoy the bitter-sweet pleasure of longing for the unattainable.

*In the US prices
start at $2055
for a frame,
and vary greatly
worldwide.*

merlin

U S A

Merlin Metalworks

In 1986, Gwyn Jones co-
founded Merlin Metalworks
because of his desire to
build high-end bicycles
exclusively out of titanium,
a project not taken seriously
by his then employer. He and
his partners chose to build
bikes out of the then unusual material titanium because
of the difficulty of improving
on 100 years of evolution
in steel frame design and
manufacturing.
Today, Merlin has 35 full-time
employees and continues to
operate in Cambridge,
Massachusetts in the shadow
of Harvard University. Their
plans for the future are
characteristically modest: a
wider range of frame sizes
and a line of full-suspension
mountain bike frames top
the list.

Merlin Metalworks, 40 Smith Place,
Cambridge, MA 02138, USA.
Tel +1 617 661 6688
Fax +1 617 661 6673
Website http://merlinbike.com
International enquiries:
see page 145

Gwyn Jones

Titanium tubing is an essential component for hydraulic systems in aircraft, and one of the highest-performance varieties is created by alloying pure titanium with small percentages of aluminium and vanadium. Merlin Metalworks use this material in their proprietary seamless tubing, which they build into light and strong frames that have been ridden in the Tour de France, the Olympics and the World Championships. In addition, Merlin frames do not rust or show scratches, and this has endeared them to people who operate in permanently hostile conditions – among them rain forest campaigners in Africa and National Geographic scientists in Alaska.

With 47 different sizes, Merlin has available the widest range of custom titanium tubes of any manufacturer. All of the tube gauges and diameters are size-specific: they are individually selected for each frame size in each style to result in the best possible ride and lowest weight. Customers of stock sizes and styles (there are over 100) can expect a wait between two and four weeks for their frame. Custom-sized bikes – also a Merlin speciality – are produced within two weeks (customers outside the USA usually have to wait a little longer for both).

The top-of-the-line, double-butted, Merlin Extralight frame weighs a feathery 1.2kg, and the standard Merlin road frame pictured here weighs 317g more in the standard 57cm frame size. The weight difference is due to the latter's straight gauge tubing, necessary to accommodate the S&S Machine Bicycle Torque Coupling System: two precision-fitted coupling devices fastened to the frame during the manufacturing process. These allow the bicycle to be split in half and packed away into either a hard or soft-shell case for use when travelling or if storage space is tight. The 250g S&S system converts the lightweight and durable Merlin into an excellent high-performance travel bike.

giant MCR

Mike Burrows

When Mike Burrows was asked to design a racing bike for Giant, he introduced the Giant design team to the 'small is beautiful' concept: "Shrink the frame and it's lighter, because it uses less material. It's more aerodynamic. It's stiffer because the triangles are smaller, and line up better with the forces on the bike. You have a lower step-over height, and finally, the bike's even easier to put in a case for transportation. And it makes a perfect excuse to use one of my aerodynamic carbon-fibre seatposts."

The design was pushed through to production, and the Giant 'Compact Road' range is now available in either composite monocoque construction (the MCR), or in welded aluminium tubing (the TCR). The frames are sized around 10-15cm smaller than convention would dictate, yet offer a riding position identical to any other racing bike, thanks to seven sizes of carbon composite seat posts, three frame sizes and a specially designed (Burrows) adjustable stem.

Burrows-designed wheels complete the equipment. Lighter than tri-spoke or disk wheels, and less susceptible to sidewinds, they are more aerodynamic than the traditional variety, yet the plastic spokes (12 front, 16 rear) can be adjusted or replaced in the conventional manner. The front wheel is mounted on a carbon-composite fork. The TCR

weighs around 10kg complete, and the MCR weighs around 9.5kg. They are available only through Giant dealers, who fit frame and parts to the individual customer.

Burrows admits that the Compact Road bikes bear a striking resemblance to mountain-bike frames with road components. It's a fair comparison, but he points out that the conversion is not simple, or cheap, and that a good ergonomic and aesthetically-satisfying result is not easy to achieve. Giant's MCR and TCR satisfy both criteria in fine style.

Giant

Giant are the largest manufacturer of performance bicycles in the world. Based in Tachia, Taiwan, they sell bikes across the globe. Looking for innovation to keep their range fresh, they approached Mike Burrows, who agreed to join their R&D team as a designer. His input has been considerable, and alongside the TCR and MCR, he has also worked on the Giant dual-suspension mountain bike. Burrows continues to work with Giant as a consultant, making regular trips to Taiwan, and both enjoy the stimulating partnership.

Giant bikes are distributed through bike dealers worldwide. See page 142 for a list of Encycleopedia shops (not all of whom will be Giant stockists).

In Europe, frameset prices range from DM2999 for TCR to DM5999 for the MCR, and will vary worldwide.

tom board frames

UK

Tom Board

The 1940s and '50s were the heyday of the classic British racing frame. Forbidden to decorate their bikes with a manufacturer's name during competitions, frame designers came up with a wonderful variety of individualistic frames. The cognoscenti of the cycling world could then identify the manufacturer from the design details. The best-known of these were perhaps the 'curly' Hetchins stays or the Bates 'Cantiflex' tubing. Thanet, Waller, Baines – these were just a few of the once-famous makers of classic, top-level racing bikes.

These bikes have bewitched many a cyclist, and none more so than Tom Board. Ten years ago he began recreating those classics which were no longer being made. His faithful replicas are painstakingly accurate and wonderfully finished. Although there are modern versions of a few bikes, like the Hetchins, available elsewhere, he believes that he is the only framebuilder in the world to offer true replicas of the original machines. His range also extends beyond this classic era, with versatility born of experience: he has recreated cruisers from '60s America, and built low-profile racers, tricycles and tandems. His range of modern racing frames has a dedicated following of top-level athletes. He recently met one of his earliest tricycle customers, who still had the original purchase receipt for the machine. Still in regular use, it was bought in 1954.

Tom is based at Bicycle Workshop, a cycle shop run by Ninon Asuni. He works closely with her in the search for authentic components – perhaps Simplex, Osgear or Chater-Lea – to complete the machines. Many bicycles are simply ordered as framesets – finished in the authentic racing colours of the day, chromed if appropriate. These rare and exclusive designs excite the same admiration today as they did on the racetracks half a century earlier.

Tom Board

Tom Board is the epitome of a master-framebuilder in the long British tradition. Leaving the Army in 1949, he started work at Paris Cycles in Stoke Newington, learning his craft and joining enthusiastically in the racing scene at Greenford C.C., and in the days of the British League of Racing with the London-Italian R.C. Today, his quiet reputation for quality and attention to detail has brought him to the attention of keen cyclists from around the world. Some come to London just for that purpose. Tom Board's bicycles are always made to measure, and the dialogue between craftsman and customer is an important part of the framebuilding process.

Tom Board, Bicycle Workshop, 27 All Saints Road, London W11 1HE, UK. Tel +44 171 229 4850

In the UK, frame-set prices range from £480 upwards, and will vary worldwide.

In Germany, prices range from around DM3500, and will vary worldwide

Kemper Fahrradtechnik

Jet engines were the obsession of the old Michael Kemper. he was, he says, an aerospace industry wage slave with no time for his family or for himself. Then, in 1987, he decided to leave the financial security of his old job, throw over the expectations of conventional society and start up as his own boss, making bicycles and sharing the childcare responsibilities for his daughter Miriam. Taking control of his life has been good for Michael, and the success of his new business has recently forced a move to a new, larger factory in the country. Kemper are also looking for further distributors abroad.

Kemper, Rheinweg 70A, 41812 Erkelinz Grambusch, Germany. Tel/Fax +49 2431 77017 Office in Düsseldorf, and agent for Holland: see page 145.

classic pedersen

G E R M A N Y

At the turn of the century, the Pedersen was a force to be reckoned with on the racetrack, so when former aerospace engineer Michael Kemper began to recreate this classic, he put the highest priority on precise, lightweight construction which would maximise the riding performance, without departing from the spirit of the original. Mannesmann cromoly tubing is carefully brazed into a Pedersen frame optimised for lateral stiffness. While a traditional woven hammock seat is available, a very comfortable Brooks leather saddle is usually used, for a lower saddle-sling attachment. This makes the whole frame smaller and stiffer. The fork tubes pass through a laser-cut fork bridge, reinforcing the front assembly, and taller frames can be further stiffened by a specially-made, wider bottom-bracket housing.

Saddle height and angle combined define the fit of a Pedersen, and Michael Kemper custom-sizes each frame to suit the customer. The customer can specify almost any conceivable frame detail: braze-ons, internal cable-runs, or the customer's initials engraved onto the steerer tube. The customer can also choose every aspect of the equipment, and an enormous palette of colour options is available. Nickel, chrome or copper-plating are also possible.

Michael has never made two Pedersens the same. His customers have ranged in height from 1.5m to over 2.0m (4'11" to over 6'7") tall, and in weight up to 130kg (290lb). Their tastes have ranged from Woodguard-equipped machines in classic black or British racing green, to hydraulically-braked racers in sulphurous yellow.

The Classic Pedersen is built alongside Kemper's Lorri and Filibus; lightweight but stable two-wheeled load-carriers, excellent for deliveries or a cargo of children. The 15.5kg (35lb) Lorri is the smaller version, with two 20" wheels and load-carrying platforms front and rear. The Filibus is longer, with a 26" rear wheel, and a childseat can also be fitted to the large front platform. The child can sit facing you for good eye contact, or facing forward to see the world.

Michael Kemper

mountain bikes

Lift your eyes from the road
and what's there? Fields. Hills.
Mountains. Tracks. Bridleways. Way back in the dawn of cycling, Baron Karl von Drais was perhaps the very first off-roader. Bumping along the forest tracks near Karlsruhe in Germany, he could have had little inkling that one day the roads would become so good, not only for cyclists, that cyclists would want to escape again to the rough tracks of the countryside.

The first off-roaders were simply cyclists prepared to tackle 'rough stuff' – the off-road journey you made to link the road sections of a route. The 1950s and 60s saw the heyday of British 'rough stuff' cycling. The bikes were tourers, probably with handbuilt wheels for extra resilience.

Then in the 1970s, a group of American enthusiasts took the heavy American cruiser bikes, fitted the fattest tyres they could find, and began an anarchic series of race meetings in Marin County. Their bikes had grease-filled hub brakes, and moderating the furious descent created enough heat to burn it off. At the end of the day brakes would be stripped and repacked with grease. So the races became known as Repack, and they were a phenomenon. Invention was followed by innovation, and the enthusiasts began refining their heavy, essentially unsuitable machines. Soon, bespoke frames were being designed and built, lighter components added. Those enthusiasts had changed the world. They had invented the mountain bike – the brash populariser of off-road cycling. The toughest bikes in the world had been invented just in time to catch a generation for whom hedonism, thrill-seeking and living on the edge were perfectly expressed in the technicolored, consumer's world of mountain-biking.

Light, stiff frame, 26" (559) wheels, knobbly tyres, flat handlebars with climbing pegs, brake and gear levers right under your fingers, 21 or 24 gears and powerful brakes are the hallmarks of the modern mountain bike.

ATBs make up the bulk of modern bike sales, and they have been responsible for a boom in bike ownership. Suddenly, cycling has become fun again and most people can afford a bike that is built to cope with crashing down a steep forest track, without either bike or rider finishing the descent in bits.

As ATBs entered volume production, initially high prices dropped and components started to improve in quality. Steel frames are being jostled by oversize aluminium, titanium and carbon-fibre frames. Manufacturers are fighting to shave grammes off components, and the mountain-bike press reads like a gallery of technicoloured, high-priced bolt-ons.

Suspension, once a high-priced luxury, is now appearing on modestly-prices ATBs, allowing riders to take descents at higher speeds, with front forks and elaborate rear suspension to soak up the battering of rocks, ruts and tree roots. Suspension has radically changed bike design, allowing frame designers to add floating rear triangles, oddly-mounted shock absorbers and even inspiring some to replace tubes with tensioned cables.

The same bike that is designed to cope with the slings and arrows of off-road riding takes potholed urban streets with great urbanity. Big tyres, good low-speed control offered by the wide bars and massive braking power make the ATB a fine urban survival machine. The loud image portrayed by the ATB press does a disservice to the millions of people for whom the ATB was a revelation. People brought up on heavy roadsters could suddenly afford a light bike with plenty of gears, reliable brakes and the flexibility to move briskly on road and take off-road tracks with gusto.

Disapprove of anodised purple titanium alloy hubs if you wish, but do homage to the Repack inventors of the ATB. They changed the world.

In the USA, prices range from $3500 for a Bow-Ti frame, and will vary worldwide

Ibis Cycles

Ibis is based in Sebastopol, in California's wine country. The company has been dedicated to producing top-spec mountain bikes, tandems, road bikes and accessories since 1981. Founded by off-road racer Scot Nicol, the Ibis team of seventeen (all cycling enthusiasts) regard innovation and a slightly crazed sense of humour as essential to the company ethos. Ibis have the reputation for thorough engineering and offbeat ideas – look for the 'Moron' tubing (more on the ends!), and details such as carefully sculpted metal hands and feet acting as cable stops and pump brackets. The Bow-Ti frame was the brainchild of frame engineer John Castellano, who has been collaborating with Ibis for many years, and is hailed as a 'suspension guru'.

Ibis, P.O. Box 275, Sebastopol, CA 95473, USA. Tel +1 707 829 5615 Fax +1 707 829 5687 Email info@ibiscycles.com Website www.ibiscycles.com

bow-ti

USA

You don't wear this Bow-Ti to formal occasions, unless screaming downhill off-road or digging into a hard climb is your idea of formality. The Bow-Ti name describes the frame concept – a titanium rear suspension which gives 12.7cm (5") of travel without a pivot in sight, with a frame weight of 2.2kg (5lb) including the rear shock. Ibis describes the Bow-Ti as one of the most highly-evolved bicycles ever, drawing on exhaustive computer modelling and practical testing to prove the design. The result is a frame that uses twin, head-tube-to-rear-dropout 'bow-stays' that act as sprung members, soaking up the energy from bumps along their entire length and giving considerable vertical travel while minimising lateral play.

Scot Nicol, President and owner of California-based Ibis Cycles, needed some convincing, but backed Bow-Ti designer John Castellano's intuition about pivot-less suspension and titanium's qualities. The development programme was rigorous, building frames designed to break, so that the Ibis team would know where the stresses developed and where the frame needed strengthening. The testing programme for this hi-tech bike had a low-tech name: 'Riding the snot out of it'. They did find that no moving pivot means no maintenance. Ibis are keen to stress that the no-compromise material specification (three grades of titanium alloy are used in this design, matching their properties to the situation) and testing means that the bow stays are loaded well within their limits. It'll bend, they say, but it won't break!

This strenuous development, and the use of costly materials make the Bow-Ti a premium product, but Ibis does aim to bring Bow-Ti technology to an affordable level.

breezer twister

In 1977 Joe Breeze built the first frames for an activity which would later be called mountain biking. This year, his Breezer will be the first mountain bike to celebrate its twentieth anniversary. His Repack days have made him something of a mountain-bike celebrity, and yet he has not lost sight of the potential for cycling beyond the racing scene. He says that energy spent on the recreational side of the sport boosts awareness of cycling in general – and this can only be good for the longer-term future of bicycles as transport. Back in 1973 he was searching out bikes from before the turn of the century, planning to restore and display them so that people could appreciate cycling through its heritage. Then he got sidetracked with 'the mountain bike thing'. His company have made mountain bikes ever since, and one of their latest is the full-suspension Breezer Twister.

The unified rear triangle rotates around a high, forward pivot, giving 125mm (5") of travel. This geometry has been patented by John Castellano as the 'Sweet Spot' system. It gives a plush ride in the saddle, yet the suspension stiffens considerably when you're out of the saddle climbing – racers love it. Because the bottom-bracket to rear axle distance is constant, pedalling does not affect the suspension.

The Twister's front triangle is made of aluminium and the rear is heat-treated, chrome-moly, making the best use of each material. The Breeze-designed tubing is called D'Fusion – down and top tubes are D-shaped near the head tube to diffuse stresses where they are highest. Up front, the Twister uses a Rock Shox Indy XC fork and a unique integrated lower head tube bearing to widen the stance of the top and down tubes. Complete bikes weigh 12.2kg (26.9lb), and the bare frame and shock-absorber weigh 2.6kg (5.8lb), without the fork.

Joe Breeze on the very first
Breezer, at Repack in 1977

Joe Breeze Inc.

Joe Breeze launched a mountain bike racing team in 1995. He says "Publicity for recreational cycling puts cycling on public view, and something as sensible as the widespread use of bikes for transport will inevitably catch on sooner or later". Team Breezer is co-sponsored by Nexus, Shimano's hub-gear utility groupset. "Several other mountain bike race teams are sponsored by automotive transportation companies", says Breeze. "We'd rather be sponsored by a company focusing on bike transportation. In some respects, the 'recreational' mountain bike just serves as another way to burn fossil fuels."

For more information, try shops (page 142), or contact your closest national distributor (listed on page 145) for details.

In USA, prices are from about $2300 (complete) or $1400 (frame and shock). Prices will vary worldwide

recumbents

Moving into the mainstream

A 'wedgie' is a painful experience, as any victim will confirm. 'Friends' grab hold of your belt, and lift you from the floor, until the entire weight of the body falls on the crotch of your trousers. Unless this gives way, the (usually male) target can be certain to remember the experience for some time.

Now the term 'wedgie' has a new but not unrelated meaning for some American cyclists who ride recumbent. As beneficiaries of comfortable, laid-back seats, they pity those poor, misguided unfortunates who persist in using a saddle so poorly adapted to the human posterior that the effects can be as painful and potentially embarassing as the 'wedgie' of their schooldays. Yes, a 'wedgie' is an upright bicycle.

Not every recumbent rider would use that term. It's a little smug, even contemptuous. But it does illustrate perhaps the most effective argument of all in favour of recumbents: just compare sitting on a comfortable, cushioned seat to sitting on a small, hard saddle.

As a common-sense argument this is a winner. But it's not as simple as that, as any recumbent salesman will tell you. Recumbents have their ups and downs, their strengths and weaknesses. They're not the answer to everything: as ever in the cycling world, it's horses for courses, and the arguments are further complicated by reactions which have little to do with common sense. For many people, and many cyclists, the recumbent bicycle is a concept which seems ever so slightly threatening. Perhaps it is the fear of the unknown. The upright bicycle has developed over the years a certain comforting familiarity: the pleasure of refining the minutiae of frame and components rests on the certainty that the basic design is evolved perfection – indeed, in its own terms, it is. And anyone can ride a bicycle. Then along comes the recumbent. Have all those man-hours been wasted tinkering with a design unchanged since the 1930s? Can I even ride it? What horrible process has transformed our two-wheeled friend into the strange feet-first monstrosity clamouring at the bike-shop door? And why?

Well, the reasons are many

First, comfort. The seated position not only eliminates the problems of saddle (wedgie!) pain, but also takes pressure off the wrists, relaxes the shoulders, removes the strain in the neck, and supports the back. Longer rides become a pleasure not a pain. Many people whose aches and pains have forced them to give up cycling may find that recumbents can put them on the road again.

Second, speed. The 'low-profile' recumbent arrangement should, according to common sense, be faster than the upright. It can be, but the speed advantage is often minimal. What you do get is speed with comfort, without needing to crouch into uncomfortable contortions to minimise air resistance. Fairings and tailboxes (which often form useful, lockable luggage containers) smoothe the airflow and can offer some weather protection. On the flat, into headwinds and downhill these factors can add up to a considerable advantage compared to the upright racer. The 'well-known fact' that recumbents are slow on hills is perhaps true: what is not so often repeated is that overall on a hilly route they may be faster. And is it too obvious to say that it depends on the rider?

The third advantage of recumbents is safety: there is not so far to fall in the event of a spill, and if impact is inevitable, it's the feet not the head out in front. Braking on recumbents can be as sharp as you like, without the danger of going over the bars. By pushing against the seat it is possible to generate higher forces for acceleration than by standing on the pedals of a conventional bike, allowing the recumbent to shoot out of trouble when the brakes are inappropriate. Another little-appreciated advantage is that pedals will not ground when cornering or riding close to a kerb.

Wait, I hear you cry. What about visibility? It's not the bike's safety I worry about, it's whether motorists will see me!

There are two answers to that one. First, it's worth bearing in mind that a lot of bicycle accidents are caused by riders' misjudgements rather than conflict with motorists. Second, just listen to the people who have actually used their recumbents in traffic. They'll often ride a machine which puts them at a height level with or above the motorist, so that eye contact is easily made. The recumbent draws the eye of motorists, unlike a normal bicycle which can so often be 'tuned out' and ignored 'unseen' by the motorist's fume-fogged mind. A recumbent will cut a Ferrari dead for sheer head-turning impact. A partial fairing can also add enormous visibility.

So why aren't we all riding recumbents?

The most obvious reason is ignorance – not many people know about recumbents – and behind the ignorance is history and cycle politics. In 1934, the UCI (the international cycle sport organisation) decided to ban recumbents from official cycle racing, after no less than seven world records (1, 5, 10, 20, 30, 40, 50 km races) and the hour record were shattered by Frenchman Francis Foure on a Velocar recumbent made by George Mochet. Deprived of the oxygen of racing publicity, and with a tiny user-base, the recumbent remained for many years an oddity, on the edge of the cycling world. The UCI ban remains to this day, so recumbents now race outside the mainstream, under the rules of the International Human Powered Vehicle Association, an organisation set up in the 1970s to encourage all human-powered machines without artificial design restrictions.

For racing, it's one or the other; recumbent or upright. Not so for the rest of us! It's recumbent *and* upright for many people: some like hacking around town on a folder or offroad on a mountain bike, then touring at weekends on their recumbent. Others just mix and match; the riding sensations are different and complementary, and both are enjoyable. Recumbents come in all flavours: long or short, two wheels or more. Long-wheelbase recumbents traditionally offer the most comfortable ride and easy handling, and often make exceptional touring machines. The short-wheelbase variety usually feel sharper and more sporty, and comfort may be first-class with suspension. The up-and-coming design for two-wheelers is the medium-wheelbase recumbent: combining the best of both worlds.

Three-wheelers add a whole new dimension: tremendously low gears can be used to crank up hills at leisure, sitting back and watching the scenery, with the option of stopping at any time for a breather. The sure-footed manoeuverability is appealing to many, especially in wet or icy conditions. Three-wheeled stability is also excellent for load-carrying or for use with a fairing. One owner with limited space even finds that the tricycle can be usefully placed in the living room as an extra seat.

There are several newcomers to this year's recumbent section, all with their own story to tell. Most recumbent manufacturers are still enthusiastic, ecologically-aware small companies, and even the biggest make only a few thousand a year. This small-series, labour-intensive production means that they cannot compete on price with the big boys of the upright cycle industry. Recumbents are still premium products.

In Europe, the USA and Australia, public interest in recumbents has grown enormously, fed by press coverage and by the ever-growing number of recumbent enthusiasts on the streets. Even the entrenched cycle press and industry is taking them seriously at last. In time, the recumbent will be just another option for the consumer: taking its proper place as an accepted part of everyday bicycle culture.

In the UK, prices range from £1200, and will vary worldwide.

Cool Breeze UK Ltd

After many years in the British (upright) cycle industry, Tim Elsdale decided to apply his experience to making something very different. He had decided on the prone design even before he heard about previous prone HPV racers, feeling that it is a more natural way to minimise frontal area than some of the very low 'traditional' recumbents. Along with his son Ben, he has covered considerable distances on the Prone Low-Profile, and he reports that some 'very fit racers' have been putting the machine through its paces with some hard riding.

Cool Breeze UK Ltd, 194 Upper Street, Islington, London N1 1RQ, UK. Tel +44 171 704 9273 Fax +44 171 354 9641

Ben and Tim Elsdale

prone low-profile

UK

Prone recumbents have been seen on the HPV race circuits of the world for several years – never in great numbers, but with a dedicated following. It's hard to beat the prone position for unfaired aerodynamics: with minimal frontal area and a smooth profile, these are slippery machines indeed – and with the pedals at the back, the legs don't churn the airflow before it passes over the body. A further advantage is the compact drive system, which uses a standard-length chain with no power-loss through idlers.

The Cool Breeze Prone Low-Profile is, to our knowledge, the first commercially-available prone cycle. It does not pretend to

be anything other than a pure speed machine: it is the sort of bike you'd choose for exhilarating, joy-of-cycling experiences on the open road. With the head out in front and close to the ground, it's more like flying than anything else on wheels.

Careful design provides enough support for comfort and stability, without affecting the rider's breathing. Shoulders and hips rest on carefully-shaped cushions, which can be adjusted fore-and-aft for a precise fit. Hands fall naturally to the handlebar, which is adjustable for reach and angle. Clipless pedals are strongly recommended to keep feet secure.

The Prone Low-Profile frame is made from Reynolds 531 tubing, and is usually equipped with Campagnolo race components, although other groupsets can be fitted on request. Wheels are 26" (577) rear and 24" (520) front, with narrow-section rims. Complete machines weigh around 11kg (24lb).

adagio

How do you give a pothole an inferiority complex? Ignore it and ride over it on your Ostrad. The suspension on these bikes can eat cobbles and sunken drain covers for breakfast, and won't balk at riding over a curb or two for good measure.

It's a design philosophy which puts comfort above speed, and which Ostrad have been refining for more than eight years. Their Adagio (LWB) model epitomises their thinking: the custom anti-dive suspension at the front is matched to the Ostrad rear swing-arm, shared by all bikes in their range. The 120mm (4.7") of travel at the back can be adjusted in five stages for hardness, or the polyurethane shock-absorber can be changed for a softer or harder model, for example when going on tour with a substantial load (carried on the stainless-steel carrier rack, included as standard). The mesh seats can be adjusted for angle, or moved along the frame for leg-length.

Dual-stage transmission provides a tremendous range of gears: a typical setup can cover from 1.2m to 8.0m development (15" to 100"), over a well-spaced set of 40 ratios. All components subject to wear are standard items, so eventual replacement should cause no problems.

The Adagio shares these features with the Ostrad Presto (SWB), which uses AMP front suspension. An 'Avanti' version of the SWB bike with above-seat steering and single-stage Sachs 3x7 transmission is third in the Ostrad line-up.

The same transmission is used on the Janus tandem. The name reflects one advantage of the back-to-back layout: it's like having eyes in the back of your head to warn of approaching traffic. You also have your heads close together for conversation, it's aerodynamic, and the layout gives this tandem a short wheelbase and a turning circle not much wider than a solo bike. It's one of those bikes you have to ride to appreciate.

Ostrad

Ostrad have been turned away from tandem races for riding the recumbent Janus, then banned from recumbent events because it's a tandem. Conventional rules don't seem to fit these enthusiasts from former East Berlin. Ostrad (literally 'East Bike') is a collective: Ecki, Tomas, Ernst, Enrico, Dan and Frank have been designing, producing and marketing recumbents since 1989. They also run the only 'recumbent' cycle shop in Berlin, also specialising in high-quality tourers and city bikes. Visitors can test-ride bikes by arrangement.

Ostrad GmbH, Winsstr. 48, 10405 Berlin, Germany.
Tel +49 30 443 413 93
Fax +49 30 443 413 94
Email OstradGmbH@aol.com
UK: see page 145.

In Germany, prices range from around DM3650 for the Adagio or Avanti, DM3980 for the Presto, and DM8000 for the Janus tandem, depending on equipment. Prices will vary worldwide.

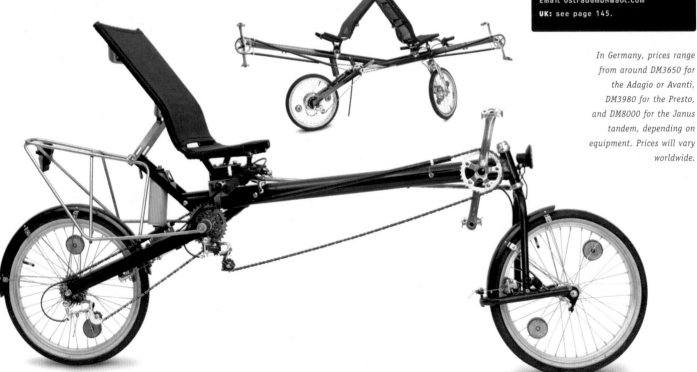

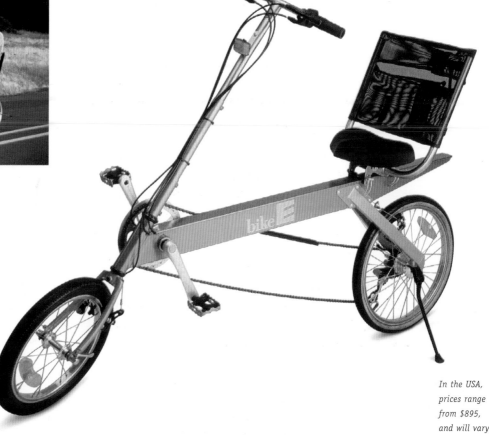

In the USA, prices range from $895, and will vary worldwide

BikeE Corp.

BikeE's inventors bring an impressive array of skills to their products. When he is not trying to overturn cycling orthodoxy, David G. Ullman is Professor of Design and Mechanical Engineering at Oregon State University. Richard Rau has turned his B.Sc. in Automotive Technology to environmentally sustainable transport through being a co-founder of the BikeE Corporation, and Paul Atwood, the third BikeE co-founder, can boast more than 30,000 miles (50,000km) ridden on recumbents. The BikeE is available through bike dealers throughout the USA – or contact BikeE direct. A wide range of accessories are available.

BikeE Corp., 5460 SW Philomath Boulevard, Corvallis, 97333-1039 Oregon, USA.
Tel +1 541 754 9747
Fax +1 541 753 8004
Email BikeEvol@aol.com

bikeE

USA

The BikeE wants to do for recumbents what the Model T Ford did for cars – make them popular, and the stuff of everyday transport. The BikeE can have you cycling in seated comfort for the price of a good conventional bicycle.

The BikeE's virtues stem not just from its low cost, but from the fact that it is a remarkably rider-friendly machine – it was designed to bring recumbents to the masses. The idea was that a rider would feel at home from the first ride, comfortable in the seat and holding ergonomic flat, above-the-leg handlebars. The BikeE's simple aluminium spine holds cro-moly forks with 16"

(359) front and 20" (406) rear wheels. Pannier racks are slung underneath the seat, with the load's centre of gravity kept low. The running gear is easy-to-use Sachs 3x7 for more ambitious riders, or Super-7 hub gears for commuting. The gears are worked by twistgrip shifters, reflecting BikeE's philosophy that recumbents should not be niche products, but accessible and low-maintenance. Cantilever braking means they're also safe.

Unlike the Model T, the BikeE can also be bought in red, blue and violet. Given the BikeE's departure from orthodox recumbent design, the BikeE team are reluctant to use the 'R'-word. They want the machine to take recumbents out of obscurity and into mainstream cycling, intending its low cost and acclaimed rider-friendliness to prise upright cyclists from their uncomfortable perches.

rubicon

Ray Watering

'No turning back' is the Rubicon slogan – and one year on since their last appearance in Encycleopedia, progress has been strictly forwards. 'A 12-month evolution' was how Rubicon 'test-pilot' Peter Cox describes it: he has been working with Rubicon founder Ray Watering to keep up the design momentum, 'trying to break' a Rubicon with some seriously strenuous testing in the Lake District of England. He is happy to report that he failed.

One of the more positive fruits of his labours is a completely revised steering geometry. It boasts two settings – very direct steering for round town, or a more stable setup for those longer, faster journeys. Rearranging the steering tie-rods to change the setting takes just seconds.

The seat has evolved too: the fibreglass shell has been subtly reshaped, and water-bottle mounts are integrated onto the back, within easy reach. There's also now a touring kit comprising mudguards, carrier rack and panniers, and a Zzipper front fairing is optional.

The 18" front wheels have been changed to 20", allowing a wider choice of tyres. The Hope disk brakes are the latest redesigned and improved version, and are applied equally by a single lever on the joystick-style control column. Remarkably low lever pressure is enough to provide stopping power to the limits of the tyres' adhesion.

Stopping's not the point, though. Fly the Rubicon and you won't want to stop, let alone turn back. Push into the pedals and the frame's stiff enough to kick you forwards, the road rushes up to meet you, and you flick up the gears into a corner, daring a wheel to lift. This is what recumbent triking is all about: once you're bitten, there's no turning back!

Extreme Engineering Ltd

Stainless steel does not corrode, welds well, and needs no expensive paint job to look good. It can even be recycled, and is widely used in the food industry, where 'hose-down' equipment is de rigeur. When Ray Watering caught the recumbent trike bug and decided to build his own, stainless steel was the natural choice. He's a long-time engineer and manager in the food business, and perhaps the design was also influenced by his other sport: flying microlight aircraft. He's not the first to find that the thrills of cycling are a perfect match for the thrills of aviation.

Extreme Engineering Ltd,
14 Fairways, Toft, Bourne,
Lincolnshire PE10 OBS, UK.
Tel/Fax +44 1778 590 339
USA: see p.145

In the UK, prices range from £2500, and vary greatly worldwide

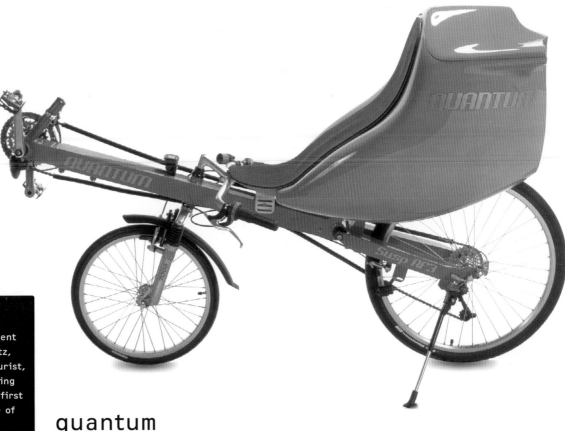

In Germany, prices range from DM1920 for a frameset, or from DM2720 for complete machines. Prices will vary worldwide.

Arved Klütz

Damaged wrists and student poverty drove Arved Klütz, an enthusiastic cycle tourist, to experiment with building his own recumbents. His first attempt had a wheelbase of around two metres: and manoeuvring around town was, he says, a challenge. Further prototypes were developed, with the wheelbase becoming shorter and the construction more sophisticated as Arved completed his degree course in mechanical engineering. He put his metalcraft business on the back-burner, and began series production of the Quantum. He now looks forward to expanding his dealer network. Visitors are welcome to visit his shop in Elmshorn for test-rides or weekend hire.

Arved Klütz, Steinstr. 5, 25364 Hornerkirchen, Germany. Tel +49 4121 483898 Fax +49 4121 483899

quantum

GERMANY

When your suspension bearing wears out half-way across India, it's not good news if the only possible replacement is custom-built in a German workshop. It's the same when you rely on your bike for commuting – you want to be able to go to any standard bike shop, get a replacement on the spot, have it fitted with standard tools, and be on your way. That's what the Quantum is all about: standardisation.

Arved Klütz, manufacturer of the Quantum, points out that everything apart from the frame, chain tubes and seat mounts is a standard cycle component. Even the seat has its place in the philosophy of interchangeability: any rigid recumbent seat can be fitted to the Quantum. In a clever bit of design, the seat fixing plates allow quick adjustment of seat height (55 to 70cm) and angle (35-55°) – the lower seat height settings will be particularly welcome for smaller riders. A mesh seat is also available, as is an above-seat steering option.

The TIG-welded aluminium frame is powder-coated, adjusts for length to fit riders from 1.5m (4'11") tall, and has fixings for bottle-cages, carrier racks and the optional front or rear fairings. The suspension comes in three levels of hardness, and there is an optional 'fine-tuner' kit. The pivot for the suspension is a standard cartridge bottom-bracket unit. Wheels are 20" (406) front and 26" (559) or 28" (622) rear. The Quantum is available with any reasonable choice of components, or as a frameset.

When Arved Klütz designed the Quantum, he didn't want to create a "high-tech experiment, which would be shown as a curiosity in the bike shop window, admired and unridden" – he wanted to make a bike which he would see in daily use: sport, commuting, shopping, touring and more. And it had to be fun!

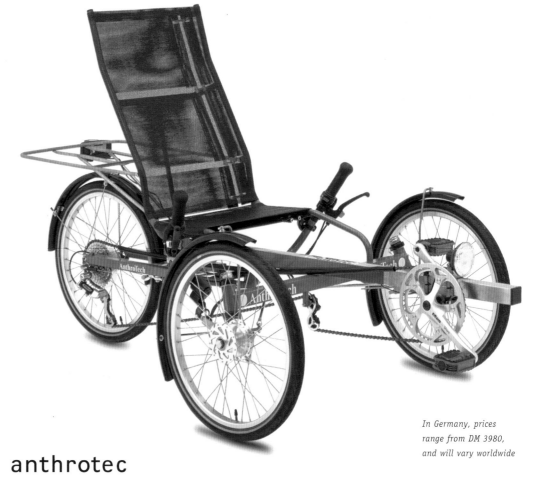

In Germany, prices range from DM 3980, and will vary worldwide

anthrotec

AnthroTech

The AnthroTech team of Matthias Krauß and Walter Scheidt are happy to have their hands full keeping up with demand. The AnthroTech has been in production since 1993, and almost all the manufacturing is done in their own workshop, aside from the powder-coating. They've hardly needed to advertise over the years: ecologically-minded cyclists recognise the practicality of the AnthroTech, often seeing it as a motor-car alternative. Long hours in the workshop, though, mean that Matthias and Walter have had little time to pursue their long-term aim: the development of a full fairing.

AnthroTech Leichtfahrzeugtechnik GmbH i.G., Rothenbergstr. 7, 90542 Eckental-Frohnhof, Germany.
Tel +49 9126 288 644
Fax +49 9126 288 321

GERMANY

When snow and ice cover the streets, most bicyclists wisely go into winter hibernation. This is when the AnthroTech comes into its own. With full mudguards, carrier and lighting fitted as standard, this is a machine for all seasons, and it remains reassuringly stable whatever the conditions. This makes it great for carrying a child, for example. There's plenty of room for this or other valuable cargoes on the large carrier rack behind the seat, and both load and rider benefit from the elastomer rear suspension.

Riders of all sizes and ages feel comfortable on the AnthroTech, and the gearing gives plenty of low ratios. You can decide between the Sachs 3x7 system, or a conventional 21-speed derailleur setup. Clothing is protected by a plastic tube on the top chain run.

The seating position is relatively high for a recumbent tricycle, so that the rider's eyes are level with those of car drivers. The steering geometry isolates the handlebars from road shock and gives light, controlled handling, and the balanced drum brakes on the front 20" wheels give all-weather stopping power.

The frame is made of steel, sandblasted and powder-coated, and the main boom, carrier and bottom-bracket housing are all stainless steel. The position of the bottom-bracket can be quickly adjusted for leg-length without having to alter the length of the chain – thanks to a second tensioner below the cross-beam. The AnthroTech weighs around 22.5kg.

Its carrying capacity makes it a fine tourer, and the carrier at the back could easily take a full expedition rucksack and tent. The AnthroTech uses mostly standard cycle components, so finding spares away from home is usually no problem.

Matthias Krauß and Walter Scheidt

lepus

GERMANY

'Lepus' means 'hare' in Latin, and in German, a hare is 'Hase'. Marec Hase seems to have a flair for naming his products – his 'Periscop' upright/recumbent tandem appeared in last year's Encycleopedia.

The Lepus is a wonderfully practical replacement for the car in town or for touring. Although it's popular with disabled riders or those with balance problems, this is not its main purpose. It's a comfortable, practical vehicle for life.

The weight is relatively low for such a trike (22kg fully-equipped). It's no speed machine, but lolloping along on the Lepus is a surprisingly sporty experience. The handling is stable yet responsive, and the brakes are superb. The seating position is high enough to give an imposing road presence and a clear view in traffic without sacrificing cornering ability, and the steering didn't seem to be affected as we took 20kg or so of Encycleopedias across York in the rear carrier. Two-stage, 21-speed gearing takes care of hills.

When you reach your destination, two other aspects of the design become apparent. First, the width is carefully calculated to pass through a standard 90cm doorway. Then, the whole rear end pivots underneath (the same motion which provides suspension), and the seat folds down, reducing the Lepus to a fraction of its original size. The process is quick and easy and requires no tools. It's possible to pack a Lepus right down to 120cm x 85cm x 66cm.

The Lepus fits any rider from 1.3 to 2.0m tall, thanks to the telescopic boom. 5cm of adjustment either way is possible without altering the chain length. You can also adjust the angle of the seat and the position of the handlebars.

The Lepus is the much-evolved and improved descendent of the Hase 'Easy-Glider', which appeared two years ago in Encycleopedia. What will follow the hare on the evolutionary ladder? Maybe we'll find out next year.

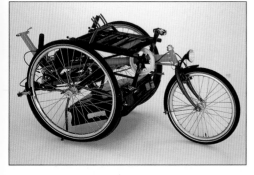

In Germany, prices range from DM5050 and vary greatly worldwide.

Firma Marec Hase

Marec Hase's other main products are the Periscop – a tandem with the recumbent stoker at the front and an upright captain at the rear, and the 'Nimbus' two-wheeled recumbent. He continues to work closely with organisations for the disabled, undertaking a lot of custom-building, and providing a wide range of specialised equipment to adapt his machines for those with special needs.
Marec also works with the industrial testing company EFBe to offer a laboratory testing service to manufacturers and importers (static, dynamic and fatigue tests to DIN standards) for frames and forks in his factory in Bochum.

Firma Marec Hase, Karl-Friedrich-Str. 88, 44795 Bochum, Germany.
Tel +49 234 946 9050
Fax +49 234 946 9099

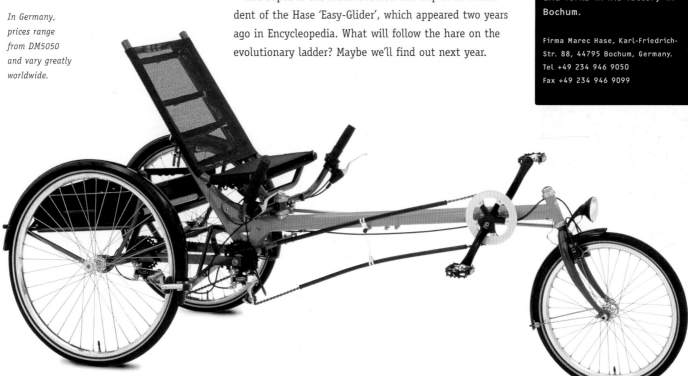

advanta SR-1

Clive Buckler

Somewhere between an upright bike with its height and handling and a recumbent with its comfort and power lies the perfect bicycle. Descended from the Northern California 'polo bikes' of the late 1980s, the Advanta SR-1 is designed to approach this ideal. It's an all-purpose 14kg bike which is great fun to ride.

The SR-1 is longer and lower than its polo-playing predecessors, still agile but more stable. The frameset is made of 4130 chromoly tubing, finished in black and silver powder coat. The Sachs 3x7 transmission combines a three-speed hub gear and a seven-speed derailleur cassette. The 26" rear wheel is stopped by a Dia-Compe Bigdog calliper brake, and a Sachs drum brake graces the 16" front wheel, which is positioned well clear of the rider's heels.

The dual-density foam seat is about 85cm above the ground, for good visibility on crowded streets. The seat back adjusts through 45 degrees, even while riding, offering a forward position for power climbing or a laid-back position for cruising. Brake levers and twist grip shifters on the handlebar ends give good control and leverage. Dismounts are easy and safe: you simply step forward off the seat. One rider, using an earlier version with a quick-release front wheel, forgot to close the lever, and simply found himself dumped to his feet, chasing the runaway wheel down the street!

Learning to ride the Advanta takes about two minutes. 'Flight training' is how the designer describes it. "People call it the closest thing to flying on two wheels", he says, "And a lot of pilots love it."

Coming soon is an Advanta SR-2 for tall people and a SR-3 for smaller cyclists.

Ride-Rite Bicycles Inc.

Clive Ernest Buckler (hence 'Ernie') is a 55-year-old machine designer from Veradale, Washington, who has spent more than 12 years developing the Advanta SR-1. After working through various long and low designs, he began to see the potential of high-seat, medium-wheelbase designs. Five basic designs and numerous prototypes later, he patented the present curved-frame model in 1994, and started Ride-Rite Bicycles, Inc. with four partners in 1995. Advanta bicycles are ordered direct or through shops, and are then shipped to the customer's local bike shop for assembly and final adjustments.

Ride-Rite Bicycles Inc., 6322 114th Avenue S.E., Bellevue, Washington 98006 USA.
Tel +1 206 228 8006
Fax +1 206 271 4017
Email Bob_Riley@msn.com
Website http://www.BikeRoute.com/RideRite.htm
Canada: see page 145

In the USA, prices range from $1495 plus shipping, and will vary greatly worldwide

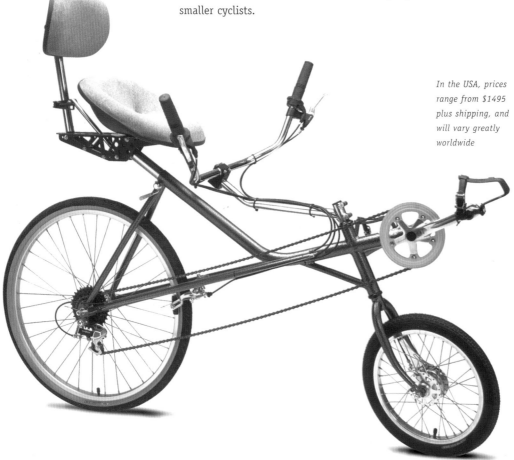

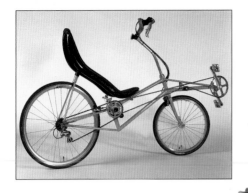

In Germany, framesets cost from DM1000 (Horizont-swing) or DM1200 (Horizont-fast), and complete bikes cost from DM 2800 (Horizont-swing) or DM4800 (Horizont-fast, with Shimano 600). Prices will vary greatly worldwide.

horizont-swing, horizont-fast

GERMANY

Zweirad & Zukunft

Zweirad & Zukunft ('Two-wheelers for the Future') began in 1990, after seven years as part of the Altona Training Workshop, a charitable organisation for youth training and education. At any time, Z & Z train twenty or so apprentice cycle mechanics on a three and a half year course, ending with qualification for nationally-recognised Journeyman status. The students play an enthusiastic part in the development of the recumbents, and particularly enjoy successful participation in international solar-bike races and HPV events. An associated cycle shop distinguishes itself by providing two 'self-service' workstands, where, for a small sum, customers can use the shop's tools to maintain their own machines.

Zweirad und Zukunft, Gauss Str. 19, 22765 Hamburg, Germany.
Tel +49 40 395 285
Fax +49 40 3902 302

Suspension experts, bred on cars or motorcycles, usually insist that the key to high performance is to minimise unsprung mass – so they suspend the wheels. When it comes to the bicycle, which weighs just a fraction of the rider's own weight, priorities are changed because the complication and weight of the suspension mechanism also make a difference. Zweirad & Zukunft threw away the rulebook and suspended the rider, ending up with a comfortable, high-performance recumbent weighing just 15kg.

The Horizont-swing seat is cushioned by 65mm of suspension travel, and the integral luggage-carrier is part of the suspended beam. The seat itself is highly-adjustable: both the angle and position of the various supports can be altered. With the fore-and-aft adjustment, three frame sizes suffice to fit anyone 1.65 to 1.9m tall. The underseat steering is likewise adjustable. Frames are constructed from Mannesmann cro-moly tubing, and are powder-coated. Wheels are 20" (406) front and 26" (559) rear.

Pare down the Horizont-swing by removing the suspension and tune it for competition, and you have the Horizont-fast. An ovalised top-tube for stiffness and a Columbus fork bring the frame weight to 3.0kg – and complete bikes can be under 10kg. The frame and forks are equipped with braze-ons for a full racing bike component groupset.

The fibre-glass seat is pivoted at the front, and supported by an elastomer spring at the rear, taking out the usual harshness of thin, high-pressure 20" (406) and 26" (571) racing tyres. The ultra-narrow handlebars bring significant aerodynamic advantages – vital for success in the HPV races for which the Horizont-fast is designed. As a fitting finale to its first season, Peter from the Z & Z team won the drag race at the 1996 German HPV Championships in Blenhorst last year, riding, of course, a Horizont-fast.

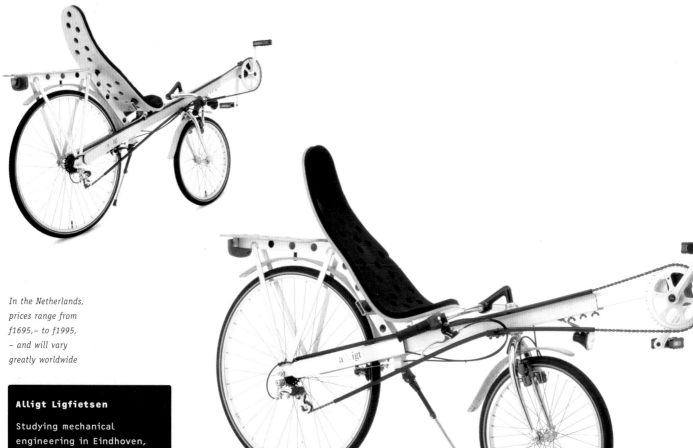

In the Netherlands, prices range from f1695,– to f1995, – and will vary greatly worldwide

Alligt Ligfietsen

Studying mechanical engineering in Eindhoven, Leo Visscher also found time to develop his own recumbent – and used the prototypes as his everyday transport. Graduating in 1994, he set up the Alligt company with the enthusiastic support of his family.

Plans for 1997 include a child's recumbent and a low-rider and then for the future, a transporter bike. Leo estimates that recumbents will capture about 5-20% of bike sales in all market segments in the Netherlands, but admits that this won't happen for some years yet.

Alligt Ligfietsen, Postbus 6494, 5600 HL Eindhoven, Netherlands. Tel/Fax +31 40 251 5728

Leo Visscher

alligt classic

NETHERLANDS

Alligt's design philosophy is to combine daily practicality with simplicity of form – no easy task when you consider all the extra accessories that a true everyday bike needs. The Alligt solution is to use elegant and durable curved wooden fittings, married to a simple aluminium frame. The result is a very usable bike that has real class.

The Alligt's appearance has been drawing the crowds at cycle shows for several years now, but only recently has it been on sale in sufficient numbers for its good handling to be widely appreciated. The mid-height seat (60cm off the road) gives the kind of stability and visibility which you need in urban traffic. It's well thought-out, right down to the nylon chain tubes which protect the rider's clothing.

There are three standard specification levels available – the Basic, Modern and the Classic, although Alligt will happily tailor bikes to an individual customer's requirements. Gearing is usually provided by Sachs, using twistgrip levers, and the 20" front wheel has hydraulic braking as standard. A strong carrier is integrated into the frame above the 28" rear wheel, and the whole frame carries a five-year guarantee. Weight is around 14-17kg, depending on equipment.

The Alligt isn't just an urban runaround – it also makes a fine touring machine. Custom-made luggage bags fit neatly over the rear carrier. The foam seat is extremely comfortable and waterproof. One of the Alligt team rode the bike pictured here through the rain from the Alligt factory in Eindhoven to us in York – and still came in smiling.

tandem touring trike

Ian Sims

Speed and sociability are the twin pleasures offered by Ian Sims' Greenspeed Tandem Touring Trike (TTT). With little more aero-drag than a solo, yet twice the power, this machine can fly. For many, though, speed is not the main issue – wonderful possibilities are opened up thanks to the versatility of that second seat. It can transport a child, a second adult, empower a disabled rider, or even carry a week's shopping. About six inches of adjustment are available for each pedaller, and the rear position can be adjusted for children.

Tourers need wide gears, and the TTT serves them up in plenty, providing up to 72 speeds from 15 to 125 inches, from a menu of three chainrings, eight sprockets and the Sachs 3x7 hub gear. Stress on the transmission is halved with the cranks set 90° out of phase. Two perennial tandem headaches – starting and stopping, and stoker comfort – are also overcome in fine style. Sitting comfortably, you don't even take your feet off the pedals as you draw to a standstill.

Fast cornering and braking are a delight: hydraulic disk brakes in 20" wheels give tremendous stopping power, and the centre-point steering combines pin-point accuracy with stability. The 7.3m turning circle is less than the width of most roads.

The TTT frame is made from Reynolds 531 tubing. All-up weight is around 29kg, length is 3.5m and the track is 90cm. For riders under 183cm tall, the length and weight can be slightly reduced.

Greenspeed are now working with composites specialist Don Elliot on a fairing for their solo recumbent trike – Ian Sims says that this is the only way that he will be able to keep up with his 25 year old son.

In Australia prices range from A$6000, and vary greatly worldwide

Greenspeed

Ian Sims is an Internet enthusiast. The Greenspeed World Wide Web site is an instant alternative to sending paper catalogues around the world. The medium allows the full range of Greenspeed's activities to be detailed – from their special needs vehicles to the latest product developments – alongside comments from customers and the press. Another benefit is cheap and easy dialogue via e-mail with owners around the world: a great source of feedback and encouragement for the Greenspeed team.

Greenspeed, 69 Mountain Gate Drive, Ferntree Gully, VIC 3156, Australia.
Tel +61 3 9758 5541
Fax +61 3 9752 4115
Email greenshp@ozemail.com.au
Website http://www.ihpva.org/com/Greenspeed/

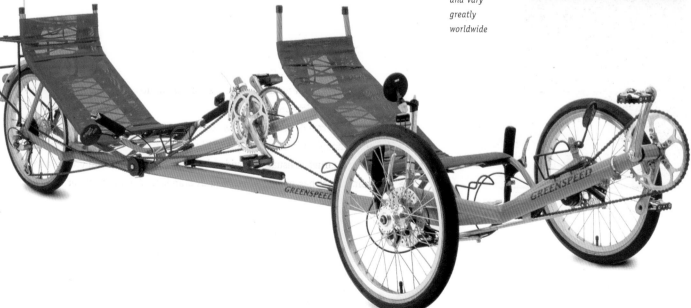

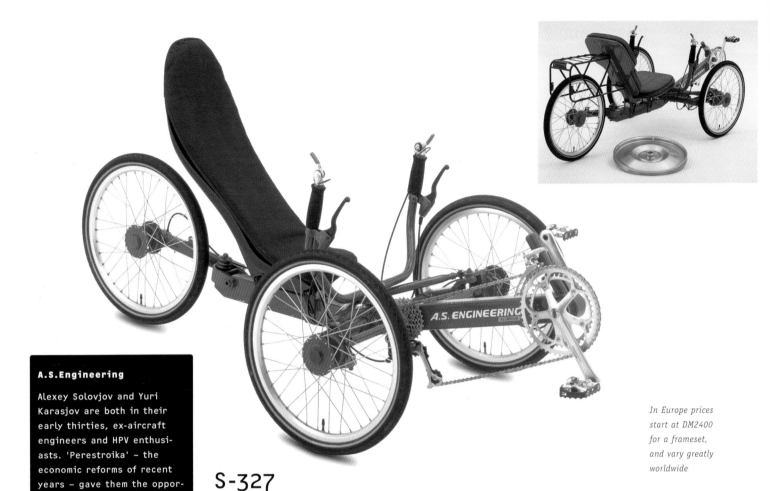

*In Europe prices
start at DM2400
for a frameset,
and vary greatly
worldwide*

S-327

RUSSIA

A.S.Engineering

Alexey Solovjov and Yuri Karasjov are both in their early thirties, ex-aircraft engineers and HPV enthusiasts. 'Perestroika' – the economic reforms of recent years – gave them the opportunity to start their own business as the aviation and defence industries of Russia collapsed around them.
A.S. Engineering normally supply framesets (the frame, all non-standard parts and a special toolkit) for the S-327, but their agents can also supply complete machines.

A.S. Engineering, c/o TNT Mailfast, MOW/MOW/10012/14, P.O. Box 66, Hounslow TW5 9 RT, United Kingdom. Fax +7 095 430 3897
Email ykpro@aha.ru
Germany, Benelux, Denmark: Mark Salman Tel/Fax +31 23 53 87 015;
Canada: Bob Simons Fax +1 604 537 4221. Full details page 145

Aircraft aluminium (80%) and titanium (15%) make up most of the S-327. Perhaps the final 5% is pure inspiration. The designers clearly started with no preconceptions, for the description of this trike reads like a catalogue of invention. First and most obviously, the drive is to the 20" front wheels, without a differential but with freewheels in the hubs – which also house the custom-built hydraulic drum brakes. One advantage is that a standard chain and transmission can be used, and another is excellent traction on wet, frozen or loose surfaces.

At the back, the monoblade suspension uses an inverted design, and there's even the option of an aluminium disk wheel for extra durability and style. As at the front, the hydraulic hub brake is integrated with the frame. The brakes are compatible with the popular Magura brake levers, and a parking brake has not been forgotten.

The seat (available in two designs) slides along the main boom to cater for riders from 160-200cm tall, and is fixed by quick-release wedge locks. A carrier can be supplied to attach to the rear of the seat, with 40kg capacity.

According to the designers, the frameset is not designed to be as light as possible, but to be ultimately reliable and strong, and reasonably priced. The frameset weighs 11kg, and when built into a complete machine, the S-327 weighs around 17.5kg.

A customer in the Black Forest in Germany told us that he finds the S-327 wonderful in the winter snow: and recommends it highly both for everyday use and touring. According to him, it is only when climbing steeply through tight curves that the front-wheel drive pulls a little at the steering. We found another advantage of this arrangement: there are no noisy idler pulleys to disturb the calm as you pedal.

Yuri Karasjov and Alexei Solovjov

burrows windcheetah

UK

There is something magical about the Windcheetah which fascinates children, and brings out the child in a good few adult owners. There can be few examples of such a serious, purposeful machine evoking so much innocent pleasure and public admiration. Everyone can see that it's just great fun.

The Windcheetah was designed by Mike Burrows in the early '80s, and was originally intended as a training aid for HPV record attempts and for racing. It has since become a cult machine. It's still raced, bare or in a fairing, and is still on the cutting edge: a fully-faired 'works' machine set the British 'End-to-End' record from Lands End to John O'Groats at 41 hours and 4 minutes. The same rider, Andy Wilkinson, had set the previous record a few years earlier on a conventional bike – four hours slower.

The Windcheetah is not just about speed. The demand for touring and commuting accessories has been considerable, and the manufacturers have responded with a 'touring pack' custom-made to fit the machine. True to the spirit of the design, mudguards are in carbon-Kevlar, the rack does not affect the ability to mend a puncture with the rear wheel still on the bike, and the panniers are custom-made by specialists Carradice. New for this year are also a redesigned joystick yoke, a one-piece aluminium rear axle, and a recumbent-specific chainset and bottom-bracket developed with drivetrain specialists Middleburn.

Changing a classic can be a risky business. Seat of the Pants Company director Bob Dixon treads carefully, and works closely with the Windcheetah's original designer, Mike Burrows. So far, even the staunchest aficionados of the Windcheetah recognise that it's in safe hands.

The Seat of the Pants Company

The aptly-named Seat of the Pants Company took over production of the Windcheetah from Mike Burrows about three years ago, freeing him for other work. They also produce three other remarkable products: the Pickup, the Velocita and the Windcheetah Carbon Monocoque. You'll find them all in this Encycleopedia. Plans include a fairing for the Windcheetah, further record attempts, and evolution of the design to take advantage of new materials. All this is happening alongside the main production process, which has now been brought fully in-house. Exports have been growing steadily, and German and American dealer networks are now firmly established.

The Seat of the Pants Company, Unit LKR4, L&M Business Park, Norman Road, Altrincham, Cheshire WA14 4ES, UK. Tel +44 161 928 5575 Fax +44 161 928 5585 Email bobdixon@seatofthepants. u-net.com
Germany, USA, Canada: see page 145

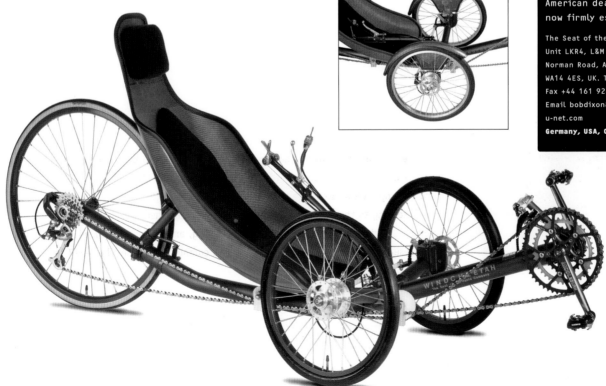

In the UK, prices range from about £2800, and vary greatly worldwide

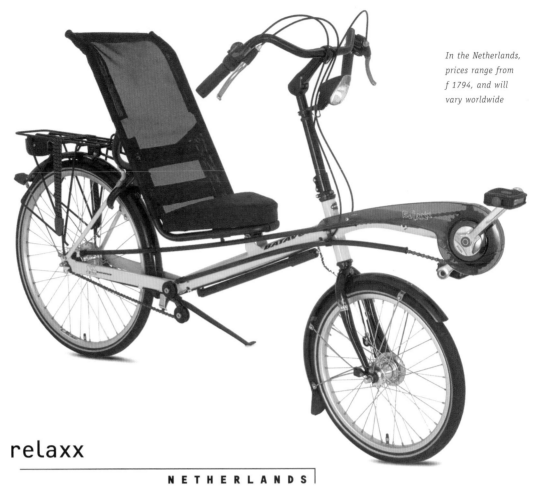

In the Netherlands, prices range from f 1794, and will vary worldwide

Batavus

The Relaxx is not the only innovation from Batavus. The 'Madison' is a city bike with a difference, making a radical departure from the diamond frame, and offering suspension and a low step-over with no compromise on stiffness. Equipped with Nexus components and full all-weather equipment, it's a very covetable bike for round town.

Batavus manufacture a wide range of cycles: children's bikes to mountain bikes, racers to roadsters. They're a major Dutch employer, major sport sponsors (not just in cycling), and have a range of schemes to help employers get their workers on bicycles.

Batavus, Industrieweg 4, 8444 AR Heerenveen, Netherlands.
Tel +31 513 63 8999
Fax +31 513 63 8262
Email info@batavus.com
Website http://www.batavus.com

relaxx

NETHERLANDS

The traditional roadster, with upright riding position and low-maintenance mechanics, is a much-loved part of everyday Dutch life – so it's no surprise that the relaxed cycling culture of Holland has given birth to the world's first production recumbent from a mainstream cycle manufacturer.

Nevertheless, it takes some imagination and boldness to be the first. Batavus have made that leap of faith, believing that only through innovation and open-mindedness can they stay ahead of the game. They brought in Johann Vrielink of Flevobike to bring his decades of recumbent experience to the design – and the result is a well-thought-out recumbent with no nasty surprises. It's perfect for the many thousands who will rely on the Relaxx for their first recumbent experience.

The Batavus Relaxx is a wonderfully easy ride – first-time riders need have no worries about stability. Just as on a traditional roadster, the rider's clothes are protected from the chain, and full, practical, everyday equipment is provided.

The seven-speed Shimano hub gearing is more than adequate for Dutch terrain, and allows a gear-change when you've had to stop or slow down on a hill – it's harder to change a derailleur gear in these circumstances. Nexus roller-brakes stop well in all conditions. 'Anti-Slip' pedals, puncture-resistant Vredestein tyres, mudguards, rear carrier, stand, an adjustable stem and built-in AXA lock complete the equipment. The frame adjusts to fit riders from 1.65m (5' 5") to 2.00m (6' 7") tall, and the solid build inspires confidence.

Batavus in Holland, Hercules in Germany and Dawes in the UK are all part of Atag Cycle Group, a Dutch cycling conglomerate with big plans for the Relaxx. Versions of the bike have joined the ranges of all of these companies, spreading the message across Europe that practical recumbents are credible and profitable, not exotica to be left to the specialists. That's the way it should be.

TranSport

AUSTRIA

Ergonomics is the art of making you comfortable, and the TranSport brings serious comfort, as well as lots of fun, to the task of load-carrying – if you're doing deliveries all day, it's nice not to be saddlesore as well as weary.

This is a bike with a seat to savour. The oil-damped shock absorber evens out bumps and vibration, and the wipe-clean foam plastic is formed to offer good back support. The seating position is quite high, for stability and visibility, and the seat can be adjusted to fit riders from 1.6m (5'3") to 1.9m (6'3") tall. Because it slides at an angle, shorter riders also have a lower seat, so it's easy to put a foot down. Mudguards, chainwheel protector and plastic chain tubes all help keep the rider clean. Full dynamo lighting is provided as standard.

The TranSport can accommodate loads up to around 50kg (110lb), and the loading platform is spacious enough for standard packing crates with room to spare. Placing the load low down ensures that the additional weight is evenly distributed, and has little effect on handling. The frame provides plenty of attachment points for strapping the load down, and the loaded bike remains compact and manoeuvrable through traffic.

Braking is provided by V-Brake type cantilevers on both 20" front and 26" rear wheels. The 3x7 Sachs gearing gives a good range of ratios, and the three 'hub' ratios can be selected even at a standstill: excellent for hill starts or heavy loads. Most other components are from the Sachs 3000 range. The TranSport is made from powder-coated precision chromoly tubing, with some parts of 'INOX' steel. The complete machine weighs around 22kg (49lb).

The TranSport is not intended just for serious courier duty: as an every-day bicycle it is a comfortable and very practical vehicle. For storage or transport, stem and seat assembly detach in seconds.

Paris Maderna

Young Austrian designer Paris Maderna has always had a fondness for bicycles, and with his father Alfons, he produces two machines. One is the TranSport, and the other is the Maderna City Scooter: a young-at-heart pedal-powered scooter for short distances in town, folding in seconds to a tiny package. It's like a mini bike without a saddle - fun and practical, yet carrying the message that small is beauti-ful, and that it is through simple and engaging solu-tions, rather than big-money projects, that we may all achieve a saner society. The MCS and TranSport are Paris Maderna's contribution.

Paris Maderna GmbH, Zeltgasse 12, A-1080 Wien, Austria.
Tel +43 1403 0158
Fax +43 1403 01584

In Austria, prices range from 15900 Schillings (DM 2290), and will vary worldwide

linear tandem

Putting two riders in line has aerodynamic advantages, but it can mean a very long bike. 'In-line' tandem designs are wonderful for stability and comfort, and their manoeuvrability can often surprise newcomers to the genre. With the front wheel tucked in below the captain – giving a wheelbase of just 1.78m (72") – the Linear Tandem brings all these on-road benefits, yet its compact design makes for easier transportation and storage. The folding rear end tucks under the frame to reduce length even further. The bike is then about as long as a long-wheelbase solo recumbent.

Linear's proprietary aluminium extrusion process is the work of Dirk Kann, who founded Linear in 1983. All components are bolted, clamped, or riveted to the single, anodised aluminium I-beam. The simplicity of this construction brings the weight down to only 21kg (47lb), but gives enough strength to support up to 220kg (500lb) of humanity. The aluminium-framed mesh seats are designed to provide lumbar support and to keep the back cool. Each seat has about 16cm (6") of adjustment to fit anyone 1.57 to 1.88m (5'2" to 6'2") tall. The seats fold forward for transportation.

Equipment can be chosen to suit the customer, and framesets are also available. Linears can be fitted with mudguards and carrier racks for touring or commuting, and a specially-designed Zzipper fairing is available.

Linears are among the most popular recumbents in North America. Their recumbents use standard fittings and components, and wheels are 20" (406) front and 26" (559) rear. The manufacturers produce a special tool to hold their machines in any bike shop's workstand, so that even the mechanic is comfortable.

Linear

Steve Hansel joined Linear in 1986, when it was a division of Kann Manufacturing Co., and in 1991 he bought the company and its proprietary frame extrusion technology. Linear's goal for 1996 was to ship 2000 bikes, and their success has encouraged them to build up a network of dedicated retailers for sales and service of recumbents. Their model range now includes the short-wheelbase Sonic, as well as the original long-wheelbase Linear, which remains their most popular product. The newest Linear is their version of the increasingly popular medium-wheelbase recumbent design. We hope to feature it in the next Encycleopedia.

Linear Manufacturing Inc., 32744 Kestrel Avenue, Guttenberg, Iowa 52052 USA.
Tel +1 319 252 1637
Fax +1 319 252 3305

In the USA, prices range from $2800 for the tandem, or from $1200 for a solo Linear. Prices will vary worldwide

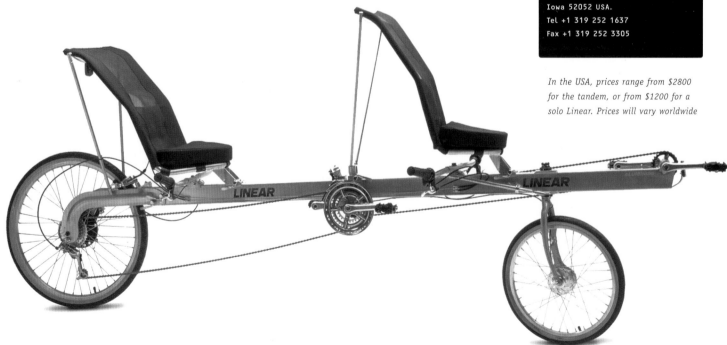

In Germany, prices range from DM5600 to around DM6990, and will vary worldwide

emotion three

GERMANY

Showme Products

Production of the Emotion Three is a dream come true for Christian Schumacher. Since his schooldays he has experimented with four-wheel HPVs, and development of the first Emotion Three began in 1991. Now 32, he produces the machines painstakingly by hand. For adaptations for disabled riders, he works closely with Berthold Müller-Schoell, who has long experience in the wheelchair industry. Showme Products also offer their modified hub-brakes for HPV-builders, with the axle supported on one side only.

Showme Products, Christian Schumacher GmbH, Bahnhofstr. 2, D-84088 Neufahrn i. NB, Germany.
Tel +49 8773 7399
Fax +49 8773 91 02 81

Christian Schumacher

Two wheels per rider: that's how most of the cycling world travels. Only a very few, though, ride sociable recumbent quadricycles. Sitting side-by-side as you ride is a special pleasure: you can see each other's faces, talk naturally, even hold hands as you travel. Couples, children with parents, or anyone riding with a disabled, blind or weaker rider all appreciate the intimacy and security of this arrangement.

It's also great fun. The Emotion Three is a stable ride, and corners with gusto. The long wheelbase evens out the bumps, and with two riders the 45kg machine can keep up a good speed. Each rider has an independent Sachs 3x7 transmission, with two chainrings providing extra ratios – you change rings by grasping the plastic chain-tube and guiding the chain over by hand. It's a neat arrangement which is easy to use, and saves weight and complication.

Balanced, hydraulically-operated Sachs drum brakes in the 20" (406) front wheels do the stopping, with an additional Magura rim-brake on the driver's side rear wheel (also 20"). The seats on the Emotion Three adjust in seconds over a very wide range, to suit everyone from small children to those up to around 1.9m (6'3") tall. Special seats for disabled riders, or for the very tall, are available on request, as is hand-crank drive on the passenger side.

The space behind the riders can accommodate a child seat, or a third full-sized seat can be fitted for pedal-powered weddings and similar events. A capacious basket or lockable box could also be placed here. A further large luggage basket can be fitted between the front wheels. Other options include a large advertising space above the vehicle and a 'rollover' roof. Overall length is 2.6m and width 1.23m.

In the UK, frameset prices range from £1095, and will vary worldwide

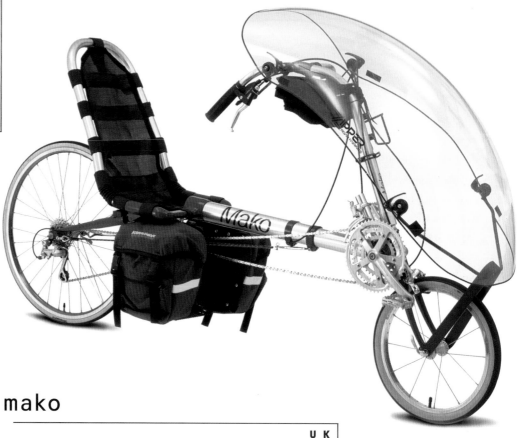

Thorpe Consulting

When the US magazine Popular Science featured the record-breaking Vector HPV, they introduced engineers around the world to the potential of recumbent cycling. Among those inspired was Richard Thorpe, then studying mechanical engineering at Boston University. His first recumbent was an elegant CNC-machined short-wheelbase machine with two riding positions, and this was followed by a fully-suspended version. Four years later, the Mako was born – with the help of the powerful computer-aided design techniques which Richard uses in his professional life as an engineering graphics consultant.

Thorpe Consulting, PO Box 250, Ruislip, Middlesex, HA4 8UU, UK.
Tel +44 0976 800 682
Email flashgd@msn.com
USA: Angle Tech, 318 N. Hiwy 67, Woodland Park, CO 80863, USA.
Tel/Fax +1 719 687 7475.
Email anglezoom@aol.com

Richard Thorpe

mako

UK

Craftsmanship in the finest tradition lives on in Richard Thorpe's workshop, where he builds the far-from-traditional Mako from raw tubes and castings. Richard carries out almost all of the machining processes himself – and, he says, the hours he spends in the workshop are fully justified by the pure satisfaction of creating this clean-lined, purposeful bicycle. He points out that even with the fairing, the Mako is as compact as many SWB recumbents, yet doesn't have most of its weight on the smaller front wheel.

Comfort then speed were the design criteria: comfort comes from the 7.6cm (3") of rear suspension and adjustable foam-padded mesh seat, which slots into the large rear casting and forms a structural part of the frame. Speed dictated the mid-low seat height, high-pressure 26" and 20" tyres, and Zzipper fairing option.

With panniers mounted on the optional carrier, it becomes a fine machine for touring or fast commuting. The 'medium-wheelbase' design, with the front wheel between the cranks, gives a comfortable and stable ride without sacrificing compactness.

The Mako is constructed from large-diameter 6000-series anodised aluminium tubes, bonded and riveted into cast aluminium lugs manufactured by suppliers to the aircraft industry. The 2.5" (63.5mm) main tube telescopes in two stages for length adjustment. The rear swing-arm is fillet-brazed, powder-coated cromoly steel, and the easily-adjusted suspension element is 'Dyneema' cord – familiar to climbers as a flexible, lightweight, high-strength and shock-resistant alternative to steel wire. Elastomer or oil-damped coil spring suspension is optional.

Although it's not principally designed as a folder, the Mako collapses in a few minutes to fit into a large bag, making it a practical vehicle for fly & ride touring expeditions around the world. Excluding the wheels and fairing, folded dimensions are 28 x 40 x 70cm (11 x 16 x 27").

culty

Hubert Meyer and Thomas Poreski

Riding the Culty is a unique experience: it's an exhilarating mix of bike and trike which combines the best of both. Flying down a series of hairpins, you lean to steer just like a bike, with body-weight shifts providing the dynamic control. Then travel through town with a child and your shopping on board, and you benefit from trike-typical stability and poise.

The secret of this happy duality is that the front part of the trike can be leaned to suit the curve and your speed, controlled by body movements and support from the handlebar, just like a bicycle: and when you turn the handlebar the rear steering takes care of sharper bends. It's easier than it sounds – most riders master it within minutes – and the result is a very nimble machine with excellent straight-line handling, and a thrilling performance through the bends. Full suspension allows the use of high-pressure 20" (406) tyres without discomfort.

The parking brake locks the leaning mechanism, so that children or luggage can be loaded up onto a solid platform. There are three spacious luggage areas: under the main beam, between the rear wheels, and behind the seat. This last is an ideal location for a childseat, or two at a pinch.

Shorter than a mountain-bike, and with a track of just 65cm, the Culty is compact, and weighs around 20kg complete. The seat height is 63cm, for good visibility in traffic. The frame is made of cromoly and stainless steel, suits riders from 1.5 to 2.0m (4'11" to 6'7") tall, and is equipped with seven or twelve-speed hub gearing from Sachs, optionally combined with a Mountain Drive bottom-bracket gearbox (featured elsewhere in this Encycleopedia). Quality dynamo lighting complete the standard equipment, and options include hydraulic braking and partial fairings.

Culty

Thomas Poreski and Hubert Meyer are each the father of two small children, which meant that when they decided to construct their dream machine, it had to be practical. Thomas is an inventor and long-distance cyclist, and Hubert is a professional toolmaker: together they build Cultys at Hubert's workshop.

They report that demand for the first production run of fifty was overwhelming: many customers make firm orders after just a few minutes test-ride. They are very willing to adapt the Culty to customers' particular needs.

Orders and enquiries should be directed to Thomas, who speaks good English. In the UK, the machine is distributed by John Prince as the 'Culti'.

Culty, c/o Thomas Poreski, Herderstr. 29, 72762 Reutlingen, **Germany.** Tel +49 177 2777 592 Fax +49 7121 231 51
UK: John Prince Tel +44 1452 760 231. Full details page 145.

The Culty prototype: photos of production machines were not available as we went to press.

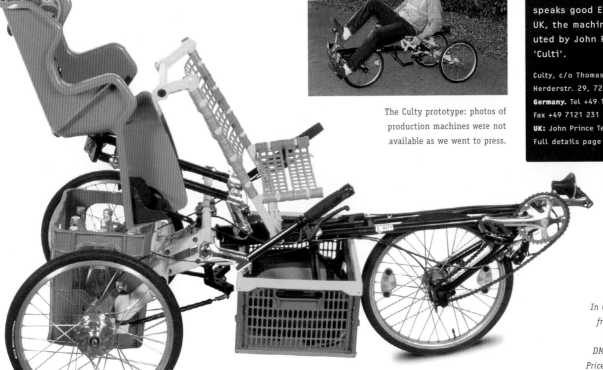

In Germany, prices range from DM 3700 complete (seven-speed) or from DM 3950 (twelve-speed). Prices will vary worldwide.

haluzak

USA

'The Ultimate Sub-Urban Assault Vehicle' is how Bill Haluzak describes his Traverse. It's one of the first recumbents specifically designed for off-road riding. While it doesn't bunny-hop or climb like an upright mountain bike, it comfortably handles the deep potholes, steep curbs, and loose gravel of city streets and country paths – obstacles more severe than the majority of mountain bikes ever encounter.

The design is based on Haluzak's all-purpose Horizon recumbent, modified with mid-frame suspension to absorb bumps evenly between its 20" (406) front and 26" (571) rear wheels. To impress visiting prospective customers, Bill and his co-workers often ride their Traverses from the back of their factory, off the concrete platform and onto the gravel driveway 18" (45cm) below. Bill also tests his Traverse on off-road rides through the nearby hills, pulling the most punishing bike stunts he can think of. He hasn't broken a frame yet. He's even built one for a customer 6'8" (2.03m) tall and weighing 290lb (129kg) – and it's still going strong. Though it's not the fastest recumbent on the market, the 32lb (14.2kg) Traverse's durability and comfort certainly inspire confidence, particularly for former mountain bikers and urban cyclists.

Haluzak recumbents feature sling-mesh seats, braze-ons for lights, pumps and bottle cages, and ball-bearing idlers. All are custom-built, and there's a lifetime warranty on the frame. Along with the Horizon and Traverse, Haluzak produces the high-performance Hybrid Race, the small-wheeled Leprechaun, and the long-wheelbase Storm.

Bill Haluzak

Bicycles by Haluzak

Bill Haluzak is a machinist, contracting engineer, and lifelong cyclist who built his first recumbent for his teenage son Erik in 1991. A year later, with encouragement from friends and local bike makers, he started Bicycles by Haluzak, basing the enterprise just north of California's Mount Tamalpais, birthplace of the mountain bike. Bicycles by Haluzak are sold direct, and through more than 20 shops in the US.

Bicycles by Haluzak, 2166 Burbank Avenue, Santa Rosa, California 95407 USA.
Tel +1 707 544 6243

In the USA, prices range from $1095 for the Leprechaun to $2195 for the Traverse. Framesets range from $900 to $1600. Prices will vary worldwide.

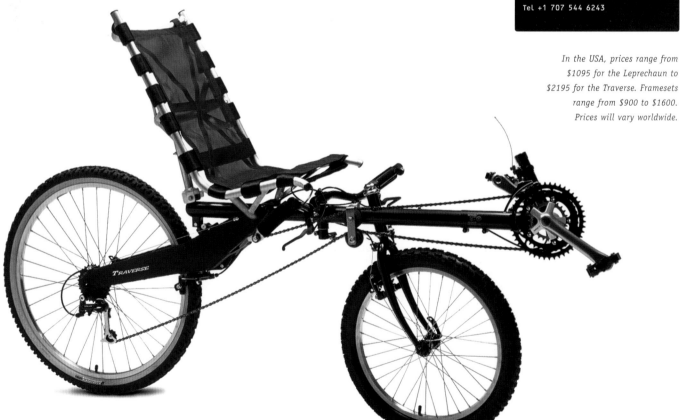

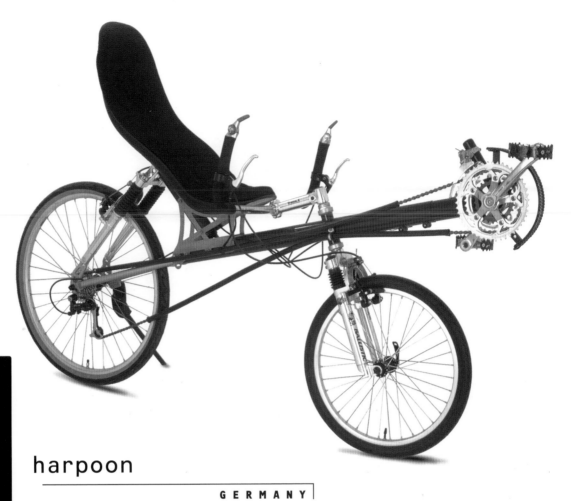

In Germany, prices range from DM2518 for a frameset or from DM3450 complete, and will vary greatly worldwide.

PIVOT-Liegeräder

Wolfgang Heinrich, Andreas Kaspar and Michael Fischer have been producing Pivot recumbents for many years – and they are best-known for their short-wheelbase 'Pure Race' and 'Pure Tour' recumbents. Andreas concentrates on the design, Wolfgang works mostly with production – both come from mechanical engineering backgrounds, and each have more than 11 years of experience in the development of human-powered vehicles. Michael, meanwhile, takes on the marketing and distribution.

PIVOT-Liegeräder, Ahornstr. 15, 88069 Tettnang, Germany.
Tel +49 7542 54656
Fax +49 7542 5981
Email pivot.liegeraeder@t-online.de
Website http://home.t-online.de/home/pivot-liegeraeder

See shops: page 143

harpoon

GERMANY

Take state-of-the-art mountain-bike technology, re-arrange it for a lie-back position, and you end up with the Harpoon recumbent. Then ride past any bike-literate onlooker and you'll excite instant admiration. The suspension is not discreetly tucked away, but displays itself handsomely, daring you to test it out. Polished, bare metal ensures that there's no mistake: this machine means business.

Despite its off-road ancestry and up-front appearance, this is also a totally civilised machine for the road. High-pressure 20" (406) and 26" (559) wheels roll easily, and any harshness is taken out by the suspension: 'Ballistic' forks at the front and elastomer units at the rear, both adjustable. This is complemented by a dual-density foam cushion on the seat. It's a fine touring combination – with the two main tubes bolted rather than welded together, there are plenty of attachment points for low-rider and standard carrier racks.

The tubing is steel, fittings and supports are stainless steel, and the aluminium rear swing-arm and 'Aheadset' stem keep the weight down to 16kg complete. Forged aluminium gives maximum strength on the drop-outs, fork crown and brake bridges, and the rear suspension pivots on a three-ply, composite, self-lubricating bearing.

A telescopic front extension caters for almost every size of rider. Lighting, mudguards, stand and computer mountings are all available – and 35 or 95 litre rear fairings can be fitted for waterproof and secure storage. The seat is an integral part of the carbon-composite 95-litre version, which weighs just 2.5kg and brings improved aerodynamics into the bargain.

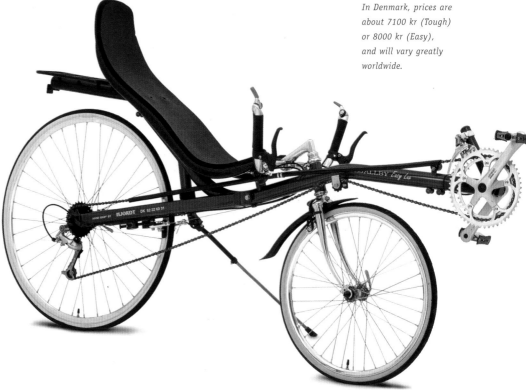

In Denmark, prices are about 7100 kr (Tough) or 8000 kr (Easy), and will vary greatly worldwide.

Bjällby Recumbents

Cost control comes naturally to Curt Bjällby, a long-time control systems engineer. When he started making recumbents back in 1984, it was always the cost that made them difficult to sell, and so he carefully analysed both the product and the production process. As often happens, this reappraisal not only reduced production costs but also improved the whole design, removing unnecessary complication and wasted material. The bikes are made in the workshop of Uffe Hjordt Brink, and alongside the production line there are also prototypes under development, including a recumbent tricycle. We await developments with interest. Meanwhile, Curt continues to be heavily involved in the Danish HPV club, and his machines are active on the racetrack.

Bjällby Recumbents, Stationwej 10A, DK-3520 Farum, Denmark.
Tel +45 4295 6005
Fax +45 4362 8783

Curt Bjällby

bjällby easy and tough

GERMANY

The aesthetics of a bicycle are always a matter of personal taste – but the gracefully curving main tubes of the Easy and Tough recumbents give them an appeal which is not only artistic but also functional. Both machines are highly versatile as everyday transport, long-distance tourers or competitive racers. A rear rack and mudguards can be quickly removed for speed, or you could leave them on for a weekend break or an extended tour. The wheels are 20" front and 28" rear, and there's a wide range of tyres available for racing or touring. The Tough, weighs 12kg, or 13kg with touring equipment. Progress will be even smoother, of course, if you go for the 'Easy' model: at the cost of about an extra kilo of weight, an excellent rear suspension irons out the bumps.

You can choose the precise position and angle of the fibreglass seat – the mounting holes are simply drilled in slightly different locations. A telescopic section in the main tube takes care of leg-length adjustment. Among the options are above-seat steering, and framesets are also available. Components are usually fitted to the customer's specification, and almost anything is possible – including hub gears.

The Danish used to give their recumbents the nickname 'Sofacykel': an amusing viewpoint, but hardly true of Curt Bjällby's machines, which combine comfort with real performance. Even the Easy is fast, and the Tough is comfortable – and choosing between them is a pleasure to be savoured.

red pepper

GERMANY

D etails can reveal a lot about a bicycle. The Red Pepper from Radius withstands close scrutiny, from the neatly-sculpted elastomer shock-absorber to the carefully-calculated frame reinforcements. And if the details are good, that's an indication that the reliability, handling and safety of the product have received similar attention.

These qualities are particularly important for a product like the Red Pepper, designed to be used as an everyday, all-purpose machine. It's a medium-wheelbase recumbent – a format which Radius believe best combines the benefits of compact and easy to ride conventional upright bikes with a recumbent's stability under braking, comfort and aerodynamics. The cranks are carefully positioned to avoid contact between foot and front wheel.

The mesh seat adjusts for position and angle, and three frame sizes are available. The above-seat steering can also be adjusted over a wide range, and provides ready access to the Sachs 3x7 twistgrip changers, bell, and cantilever brakes – and it's a good visible location to mount a cycle computer. So far, riders from 13 to 83 years of age have ridden the Red Pepper in comfort.

Radius' attention to detail extends to the mudguards: these are the full-length type, equipped with stainless stays and the ESGE Secu-clip safety release. Dynamo lighting is also standard. And if you're nipping down to the shops one night in the rain, a bag which fits neatly behind the seat might also come in handy. The elastomer suspension irons out potholes on the way, and an adjustable oil-damped spring unit is available as an option.

Other options include a partial fairing, a folding handlebar for easier storage, a robust pannier rack, and fixings for a child-seat. For longer trips, a rack which accommodates up to four panniers is available, and the Red Pepper can be disassembled to fit into a large suitcase for transport to the starting-point of your tour.

Radius-Spezialräder GmbH

Over the thirteen years that they have manufactured recumbents, Peter Ronge, Andreas Fortmeier and their company Radius have become the largest recumbent-makers in Germany, producing over 1000 bikes each year. They made their name with the LWB Peer Gynt, perhaps the best-known touring recumbent ever. The Peer Gynt was thoroughly updated last year, and renamed the 'Viper'. Radius also make a fast SWB recumbent, the Hornet, and they manufacture a wide range of accessories and specialist HPV parts, including tubing, framebuilding parts and a variety of fairings.

Radius-Spezialräder GmbH, Borkstr. 20, 48163 Münster, Germany.
Tel +49 251 780 342
Fax +49 251 780 358
Email radrec@t-online.de

In Germany, the Red Pepper costs from DM 1400 (frameset) or from DM1998 (complete). Hornets or Vipers cost from DM3980 complete. Prices will vary worldwide.

vision

Recumbents traditionally fall into two camps – short wheelbase (SWB) models built for speed and sharp handling, and long wheelbase (LWB) with a more forgiving ride, suitable for touring and leisure riding. If you wanted both, you had to buy both, and that would cost a lot of money. No longer. With a Vision recumbent you can have both in one machine – they convert from short to long wheelbase in about 20 minutes. Steering can be also changed from above the legs to under-seat, and a Zzipper fairing can be fitted in minutes. Other options include a briefcase-style daybag which attaches behind the seat, and a polycarbonate chainguard. Standard racks and panniers can be fitted.

Versatility without performance is a waste of time. Visions deliver, and perhaps the most common comment is that the unusually stiff frame seems to help overcome the traditional 'recumbents and hills' problem. Visions come in a variety of specification

levels, and top of the range is the 10kg VR45. Available only as a SWB machine, the VR45 can, like other Visions, be ordered with either a 16" (349) or 20" (406) front wheel. Seeing no adequate commercially available 16" tyres, Vision commissioned their own high-performance version for their recumbents – the HP16. 16" wheels are a necessity for many smaller riders, and Vision's initiative is also a boon for many small-wheeled folding bikes.

In 1996, Vision introduced the Double Vision tandem, which splits into 152cm (60") sections for ease of transport. Available in two options to suit your budget, and weighing around 20.4kg (45lb), the Double Vision includes optional Magura hydraulic brakes and the innovative Independent Pedalling System which allows either rider to pedal or freewheel, without disturbing their partner.

Vision Recumbents

Vision's recumbents are the brainchildren of Grant Bower, Joel Smith and Greg Bower. They opened their Seattle-based operation Advanced Transportation Products in 1992. Grant Bower worked for Hewlett-Packard as an engineer, and designed bikes for himself and the company HPV team. Joel Smith was a structural engineer for Boeing before he joined Vision, with a track record of designing and selling his own recumbents. Greg Bower is the financial brains. They're wary of complacency: they are now one of the USA largest recumbent manufacturers.

European distributor:
Future Cycles, Friends Yard, London Road, Forest Row, East Sussex, RH18 5EE, UK.
Tel +44 1342 822847
Fax +44 1342 826726
US manufacturers:
Tel +1 206 467 0231
Email atpvision@aol.com.
Full details p. 145.

In the USA, prices start at $995, the V45 starts at $2500 and the Double Vision from $3400. Prices will vary worldwide.

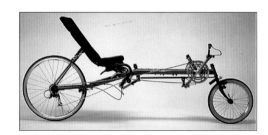

In the UK, prices range from £800 (frameset) or £1200 (complete) and will vary greatly worldwide

Kingcycle

An HPV is a complex creation, a fine balance of intuition and engineering, and a mine-field for the inexperienced. It's all too easy to produce an over-complicated machine, or to misjudge the subtleties of geometry which make up the 'feel' of a thoroughbred. The Kingsburys have mastered the art, with twelve years of riding, racing and record-breaking experience on which to base their design .(the Kingcycle 'Bean' took the world hour record in 1990, covering 75.14km.) Both father John Kingsbury and son Miles are highly-respected figures on the European HPV race circuit.

Kingcycle, Lane End Road, Sands, High Wycombe, Bucks, HP12 4JQ, UK.
Tel +44 1494 524004
Fax +44 1494 437 591
Germany: see page 145

kingcycle

U K

What starts on the racetrack often ends up as a superlative street machine, but it's rare to find a racing machine with such thorough practicality as the Kingcycle. What's even more remarkable is that the accessories which make the machine so practical are also those which make it faster. The lockable, waterproof tail fairing – with lights built in – also smooths the airflow behind the rider. On the front, the fairing incorporates a headlight, and, as well as pushing oncoming air gently aside, it keeps the rider's feet dry in a downpour.

Other options include wheel disks (for 18" front, 24" rear wheels), a headrest, and mounting brackets for a conventional carrier rack. There's also a suspension fork which can be retrofitted to existing bikes. You can even buy the full racing fairing (best restricted to the racetrack or closed roads), or buy the Kingcycle as a frameset. Most customers buy the complete machine and add accessories over a period.

The Kingcycle is based around a frame of elliptical-section Reynolds 531 tubing, hand-brazed in five sizes and complete with fixings for brakes and mudguards. A complete machine weighs about 11.5kg. The components are usually sourced from Europe – typically Sachs and Magura – and the Kingsburys are happy to undertake special orders or to alter the standard specifications within reason.

The Kingcycle's quick steering is quite intentional, and with a little practice gives a razor-sharp response. It won't suit everyone, but for those who appreciate the thrill, it's an exhilarating ride which can transform an ordinary journey into an adrenaline-charged adventure.

Miles Kingsbury

karbyk

ITALY

Paolo Cencigh

The ARES Group don't think small. They aim at nothing less than creating a whole new genre of racing vehicle, something four-wheeled, pedal-powered and fun: a lot more ecological than Formula One motor racing but just as exciting. They even organised an Italian Championship to start it all off, took over the historic Monza race-track for a day, and have toyed with racing on ice and offroad. And it doesn't stop with racing...

Although primarily designed for competition, the Karbyk has also been developed as a practical, street-ready vehicle. It is available in three versions: Road, Rent and Race.

All three versions have an aluminium chassis, and the rear wheels are driven through a differential. Individually-operated drum brakes act on the rear wheels, meaning that you can brake with the full strength of both hands. Twistgrip shifters control standard derailleur gearing. The seat is made from fibreglass or carbon fibre, and can be adjusted for leg length and for angle. The steering is controlled by sliding the hand-grips front-to-rear, so that the front axle pivots at the end of the main boom. Resilient 'hose' couplings isolate the handlebars from road shock – a simple and maintenance-free design solution.

The Road version is equipped with 20" front and 24" rear wheels, and is the 'general-purpose' Karbyk for utility or leisure journeys. Lighting and other accessories can be fitted. The 'Rent' goes for 16" front and 20" rear wheels, and is equipped to suit bike hire centres. The low-profile 'Race', with 12" front and 16" rear wheels, is the speed machine of the range. Weights range from 25 to 28kg (56 to 63lb), depending on version and specification.

ARES Group

Paolo Cencigh heads the ARES Group – a company formed from a group of HPV enthusiasts. They have organised a series of Karbyk 'Grand Prix' races in across Northern Italy for 1997 and beyond, including more events at Monza. They invite anyone interested in finding out more about these events, or even in extending the idea into other countries, to get in touch. By bringing the glamour and publicity of a 'Formula One on pedals' to Italy, they hope to improve the image of pedal-power and cycling as a whole.

ARES Group, via Guglielmo Marconi, n. 18, 33010 Reana del Rojale (UD), Italy.
Tel +39 330 545 091
Fax +39 432 857 504

In Italy, prices range from the equivalent of £980 to £1800, depending on specification. Prices will vary worldwide.

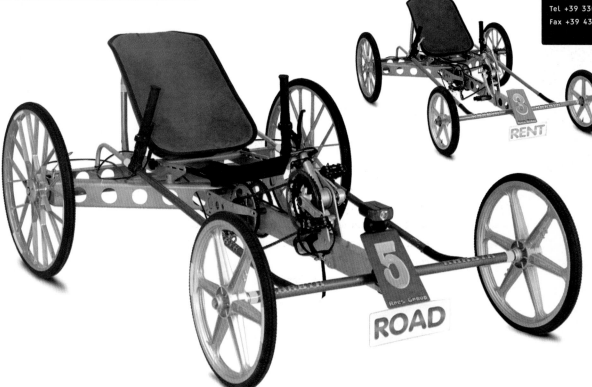

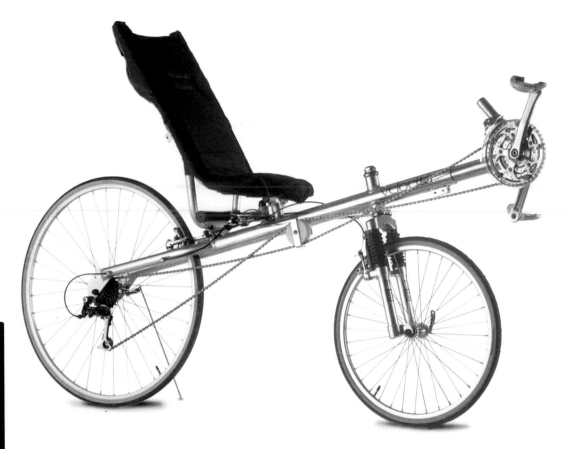

In the UK, prices range from £1600, and vary greatly worldwide

The Seat of the Pants Company

Julian Higgs, designer of the Velocita, built his first recumbent at the age of 17, and since then has lost count of the machines he's made. He's also a keen racer and upright cycle designer – and he is delighted that the Seat of the Pants Company are manufacturing and marketing the Velocita, leaving him free to experiment further in his workshop.
The Seat of the Pants Company also manufacture the Burrows Windcheetah, the Pickup, and the Windcheetah Carbon Monocoque, all of which appear elsewhere in this Encicleopedia.

The Seat of the Pants Company, Unit LKR4, L&M Business Park, Norman Road, Altringcham, Cheshire WA14 4ES, UK.
Tel +44 161 928 5575
Fax +44 161 928 5585
Email bobdixon@seatofpants.u-net.com

USA, Germany: see page 145

Bob Dixon

velocita

'Coke-can' construction – that's how some traditionists described the oversized aluminium frame tubes of mountain-bikes: chunky, macho looks contrasting with the spindly elegance of race-bred steel. It hasn't really happened that way with recumbents – possibly because the main tubes on many steel recumbents have always had that oversized look, and possibly because, among recumbent enthusiasts, traditionalists are rather thin on the ground. So are aluminium recumbents – few recumbent developers have access to aluminium welding equipment.

The Velocita is one exception. It's conceived as a touring and commuting bike, fast yet comfortable, and stable enough so that first-timers can ride with confidence. The frame is made from welded aluminium, normally left polished and unpainted. There are mountings for a carrier-rack and mudguards (the carrier is provided, although not shown on the photograph), and Shimano STX 24-speed derailleur gearing is standard. Front suspension forks improve road-holding and comfort, and the mesh seat minimises sweat. The tele-scopic front boom adjusts to fit the rider's leg-length. Cantilever brakes operate on both 20" (406) front and 700c rear wheels. It weighs around 14kg (31lb) complete.

The Velocita is built by hand on a small production line in the Seat of the Pants factory, operated by a single craftsman with over fifty years in the cycle trade and a reputation as a master wheelbuilder. The Seat of the Pants team are working with the original designer, Julian Higgs, on evolutionary changes to the design, and are considering producing a Nexus-equipped version. They've also given the Velocita their highest accolade: it's the vehicle of choice for their lunchtime journeys over to the local chippie.

In Germany, prices range from DM1495, and will vary worldwide.

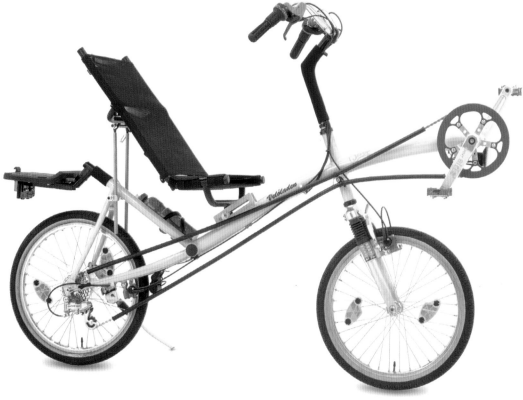

HP Velotechnik

Klaus Schröder designed the Wavey with the help of his friends at Veloladen, a cycle shop and 'bike culture centre' in Bergisch-Gladbach near Cologne. Veloladen have over ten years experience of riding and selling recumbents. After producing the first few Waves themselves, Veloladen joined forces with the manufacturers of the Street Machine recumbent, HP Velotechnik, whose recumbent fairing appears in the 'Accessories' section of this Encyclopedia. The Street Machine was featured in Encyclopedia '96. HP Velotechnik now produce and market the Wavey, and work with Klaus on product development.

HP Velotechnik, Goethestr.5, 65830 Kriftel, Germany. Tel +49 6192 41010 Fax +49 6192 910218

wavey

GERMANY

Wave at the unfortunate occupants of traffic-jammed automobiles. Smile at their frustration as you enjoy your mobility. That's your reward for going by bike, and a bike called Wavey just adds to the pleasure. It's designed as an inner-city jam-busting recumbent: agile, responsive and comfortable. And once a machine's been optimised for the cut-and-thrust of city traffic, it's usually a good general-purpose machine for touring and commuting as well. So it is with the Wavey.

The compact design, with 20" wheels and above-seat steering, keeps the bike short and narrow. The seat height is chosen so that even smaller riders can get a foot firmly to

the ground when stopping at the lights, and the fully-protected chain keeps clothes clean and presentable. Quick-releases allow fast adjustment of seat and handlebars, so that several members of a household or business can use the same machine without compromising on ergonomics or safety. Since the photographs were taken, the standard mesh seat has been slightly modified to improve comfort. The seat can be exchanged, if required, for almost any recumbent seat on the market. Seat fittings are scratch-resistant stainless steel.

Equipment can be chosen to suit most tastes: there is a wide range of options available including hydraulic brakes, front suspension, front fairings and lockable rear boxes, mudguards, stand, lights, carrier racks and more. The Wavey is usually equipped with the Sachs 3x7 system with twistgrip shifters. The main frame is made from cromoly steel, and complete machines weigh from around 16kg, depending on the options chosen.

Klaus Schröder

trice

Peter Ross

The Trice's reputation was not easily won. Hard use by hundreds of customers, over more than ten years of production, has given manufacturer Peter Ross the feedback he needed to bring the design to its present refinement. It's also relatively inexpensive, great fun, and has provided many riders with their first, positive, experience of owning a recumbent. It's a fine tourer which is also no slouch on the racetrack.

The design emphasises practicality: standard components are used wherever possible, and the frame separates into three sections for carriage. An optional rear fairing provides 120 litres of lockable, waterproof luggage storage, and a front fairing is also available.

Crystal Engineering also make the 'Speed Ross SWB' recumbent – at 10.9kg (24lb) complete, one of the lightest production machines on the market. For competition, they offer the low-rider 'Festina' recumbent: a serious contender which has earned respect on the HPV racing circuit. At the other end of the spectrum is the Gem – a sociable recumbent trike woth optional electric-assist motor, and which will eventually acquire a fairing. The chassis is 1.1m wide, no longer than a LWB solo recumbent, and the optional lockable, waterproof glass-fibre carrier box can accommodate vast amounts of luggage – or a couple of children. Each rider has his or her own freewheel, and so can pedal at their own pace, or not at all, as they please. The 30-speed gearing drives both rear wheels, and has a range of 20" to 120". The frame accepts the steering on either side. The GEM can be disassembled to fit inside its own luggage-box, and weighs around 32kg.

We look forward to reporting next year on the fully-enclosed version, which is expected to weigh no more than 50kg. Meanwhile, unfaired Gems can be custom-built to order, and a version hand-cranked on the co-pilot's side is also available.

Crystal Engineering

When most people would be thinking about retirement or tending the garden, Peter Ross enthusiastically competes in low-rider HPV races, cycles everywhere in all weathers in hilly Cornwall, and makes HPVs for a living with a gusto that seems to grow rather than diminish with time. Fifteen years of personal experience designing, building, racing and listening to customers have left him with a conviction that the HPV will not replace the car until it offers weather protection and the ability to climb hills while carrying at least two adults and a child (or the weekly shopping) in comfort. A tough target for the GEM – but if anyone can make such a machine, surely it's Peter Ross.

Crystal Engineering, Unit 1A Jubilee Wharf, Commercial Road, Penryn, Cornwall TR10 8AQ, UK.
Tel/Fax +44 1326 378 848
Email tricehpv@globalnet.co.uk
USA: see page 145

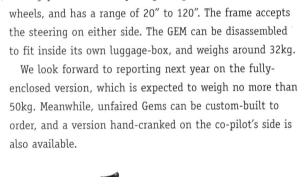

In the UK, prices range from £825 for the Speed Ross, £1499 for the Trice and £3000 for the GEM, and will vary greatly worldwide

bevo-bike

GERMANY

Klaus Beck and Hans Voss

The BEVO-Bike is a do-it-all recumbent for the masses. The makers claim that this is the one bike in the world that does not need a test ride – they guarantee that the riding position can be adjusted quickly and easily to give a superlative ride for anyone under 1.95m tall.

Indeed, the adjustment available is impressive: the angles of seat back and leather base can be set separately, and the handlebar is also easily adjusted for position. The above-seat steering feels natural for many riders, and also enhances the aerodynamics. The seating position is high enough to give visibility and stability in traffic – although it is a little lower than our picture suggests, as the rider's weight compresses the suspension.

At 1.95m long, the BEVO-Bike is only a shade longer than a traditional Dutch roadster, and with the rear triangle tucked under and the seat folded forward, it's fairly compact to store.

The front-wheel drive system is patented under the name 'Top-Drive', and keeps the transmission very compact. The chainset is mounted on the frame, and chain twist is minimised by arranging the two chain runs together, close to the steering axis. For the tightest, low-speed turns, a stop limits the steering to a safe range, although riders report that this is no significant restriction when riding the bike.

The Top-Drive system means that hub-gears are a necessity, and the Sachs 7-speed is usually fitted, although other options are available. Standard equipment includes Magura hydraulic brakes on the front wheel, and full lighting and mudguards. Wheels are 20" front and 26" rear. The standard bike weighs around 16kg.

A specially-designed Zzipper fairing is an option, as is the under-frame carrier rack. A Karrimor rucsac/bike bag can also be clipped behind the seat.

Voss Spezial-Rad GmbH

Klaus Beck and Hans Voss bring two very different perspectives to bear on the BEVO-Bike design. Klaus is an art and physics teacher from Hamburg, who encourages his students to build bikes without preconceptions. Hans, on the other hand, is a distributor of recumbents from around the world, and this has given him a clear idea of what is important in recumbent design. When the two of them teamed up, they were after a practical and pragmatic compromise, avoiding the long chainruns and awkward riding positions which, they believe, put many people off recumbents. They now promote their product with extraordinary zeal, tempting people onto the BEVO-Bike by comparing the riding position to that of an armchair in front of the television. And why not?

Voss Spezial-Rad GmbH, Tulpenweg 2, D-25524 Itzehoe-Edendorf, Germany.
Tel +49 4821 41409
Fax +49 4821 41014

In Germany, prices range from DM2680, and will vary greatly worldwide

In Germany, prices range from DM 4200 (complete) or DM 2500 (frameset), and will vary worldwide

radnabel ATL

Radnabel

Dieter Baumann is increasingly using high-tech manufacturing processes: CNC machined and laser-cut parts are consistently precise, and save much time, which he can now use for further development work. He has been developing the ATL for over eight years: in 1989 a prototype equipped with solar cells and a motor won the 'hybrid-mobil' category in the Tour de Sol. In 1994, it won the prize at the European HPV championships as the 'best everyday bike'.

Radnabel, Jakobsgasse 19, 72070 Tübingen, Germany.
Tel/Fax +49 7071 238 96

GERMANY

N eed to carry two children home from school, do some shopping, then carry the lot back home? It's a pleasure on the Radnabel ATL. A pannier can be mounted either side below the seat, so that even if the front platform and rear carrier are already occupied, there's still capacity available. And there's no need to be concerned about stopping with such a load on board: the Radnabel is renowned for its braking: drum brakes are particularly powerful in small wheels – and operate just as well whatever the weather.

Tremendous suspension is provided for the high-pressure 20" wheels – at the front with eight rubber torsion elements and 4cm (1.6") of travel, and also at the rear where a new polyurethane suspension element offers improved damping and 8cm (3.6") of travel. The seat can be adjusted in seconds with two quick-release catches, and the seat tube conceals a pump.

The Radnabel is available either as a frameset or complete with either hub or derailleur gearing. If hub gears are chosen, a completely-enclosed drive system can be created – and for a wider range of gears, a 'Mountain-Drive' bottom-bracket gearbox can be used. Complete with all basic equipment, the ATL weighs around 17.5kg.

An adjustable 'Shark' fairing for the ATL is also available. The unit attaches quickly to the front load platform, and covers a large load-carrying area. Below, it can be folded down to protect the rider's feet. A cape can then attach to the rim of the hood, providing complete protection from rain, yet leaving everything open below for welcome ventilation.

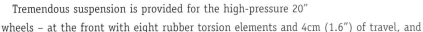

velomobiles

Velomobiles can offer a higher level of mobility than the motor car, need no fossil fuel, cause no pollution, have full weather protection, and have higher comfort and safety than a conventional bicycle. Magic machines? Maybe.

The trick is to combine a full fairing for weather protection and aerodynamics with lightweight, practical design. It is a fascinating concept, and challenges the supposed advantages of the motorcar. The velomobile is a human-scale alternative, which can catch the attention of the vast non-cycling public. Some velomobile owners ride 10-20,000 km per year: more than many car drivers. It's an idea to change people's lives.

Tobias Enke from Germany is a case in point. Making a living as a street artist selling silver ornaments, he toured the country in his fully-faired Leitra, staying with friends, often travelling over 200km in a day, under his own power, and in all weathers.

According to Tobias, his velomobile is "perhaps the smallest mobile home in the world". For someone who is concerned about the environment, their own health, and the state of society around us, the velomobile is a powerful message on wheels. Tobias again: "My velomobile makes my present lifestyle possible: no other vehicle on this wonderful planet would let me live like this."

The term 'Velomobile' covers a wide range of vehicles. Some have fairings which are removeable for fine weather, others are of monocoque design. Some have the option of motor assistance to extend their range and make hills easier. Detail is important: ventilation has to be just right, lighting is usually integrated in the design, and the weight must be strictly controlled. Most velomobiles designed for human power alone weigh in at under 30kg. The range of velomobiles available on the market has increased enormously in the last few years. Most of the activity in the field still seems to be in Northern Europe and Germany, – and in Russia.

The velomobile is a valuable step on the way towards lessening society's dependence on the motorcar.

berkut B-317

RUSSIA

The Berkut B-317 brings new thinking and new technology to cycling. Inspired by former helicopter and aircraft engineers, Berkut's innovative approach was rewarded when their B-307 was awarded a gold medal and a special prize at the invention exhibition 'MUBA 95' in Basel, Switzerland.

The velomobile is based on the Berkut range of recumbent tricycles. The drive can be to both front wheels via a differential (B-317), or via freewheels in both front hubs (B-305) for better traction in sand, mud, snow and ice, or the single rear wheel can be driven (B-301). In addition, adjustable elastomer suspension can be specified on all three 20" wheels. The chassis consists of about 90% aluminium, with steel and titanium used for highly-stressed parts. Brakes are hydraulic drums, actuated by Magura levers, and use widely-available Sturmey-Archer brake shoes. The seat adjusts to suit riders from 1.5 to 2.1m tall. The unfaired recumbents weigh around 18kg, depending on equipment.

The velomobile chassis features front-wheel drive via a differential, and a sealed oil-bath gearbox provides forward, neutral and reverse gears, giving complete control without feet leaving pedals. The reverse gear has a 3:1 reduction ratio, which is particularly good for reversing uphill.

The fairing is constructed mainly of carbon/kevlar composites, strengthened by aluminium stringers. The canopy slides forward for ventilation, or can be removed completely. A hand-lever drives the windscreen-wiper, and a large rear-view mirror is provided. Ventilation scoops under the nose ensure that overheating is not a problem. A hatch gives access to 30kg or 100 litres of luggage capacity behind the rider, and full lighting and turn indicators are provided. Steering is via a 'joystick', and the minimum turning radius is 2.5m. Complete, the velomobile weighs under 40kg.

Berkut

The Berkut team of Vladimir Shtrakin, Vadim Mazaev, Mishail Novikov, Maxim Poretsky (all graduates in mechanical engineering) and Marina Darenko (a graduate in engineering and business studies), make their innovative machines in Moscow factories which once produced aircraft and helicopters – they have plenty of space. Non-availability of modern cycle components in Russia means that prototype testing can take some time, but with the help of friends in Europe, especially their agent Manfred Klauda, Berkut manage admirably. The machines are made from all-Russian aircraft materials.

Berkut, Department of 'Outlook Ltd', adm. Marakov Street 45-91, Moscow 125 212, Russia.
Tel/Fax +7 095 452 3398
Western Europe: Manfred Klauda, Westenriederstr. 26, 80331 München. Tel +49 171 370 4970 or +49 89 290 4121 Fax +49 89 333955

Prices in Deutschmarks range from DM5000 for the B-317, and will vary greatly worldwide

carbon alleweder

NETHERLANDS

The Italians had seen nothing like it: an Alleweder crossing the Alps. The occupants were Flevobike employees Ymte Sijbrandij and Theo van Andel (above right), on their way to visiting friends in Turin, Italy, via the Great St. Bernhard Pass and carrying full camping gear. They took it slow but easy going up, with suitable gears, and going down was, they say, an adrenalin-charged delight.

Versatile the Alleweder certainly is – but it was not conceived as a machine for mountaineering. The aerodynamic bodywork, with zip-on sailcloth fabric closure to adjust for varying weather conditions, has developed over several years to form a solid, affordable and practical vehicle for all-weather commuting. In 1992, it won the '365-days bike' competition, organised by the Dutch cycle magazine 'Fiets' to encourage true everyday practicality in design.

Flevobike are active in the development of high-speed HPVs, and their experiences of new materials for racing suggested that the technology could be transferred to the Alleweder. The Carbon Alleweder offers improved aerodynamics, more luggage space, and a fully-enclosed 24-speed transmission, protecting clothing and reducing maintenance. It's also lighter, weighing 26kg complete, compared to 33.5kg for the aluminium version.

Both versions use McPherson strut suspension at the front, and a swing-arm system on the rear. Wheels are 20" (406) all round, and the joystick-steered front wheels are equipped with 110mm Sturmey-Archer drum brakes. An optional third drum brake can be fitted to the rear wheel. A rechargeable lighting system can be fitted, and almost any derailleur gearing system can be used – seven gears are standard (or 24 on the Carbon Alleweder). Around 90% of purchasers choose to assemble the aluminium Alleweder themselves – it takes 60-80 hours, but only simple tools, to complete.

Flevobike

The Flevobike name is strongly identified with the modular front-wheel-drive, central-pivot design with which they began their recumbent business. Since the original Flevobike, the product range has expanded to include the Flevotrike, with its 100-litre rear cargo module, popular with cycle couriers in Amsterdam. Flevobike also produce the 'Basic' – a rear-wheel recumbent ideal for those new to recumbent cycling. They welcome visitors to their factory in Dronten, where advice, hire, and test-rides are available. It's also a resource centre for alternative transport, with books, plans and special parts on offer.

Flevobike, De Morinel 55,
8251 HT Dronten, Netherlands.
Tel +31 321 312 027
Fax +31 321 319 350
Email flevobike@pi.net

In the Netherlands, prices for the aluminium Alleweder range from f 3495 as a kit to f 5095 complete. The carbon Alleweder costs around f 9500. Prices will vary greatly worldwide.

Leitra APS

Carl-Georg Rasmussen aims to maintain the Leitra as the 'best practical velomobile in the world'. He is himself living proof of the velomobile concept: for over 15 years and 200,00km he has lived without a car, often delivering Leitras personally to their new owners by towing them behind his own much-used vehicle. He is also pleased to share his experience in the design and manufacture of velomobiles (the Leitra has been in production since 1985). An enthusiastic participant in the Danish HPV club and at the 'European Seminars on Velomobile Design', he often pedals to HPV events across Europe. He believes that although it is the vehicle of the future, we will be well into the next century before the first mass-market velomobile is introduced. Meanwhile, the Leitra serves admirably.

Leitra APS, Box 64,
DK-2750 Ballerup, Denmark
Tel/Fax 0045 4218 3377

Carl-Georg Rasmussen

leitra

DENMARK

Prices are usually in Deutschmarks: DM10–12,000 for the faired version, or DM6–7,000 unfaired. A do-it-yourself kit is sold for DM4,500–5,000

The rain pours down, and your fellow-cyclists in their waterproofs are being buffeted by the icy wind. It's winter out there, but you're dressed in normal indoor clothing, and your shoes are clean and dry. You are in a Leitra.

The Leitra is a true all-weather velomobile. It is the realisation of many cyclists' dreams: on those cold, wet and windy days you can sit back, and enjoy the ride in your own dry, warm personal space.

The space-frame chassis surrounds you, giving protection from all directions: no-one has been injured in a Leitra after over several million kilometres in traffic. Arms rest comfortably on the frame, and the control sticks fall easily to hand. Carbon fibre leaf springs provide full suspension, and three drum brakes do the stopping. Powerful 6-volt lighting is fitted as standard, and 100 litres of luggage can be carried inside the fairing, protected from the weather.

The fairing can be removed for summer riding, or the top can be taken off. However, most riders prefer to leave the fairing on as protection against the sun's rays. Ventilation inlets can be opened to create a cooling air stream through the fairing. Take off the fairing and you have a recumbent tricycle – ready to fit a childseat or a trailer. The 600g seat can be removed to make the Leitra unridable – effectively preventing theft. The Leitra can even be taken as personal luggage on a train or aeroplane. The frame and suspension disassemble in minutes.

The Leitra is a remarkable piece of lightweight engineering. It makes possible life without a car in a car-oriented society. It can even be free – several owners have recouped the original cost in a few years by selling advertising space on the fairing. Wonders never cease.

accessories

and components

A bicycle is more than the sum of its parts, but what a difference the parts can make! Cycling satisfaction is a complex thing, and good times can be had on almost any bike, but one of the joys of cycling is to let your bicycle (or trike, or bicycles, or both!) evolve to fit your needs precisely.

To do that, you'll end up searching out components and accessories to tune your bike to your life. There is a bewildering array of components and accessories available today, among them some real gems. We've tried to bring a few of these together in this section.

All of these products go a little beyond the ordinary, serving a particular, practical use. We chose them because they caught our eye as being sensible, answering real needs, and being well-implemented designs.

MP200 'stealth' pedals

The designer of these pedals, Jon Heim, believes that at 225g per pair, they are the lightest double-sided SPD-compatible clipless pedals in the world, and the only ones to offer both adjustable float and adjustable release tension. The simple design has about half as many parts as typical SPD pedals. The platform is one of the largest available for clipless pedals – and because it's uncluttered mud has nothing to cling to.

The oversize aircraft alloy axle is hard coated with a lubricant film, and has some of the largest bearings ever used in a bicycle pedal. Cleats are supplied, or any SPD cleats can be used. He reports that every component has been optimised using finite element analysis to remove every gram of unnecessary weight, and then rigorously tested in NORBA racing and extreme MTB riding to ensure real world durability.

In the USA, prices range from $190, and will vary worldwide.

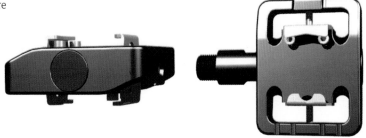

Montara Mountain Bike, 61 Clarendon Road, Pacifica, CA 94044, USA. Tel +1 415 359 1326
Email mtb@montaramtb.com
Website www.montaramtb.com

timbuk2 bags

Timbuk 2 bags are made in 1000 dernier Cordura, lined with a single piece of 14oz vinyl 'truck-tarp'. They're comfortable, with an adjustable 'stabiliser strap' holding the bag close against your back, so that it won't swing around as you weave through the traffic. Internal and external pockets, reflective tags and high-impact Delrin buckles complete the package – and you can choose any three colours from a range of 12. Options include a padded shoulder strap, a strap pouch and a radio holster, and there are four sizes, from 900cu. ins to 3300cu. ins (14 to 54 litres).

In the USA, prices range from $49.95 to $79.95, and will vary worldwide

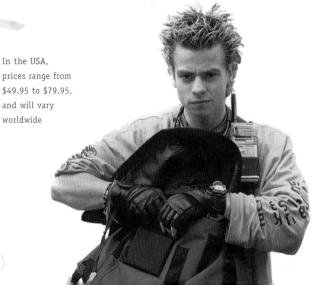

Timbuk2 Designs, Inc., 5327 Jacuzzi Street 3E-2, Richmond, CA 94804, USA. Tel +1 510 526 0597 Fax +1 510 526 0599. USA/Canada (toll free): Tel 1-888-Timbuk2 Fax 1 -888-TimbukX. Email brennan@timbuk2.com Website http://www.timbuk2.com

International agents:
UK: Wheelie Serious Imports Tel +44 181 543 5255
Sweden: GBS Sports +46 823 1100.

See also page 145.

woodguards

Wood is a fine material for mudguards: strong and light, and with a timeless elegance. These hand-crafted guards, made by Johannes Rességuier in his Bremen workshop from Swedish birch, are carefully laminated in nine layers. Johannes has recently introduced a new version – curving round the tyre profile with wonderful grace. Such double curves are no easy matter in wood.

In the 1880s, beechwood was widely used for the rims of bicycle wheels. Lighter than aluminium alloy, Woodguard rims are made in Italy by traditional methods, then brought to Bremen to be stained and coated. Naturally, rim brakes are out, but Johannes says that the rims cope well with heavy loads, using the flexibility of the wood to advantage.

Carrier racks, chainguards, grips and lights complete the range. Woodguards parts are most often seen on classic Pedersens, but bestow a functional distinction on almost any quality bicycle.

Woodguards, c/o KGB, Donnerschweerstr. 45, Oldenburg 26123, Germany. Tel +49 441 885 0389 Fax +49 441 885 0388

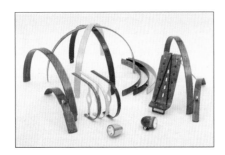

Mudguards cost from DM195, complete with fittings, and rims cost from DM120, or assembled as wheels from DM350.

EGS synchro shift

In France, prices range from FF250 to over FF680, and will vary worldwide

The French gave us the derailleur, that lovely but awkward collection of levers, cables and sprockets, and now they've made it an ergonomic delight with the Synchro Shift. The French company Effective Gear Systems (EGS) has produced a cyclist-friendly single twistgrip gear shifter that lets you change up and down through the gears with a single action. No more remembering whether it's time to shift at the front or at the back, and no looking down to see which gear you're in. The patented Synchro-Shift moves front and rear derailleurs in sequence, avoiding duplicates and extreme chainline positions, and ends up with twelve evenly-spaced gears. A spring-loaded assistance mechanism (likewise patented) ensures that the action remains light, and a clear display shows which gear you're using. Versions are available to suit almost any available transmission.

EGS, B.P. 476, 86106 Châtellerault, France. Tel +33 549 214242 Fax +33 549 853542.

mountain-drive

Florian Schlumpf's Mountain-Drive is a super-smooth bottom-bracket planetary gearbox, available in two versions, and you change gear by lightly tapping a button with your heel. There are two versions: the Mountain-Drive I shifts from direct drive to a reduction ratio of 1:2.5 – the equivalent of switching from a 46 to a 19-tooth chainring. Even combined with seven-speed gearing at the rear, there is no overlap between ratios, and the range achieved is greater than anything possible with standard triple-chainring setups. Any standard chainring can be fitted, and it weighs 890g, including bottom-backet and bearings but without cranks and chainrings.

The new 'Triangolo' Mountain-Drive II takes its name from the arrangement of its bearings, braced in a strong triangle. It's an 1:1/1:1.65 overdrive unit, ideal for bikes with a small rear wheel or for racing. Shifting is instant, while pedalling or at a standstill, and Florian reports that downhill mountain-bike racers have been using the system successfully. For further details, and information about the many options, please contact Florian Schlumpf direct.

In Switzerland the Type 1 Mammouth costs SFr439 and the Type 2 Triangolo costs SFr649

Florian Schlumpf
Spezialmaschinenbau,
Dorfstr. 10,
CH-7324 Vilters,
Switzerland
Tel +41 8172 38009
Fax +41 8172 38364
Email schlumpf_ing
@bluewin.ch
Website www.schlumpf.ch

kunst & leder products

Stephanie and Gerhard Schulz Rothemund, who hand-craft the Kunst & Leder range, are aiming at cyclists who want quality bags to withstand a lifetime of use – often on a Pedersen, a Galaxe, or a Moulton. There are specially-designed Kunst & Leder bags and accessories for each of these classic designs – and for others. The colourful 'Selle Crocal' saddle, and Pedersen saddles (narrower than standard, and with a rainproof pocket) – are specialities. All products can be ordered with decorations or personal mono-grams, elegantly punched into the surface of the leather. These bags are saddle-stitched by hand from high-quality, naturally tanned leather: they are waterproof and extremely durable. Each seam runs in a notch in the leather, so that it does not project above the surface, where it would be vulnerable to scrubbing or wetness. Where buckles are used, paintwork is protected by a thoughtful leather flap.

In Germany, prices range from DM 150 for a tool bag to DM 550 for the largest Pedersen bag, and will vary greatly worldwide

Kunst & Leder,
Esbacher Str. 2,
91746 Weidenbach,
Germany.
Tel +49 982 69446

In the Netherlands, prices are f59.90 for the 'Egg bag', f64.90 for the 'Shopping bag', and f69.95 for the side pannier, and will vary greatly worldwide.

UBiCS

The Urban Bike Cargo System (UBiCS) is the first in what promises to become a range of innovative cycling products from Holland-based URBICO (Urban Bicycle Concept). A city bike and further accessories are on the horizon.

The universal 'panniers' take just about any load: a business briefcase, a bag of shopping, even a football. You simply pop it in: the binding stretches to fit.

Then, at the front or rear, you can fit one of the UBiCS bags (two sizes: 5 litre 'Egg bag' or 10 litre 'Shopping bag'). An ingenious 'Pocket-fix' system provides quick release and secure attachment. The zips run right round for easy loading.

The UBiCS microporous material (black or khaki) is light, hard-wearing and waterproof, and the bags are equipped good-quality zips, buckles and reflective trim. Designed for sale by mail-order, and to take up minimum room on dealer's shelves, the bags are available through shops or direct from the manufacturers.

Urbico B.V., PO Box 160,
6190 Ad Beek (L), Netherlands.
Fax +31 46 437 9342
Email urbico@ilimburg.nl
Shops: see page 142

In the US, prices range from $130 to $550, and vary greatly worldwide

angle tech super zzipper P-38 fairing

Ovalised tubing, low handlebars and aero spokes can shave fractions of a second from world-record times, though often at the expense of comfort and affordability. Streamlining the frontal area of bike and rider can make a far more significant difference. The Angle Tech Super Zzipper P-38 fairing, which fits most short wheelbase recumbents, is designed to reduce drag by up to 30%, increasing average speed by around 10%. Made from shatter-proof polycarbonate, the fairing together with the 'P-38' mounting system weighs only 1.95kg, and can be adjusted for height and foot clearance with a 5mm Allen key. The system also provides extra visibility in traffic and protection from inclement weather and flying debris.

Zzip Designs, PO Box 14,
Davenport, CA 95017, USA.
Tel +1 408 425 8650 or
(US only) 888-WINSCRN
Fax +1 408 425 1167
Website http://www.diskspace.com/zzip/

trailfix tools

Walking home is not most cyclists' favourite pastime. Self-reliance is much more fun – and the essential toolkit can be lightweight and unobtrusive. The 15g Trailfix puncture kit replaces the traditional three tyre levers with one: hook it under, then slide round to remove. 'Self-Seal' glueless patches are stored in the lever body, and spares are available separately.

The single-lever design and patches are also part of the 150g 'Trailfix Toolkit', which addditionally provides a chain tool suitable for any chain, 3,4,5,and 6mm Allen keys, and a screw driver. Spoke keys (3.4 and 3.5mm), and 8, 10, 14 and 15mm spanners are all part of the multitool which slides neatly into the lid. All tools are hardened steel, and the Toolkit can be mounted under the saddle using a velcro strap.

Try your local bike shop (see page 142), or contact Weldite Products Ltd, Harrier Road, Barton-upon-Humber, North Lincs DN18 5RP, UK. Tel +44 1652 660000 Fax +44 1652 660066

In the UK, the tool kit costs from around £12, and the puncture repair kit from £3

monte carlo tyres

In 1993 Vredestein took note of the needs of the recumbent world for fast and comfortable small tyres and began making their Monte Carlo tyre in the 37-406 (20") size. It opened up the options for manufacturers of quality small-wheeled bikes everywhere. The Monte Carlo has an outstanding resistance to punctures and a long life thanks to the specially developed rubber on the tread surface.

The carcass is woven by winding a single fibre around. This gives better rolling resistance than is offered by tyres based on the usual method of layering, and the rounded profile makes for a comfortable ride.

Monte Carlos are available in sizes 35-559, 37-622, 37-406, 47-622, 32-622, 28-622: all with reflective bands.

Vredestein Fietsbanden b.v., Postbus 24, 7000 AA Doetinchem, Holland. Tel +31 314 370 555 Fax +31 314 370 500

In Germany, the 20" (406) tyre costs around DM41

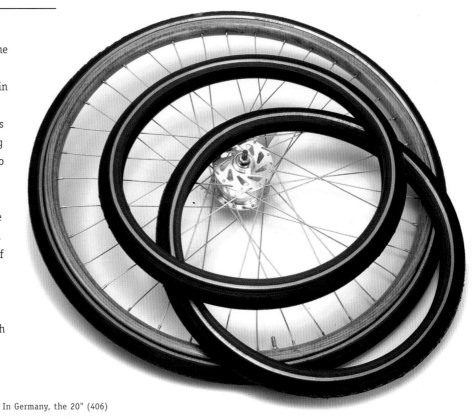

streamer fairing

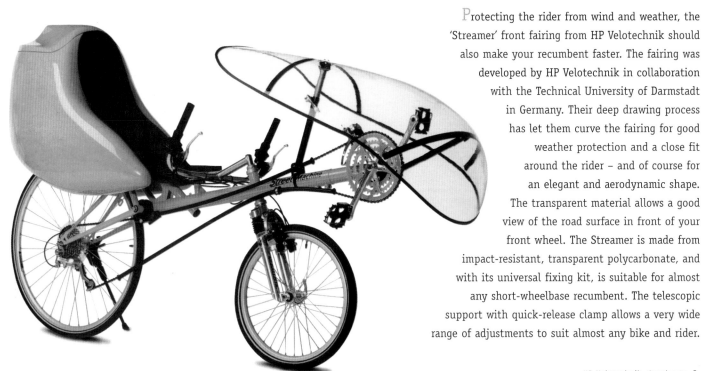

Protecting the rider from wind and weather, the 'Streamer' front fairing from HP Velotechnik should also make your recumbent faster. The fairing was developed by HP Velotechnik in collaboration with the Technical University of Darmstadt in Germany. Their deep drawing process has let them curve the fairing for good weather protection and a close fit around the rider – and of course for an elegant and aerodynamic shape. The transparent material allows a good view of the road surface in front of your front wheel. The Streamer is made from impact-resistant, transparent polycarbonate, and with its universal fixing kit, is suitable for almost any short-wheelbase recumbent. The telescopic support with quick-release clamp allows a very wide range of adjustments to suit almost any bike and rider.

In Germany, prices range from DM590 (complete with fittings) or DM450 (fairing shell only).

HP Velotechnik, Goethestr. 5,
D-65830 Kriftel, Germany.
Tel +49 6192 41010
Fax +49 6192 910218

carradice saddle bags

It's not just the sensible, traditional British style which has made Carradice bags so internationally popular, but also the use of traditional materials. The fabric is cotton duck, the straps leather and the stiffening bar is wood. Should you ever manage to wear one out, you can be sure that it is biodegradable.

Cotton Duck is the original performance material, once much favoured by the military. Now Carradice have it specially made. The cotton is breathable, and waxed to make it waterproof, while the sewing thread swells when wet to close any holes. This makes Carradice bags very useful for everyday wear, especially for saddle bags which are permanently left on the bike, come rain or shine.

Carradice produce a modern version of the capacious saddlebag, with bright red polypropylene straps and trim, and quick-release fasteners. This bag has internal compartments for documents and smaller items. There's a quick-release saddlebag support available for saddles not fitted with bag loops, or for anyone who likes to take the bag off quickly.

Carradice of Nelson Ltd,
Westmoreland Works,
St. Mary's Street,
Nelson, BB9 7BA, UK.
Tel +44 1282 615 886
Fax +44 1282 602 329

In the UK, classic long flap saddlebags start at £38:45. The modern 'Super C' saddlebag costs £45:95, and the quick-release support costs £23:95

'W' performance products hubs

Long-time builders of tandems and tourer frames, Geoff Wiles Cycles have now developed some fittingly durable hubs. These hubs, with oversized axles, can also contribute considerably to suspension fork rigidity. The alloy hub shell has wide flanges for spoke support and strength, double-sealed industrial bearings, and at the rear, an alloy freewheel boss. This, like every other component, is replaceable individually, so that a stripped freewheel boss (a common problem on tandems) no longer means a whole new wheel. Axles are 15mm stainless steel, fitted with stainless Allen-bolt end caps, and also accept a quick-release. The rear axle is threaded, and two locknuts position the hub shell laterally – ideal for creating wheels with minimum dish. Any drilling or spindle length can be accommodated. An adaptor for interchangeability with freehub cassettes is under development.

In the UK, hubs cost from £149:95 per pair, including VAT and free delivery worldwide

Geoff Wiles Cycles, 45-47 Cuxton Road, Strood, Rochester upon Medway,Kent, ME2 2BU, UK. Tel +44 1634 722586/727416 Fax +44 1634 727416

nightsun XC

Nightsun burst onto the scene in 1986, with the first ever high-performance rechargeable lighting system for cyclists. Much imitated, Nightsun have since stayed ahead of the game with ever-more powerful and long-lasting lights, all designed and manufactured in-house at their California factory.

The latest Nightsun light is the 1.07kg (2.36lb) XC, intended for off-roading at night. The twin lights are mounted on quick-release brackets, moving them well clear of handlebar clutter, and it's all made from powder-coated aircraft-grade alloys. The 40Wh nicad battery is good for up to four hours of light. The 10W floodlight lets you see the lie of the land, then flick on the 35W spotlight and with 45W of combined power you'll see why it's called Nightsun.

In the USA, prices range from $200, and will vary worldwide.

Nightsun Performance Lighting, 995 South Fair Oaks Avenue, Pasadena, CA 91105,USA. Tel +1 818 799 5074 Fax +1 818 799 0923 Website www.night-sun.com

pitlock

Lock a bike with the most impregnable ironmongery imagineable, but it won't help. Thieves just take the components. The brute force approach to security is fine, but it's worth being a little clever too.

Enter the Pitlock system to protect quick-release wheels, seatposts and Aheadset stems. The 'code nuts' and matching keys each have one of 256 coded shapes, which can't be opened by any other tool. The nuts are protected by a tapered cylinder – pliers and similar implements simply slide off. Available for all axle lengths (including tandems and hub gears), Pitlock components are also lightweight: the whole system weighs just 122g in stainless steel, or 70 grams in titanium. That's often less than the original components.

Peter Busse is always working to improve the system, and a new development is in the offing – more details should be available after April 1997.

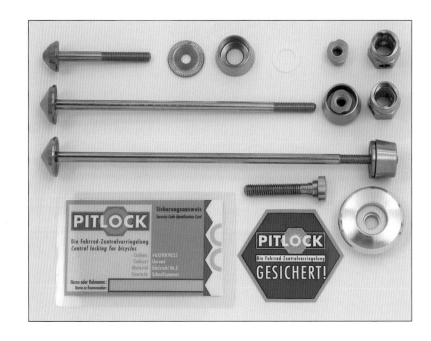

Peter Busse-Sicherheitstechnik,
Liegnitzer Str. 15,
10999 Berlin, Germany.
Tel +49 30 611 2092
Fax +49 30 611 2093

In Germany, complete systems cost from
DM129 (steel) or DM279 (titanium).
Prices will vary worldwide.

pamir tools

Cyclists on tour have always had a problem with drive-side spoke breakage. No longer! Weighing just 28.4 grammes, the 'Hyper-Cracker' removes Shimano (and Sachs, Campagnolo etc.) Hyperglide-style cassette lockrings, bracing itself against the frame and using the bike's cranks and gear ratios instead of a long, heavy spanner. It also doubles as a spoke key. A 'Cassette-Cracker' version handles cassettes secured by a threaded outer ring.

These two 'take-with' tools join Pamir's range of workshop equipment: long-lasting tools, with comfortable handles and carefully-chosen geometry. These specialised tools can solve most problems of rear gear cluster removal in fine style.

Pamir also make the Pedal Check – a simple device to measure the straightness of pedal spindles. It'll tell you your pedals need replacing long before a doctor tells you your knees need replacing.

In the USA, prices range from $10
for the Hyper-Cracker, to around $60
for the professional workshop tools.
The Pedal-Check costs around $80.
Prices vary worldwide.

The tools are available
through cycle dealers worldwide – see Shops, page 143.
Website http://members.aol.com/pamireng

trac-pearls

In Germany, a set of brake cables costs from DM62.90, gear sets from DM99.90. Prices will vary worldwide.

Gliders, yachts and aircraft: all are applications for the 'Trac-Pearls' cable system. The same technology offers superlative performance for bicycle gears and brakes. The stiffness of the hardened aluminium segments (with full-surface contact at any angle of bend) improves shifting accuracy and braking power, in a kink-proof, zero-stretch, corrosion-resistant and long-lived system – and the smooth outer surface is paint-work-friendly. A plastic liner and stainless-steel inner ensure low-friction operation. Bending does not result in relative movement of inner and outer – this is particularly important on suspension bikes. All parts can be replaced individually should this ever be necessary. They're made in seven colours, and can be ordered to fit suspension forks and V-brakes.

Development of the 'Progress-2' brake, shown on the photograph, is continuing with a view to eventual production.

The Cutting Crew, Am Mühlberg 16, D-61348 Bad Homburg, Germany.
Tel +49 6172 92868 1 Fax +49 6172 23729.
UK: See page 145

spinskins

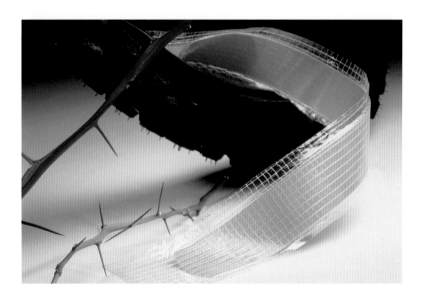

In the USA, SpinSkins cost around $39.95 a pair. Prices will vary worldwide.

SpinSkins, Warwick Mills,
301 Turnpike Road,
New Ipswich,
New Hampshire 03071, USA.
Tel +1 603 878 1565
Fax +1 603 878 4306
E-mail spinskins@aol.com
Website www.spinskins.com

When NASA's Mars Lander touches down, the airbags which cushion the landing will come from Warwick Mills. They also manufacture stab-proof clothing, and know more than most about puncture prevention. Now, their designer Charlie Howland has returned to his first love – bicycles. Ever since he built his first bike 25 years ago, he has hated punctures.

His work at Warwick Mills brought him to the answer. SpinSkins kevlar tyre liners offer protection from thorns, glass, flints and snakebite punctures, adding a meagre 34 grams to each wheel. Tyre liners have a chequered reputation, but SpinSkins claim that their patented super-close weave is far superior to any which have gone before. Tested over desert littered with cactus-spine, and used by top USA mountain-bike racing teams, SpinSkins have a practical and techno-logical pedigree to be proud of.

lyonsport adjustable stem

Cyclists with identical body dimensions may require dramatically different stem lengths, depending on their age, their sex and the flexibility of their muscles. This is the message from custom frame-builder Jeff Lyon, who has devised an elegant solution to the tiresome ritual of repeated stem changes. Lyonsport's 'Adjustable Stem' is made of square-walled 4130 cro-moly and has 12cm (4.75") of micro-adjustable horizontal travel. Jeff makes his stems in 73 degree and 90 degree versions. They are nickel-plated for scratch-resistence and tight dimensional tolerances, and two versions fit Aheadset or conventional setups.

Lyonsport, 1175 Plumtree Lane, Grants Pass, OR 97526, USA.
Tel +1 541 476 7092
email lyonsport@aol.com

In the USA, prices range from $89.95 and vary greatly worldwide

eggrings

Need some cranks shortening, a custom-chosen series of sprockets on a screw-on freewheel, or a 67-tooth chainring? If so, or for anything else imaginable but normally unobtainable for your cycle transmission, give Chris Bell of Highpath Engineering a call. He's an engineer with vast experience of supplying specialist transmission components – and if he can't find it for you, he'll make it. His best-known products, Eggrings, are rated as some of the finest, longest-lasting chainrings around, and are available round or oval to fit any crank.

Highpath Engineering, Cornant, Cribyn, Llanbedr PS,
Ceredigion, SA48 7QW, UK. Tel/Fax +44 1570 470035

quik klaws tire chains and tire cleats

Your front wheel slips on a patch of snow or ice: every winter cyclist knows the feeling of helpless insecurity which foretells disaster. An affordable first step in snow safety is to fit 'Tire Chains' from Koolstop. These, like the more sophisticated 'Tire Cleats', are designed to fit mountain-bike wheels – check your frame clearances before you ride off! The Tire Cleats provide superior traction, and have 'barrel' tensioners to ensure a good fit.

Ask your bike shop, or see page 145. In Europe, the Tire Chains cost around DM70 each, and the Cleats around DM90 each. Prices will vary worldwide.

airo-shield

The AIRO-Shield may look a simple product, but it cleverly solves a host of problems for the cyclist. First made for triathlon athletes training in all weathers, Tom Piszkin's AIRO-Shield protects the eyes from bugs, rain, freezing air and all sorts of nameless debris, making cycling a lot more fun. It's also a cost-effective and elegant solution for spectacle wearers who balk at the cost of prescription cycling sunglasses. The shields – in clear, yellow, amber, grey-smoke or mirrored-smoke tints – snap over transparent 'Airotachments' glued onto the helmet, block 99% UVA and UVB light, and are anti-fog coated.

AIRO-Series Inc., 1973 North Nellis Blvd., Suite 121, Las Vegas, Nevada 89115-3654, USA. Tel +1 702 382 7288 Fax +1 702 382 7288 email Tom@ttinet.com Website http://www.ttinet.com/tom

In the USA, the Airo-Shield costs $14.99 (Mirrored-Smoke $29.99)

kool-stop brake blocks

In Europe, Quik-Claws cost DM22.50, Stingers DM32.50

Kool-Stop continue their tradition of innovation in braking with 'Quik-Claws', designed so that the pad can be removed quickly and easily without losing brake adjustment – the pad is secured by a bolt passing through the stud. It's ideal for those who have to deflate the tyre to remove a wheel, because their brakes won't open far enough.

The 'Stinger' (not shown) is a dual-compound 'Quik-Claw'. A low-friction rear tip grips the rim smoothly, reducing chatter and squeal.

Stingers and Quik-Claws join Kool-Stop's well-proven brake block range, which now includes V-Brake type blocks.

Try your local bike shop or see page 145.

reflectalite bicycle bulb service

Reflectalite's Bicycle Bulb Service can provide replacement and upgrade bulbs and accessories for the vast majority of cycle lights in use – and their 'Bulb Finder' card identifies which bulb fits which light. Not only will they supply any shop worldwide, but if an individual customer can't find a bulb locally, Reflectalite will supply direct. In many cases this personal service is the only way to serve the cycling customer.

Alongside halogen, xenon, krypton, vacuum and LED bulbs, they offer a similar service for cycle computer batteries, a neat dynamo regulator and batteries for all types of cycle lights. Reflectalite are looking for distributors to handle some of their overseas workload.

Reflectalite, 24 Orchard Road, Brentford, Middlesex, TW8 0QX, UK. Tel +44 181 560 2432 Fax +44 181 847 2035

In the UK, bulbs usually cost under £3.99

The ones you missed

Listed below are some of the products featured in previous Encycleopedias, and which are not included in this edition. The list is not definitive, and we have taken out products which we know are no longer available. The contact details are the latest that we have available: some manufacturers may have moved without letting us know.

Alex Moulton Ltd
E94/5, E96: AM Series spaceframe cycles
Holt Road, Bradford on Avon, Wiltshire, BA15 1AH, UK. Tel +44 1225 865895 Fax +44 1225 864742

Bebop Incorporated
E96: Bebop Pedals
8570 Hamilton Ave, Huntington Beach, CA 92646, USA. Tel +1 714 374 0200 Fax +1 7143740268
Email mrbebop@bebop.com Website www.bebop.com

Bilenky Cycle Works
E96: Air Tandem
5319 North Second St, Philadelphia, PA 19120, USA. Tel +1 215 329 4744 Fax +1 215 329 5380

Bishopthorpe Bicycles
E96: Challenge Racer High Bicycle
35 Keeble Park North, Bishopthorpe, York, YO2 1SX, UK. Tel +44 1904 703413

Busch & Müller
E96: Cycle Star Mirror
D-58540 Meinerzhagen, Auf dem Bamberg 1, Germany. Tel +49 235 491 5710 Fax +49 235 491 5700

Chronos
E94/5, E96: Chronos Hammer
2936 Avenida Theresa, Carlsbad, CA 92009, USA. Tel 1 619 942 9049 Fax +1 619 942 9049

Dynrad
E93/4: Duo upright/recumbent tandem
c/o Radius Spezialräder, Borkstr. 20, D-48163 Münster,Germany. Tel +49 251 780 342
Fax +49 251 780 358 Email radrec@t-online.de

Easy Racers Inc
E96: EZ-1 recumbent
2891 Freedom Blvd, Watsonville, CA 95019, USA. Tel +1 408 722 977 Email tooeasy@aol.com
http://www.easyracers.com

Fateba Fahrradtechnik
E96: Fateba Long Bike recumbent
Bachmann & Co, Rosenstr. 11, CH-8400 Winterthur, Switzerland. Tel +41 522 126 911 Fax +41 522 137 841

Firma Veit Lehmann
E96: Tetrad hand-and-foot powered bike
Laubenhöhe 10, 69509 Mörlenbach, Germany.

Flux - Fahrräder
E93/4: ST-2 recumbent
Schubertstraße 2, 8038 Gröbenzell, Germany. Tel +49 8142 60470 Fax +49 8142 8792

Freedom Bikepacking
E93/4: Commuter and Limpet pannier bags
The Barn, Church Lane, Clyst St Mary, Devon EX5 1AB, UK. Tel +44 1392 877531 Fax +44 1392 877872

FutureCycles
E94/5, 96: Streetglider recumbents
Friends Yard, London Road, Forest Row, East Sussex RH18 5EE, UK. Tel +44 1342 822847
Fax +44 1342 826726

G. Wehmeyer Zweiradteile
E96: Weco 3BS-Synchro hubs
Engerstr. 47, D-33824 Werther, Germany.
Tel +49 520 3225/6/8 Fax +49 5203227

George Longstaff Cycles
E93/4: Tandem Trike
Albert Street, Chesterton, Newcastle under Lyme, Staffs ST5 7JF. Tel +44 782 561 966 Fax +44 782 566 044

Harig Liegeräder
E93/4: Aeroproject recumbents
Richard-Zanders-Str 48, Bergisch Gladbach, Germany D-51469. Tel/Fax +49 22 02 38455

Islabikes
E93/4: Trailerbike
252 Halesowen Road, Cradley Heath, Warley, West Midlands B64 6NH, UK. Tel/Fax +44 1384 566630

Jack Wolfskin
E96: Diogenes & Royal Flash bags and jackets
Postfach 1454, 64529 Mörfelden-Walldorf, Germany. Tel +49 610 593 3787 Fax +49 62322 6415

Lightning Cycle Dynamics
E94/5: Lightning P-38 E96: P-38, Stealth, R-84
312-Ninth Street, Lompoc, CA 93436, USA. Tel +1 805 736 0700 Fax +1 805 737 3265

M5
E96: M5 recumbents
Brak Straat,11, 4331 - TM, Middelburg, Netherlands. Tel +31 118 628 759 Fax +31 118 642 719

Mirrycle Corporation
E96: Mirrycle Mirrors & Bells
6101 Ben Place, Boulder, USA, Co 80301, USA.
Tel +1 303 4423495 Fax +1 303 4479273

Montague Corporation
E96: Triframe folding tandem
432 Columbia St., Ste 29, Cambridge, MA 02140, USA. Tel +1 617 491 7200 Fax +1 617 491 7207

Mühlberger
E93/4: Cool Team insulated bags
Bonner Wall 118, 5000 Köln 1, Germany. Tel +49 221 386056 Fax +49 221374978

PJ Taylor Cycles
E93/4, E94/5: Victorian E96: Discoverer mobility tricycles
375 Birchfield Road, Redditch, Worcs, B79 4NE, UK. Tel/Fax +44 1527 545262

Radical
E93/4: Radical suspended town bike
Damsterdiep 31B, NL-9711 SG, Groningen, Netherlands. Tel +31 503184483 Fax +31 503121123

Roberts Cycles
E93/4: Small-sized frame
89 Gloucester Road, Croydon, Surrey, CR0 2DN, UK. Tel +44 181 684 3370 Fax +44 181 683 1105

Schmidt Maschinenbau
E96: Schmidt's Original Nabendynamo
Königswiesenweg 4, 89077 Ulm, Germany.
Tel +49 731 387533

Schramm Spezial-Fahrräder
E96: Triset modular load-carrying trike
Richthofenstrasse 29, 31137 Hildesheim, Germany.
Tel +49 5121 76 0373 Fax +49 5121 760326

Sinner
E96: Record recumbent
Walkumaweg 6, 9923 PK Garsthuizen, Holland.
Tel 0031-595464318 Fax 31-595464318

St John Street Cycles
E96: D.O.G full-size folding racer; Thorn Kiddy Cranks for tandems, Thorn Discovery expedition tandem
91/93 St John Street, Bridgwater, Somerset, TA6 5HX, UK. Tel +44 1278 441502 Fax +44 1278 431107

Steco Metaalwaren-fabriek bv
E96: Attache-Mee pushchair carrier
Wolweg 34, NL-3776 LP, Stroe, Holland. Tel +31 34 2441441 Fax +31 34 2441584

Thijs Industrial Designs
E93/4: Thys Funfiets
Koorkerkstraat 10, 4331 AW Middelburg, Netherlands. Tel/Fax +31 118 634 166

Tubus Transport Systems
E93/4: tubular steel carrier racks
Overbergstrasse 22, D-48145 Münster, Germany.
Tel +49 251 131781 Fax +49 251 131783

Velocity
E93/4: Velocity electric-assisted bicycle
Burweg 15, CH-4058 Basel, Switzerland. Tel +41 616 934 358 Fax +41 616 934 332

Vitelli Velobedarf
E93/4: Camping and Buggy Trailers
Dornacherstr. 101, CH-4053 Basel, Switzerland.
Tel +41 61 361 7070 Fax +41 61 361 5770

Worksong Cycles
E93/4: Worksong full-size portable
8 Dagmar Road, Wood Green, London, N22 4RT, UK.
Tel +44 181 888 5650

For information about ordering any of the three previous Encycleopedias, see page 137

The Challenge High Bicycle from Encycleopedia 96

Bike Culture Quarterly

The publishers of *Encycleopedia* also publish *Bike Culture Quarterly*: an independent subscriptions magazine, published by cyclists for cyclists. It gives you intelligent, open-minded writing – practical and off-beat, traditional and radical. You'll find cycle design and technology, people-profiles, cycle touring, politics, cycling art and literature, and much, much more. We bring in big issues, ideas and insights – helped by the fact that we are an international publication: there's even a full German language edition. There are also specially commissioned illustrations from David Eccles and many other noted cycle artists and photographers. BCQ lives by the quality of its editorial alone: it carries no advertising. BCQ is larger than A4, and usually carries about 60 pages mostly in colour, using high quality paper. Our aim is to give you a good read. At the same time we help raise the cultural status of cycling. Each subscription increases BCQ's power and influence in the world – we go out of our way to make sure it is read by decision makers in matters of cycling, transport and the environment.

You can order BCQ either as a single issue, or as a four-issue subscription, or in conjunction with the next Encycleopedia. Details of our agents around the world are on page 139.

Plans and promises

Bike Culture Quarterly

The publishers of this book also publish Bike Culture Quarterly: a magazine which acts as a forum for new ideas in cycling. It carries no adverts, is mainly in colour, goes out in English and German-language editions, and covers themes not usually found in other publications. To give newcomers a taste of BCQ we include here a section which shows the kind of material BCQ carries (although we cannot include here the lively letters pages and readers' technical 'feedback' material). The following is an 'extra': it will not be published in BCQ. You can find out more about BCQ on page 137, and ordering information is on page 138.

Amsterdam, where the Dutch roadster rules supreme. The ubiquitous back-pedal brake means that there are often no brake levers on the handlebars.

Jim McGurn examines the cycle cultures of Northern Europe

For half a century the larger countries of Europe have given themselves heart and soul to motor-culture, with motorways, car factories and the car service industry all woven into the very fabric of their economies. We have now begun to realise that the result is a tapestry of troubles.

It has, at last, become socially acceptable to challenge the old order with arguments for real personal independence and appropriate mobility. But all the while, the smaller, nimbler, countries of Northern Europe – Holland, Denmark, Sweden, Norway, Switzerland – have been trying out new ideas and solutions, avoiding, with some success, the dead hand of a major road lobby and automotive industrial base. It was the Netherlands, Denmark and Switzerland which reacted most profoundly to the 1973 oil crisis, bringing in planned, comprehensive, integrated sustainable transport systems that are now quite mature, with a cycle culture as a part of everyday life for many people.

Despite its overt automania, Germany has long outstripped Britain in its enthusiasm for cycling. It has decent bike paths, especially in the flatter lands of the North where the Dutch/Flemish cycle culture exerts some influence. The hillier areas of the South are not lost to cycling: many scenic valleys have cycle paths down by the river, with dedicated tourist facilities servicing thousands of well-to-do touring cyclists. Many Germans are quite surprised when told that their country boasts 120 signposted long distance cross-country cycle routes, with a total length of 30,000 kilometres

(18,700 miles) and that half of these routes have been built since 1990.

While these facilities were being built up, the British government was hoping that cyclists would put away their bicycles and make their way to the nearest car showroom. In 1991, the House of Commons Transport Select Committee described cycling as 'too dangerous to encourage' because of the perceived risks inherent in a roads network that has done nothing to encourage cycling for 35 years. In Britain the official cycle usage figure varies between 1.8% and 2.3%. In Germany, with a similar climate, topography and outlook, around 8% of journeys are made by bicycle. The Germans also spend about twice as much on each bike as the British.

However, all is not well in either country's cycle industry. The value of cycle sales in Germany has dropped by about 20% over the last three years. This is partly due to the German economic recession, but also, perhaps, due to a degree of market saturation at the higher value end of the market. There is no sign that expenditure on cycle-related activities, such as cycling holidays or club membership, has fallen off: Weekend cycle tours are hugely popular, and Austria, Switzerland and Italy benefit from the custom of German cyclists from the professional classes travelling south for their holiday.

In Britain cycle sales have remained fairly stagnant over the last three years. This may change soon. Although Britain is 20 years behind its Northern continental neighbours in cycling provision, there are now rapid changes underway, and funding for cycling schemes is at an all-time high – £15 million ($24m) in the year 1995-96. This is still, however, only 20 pence (32 cents) per head of population, compared with a £20 ($32) per head expenditure currently recommended by the German government for its own citizens. Having discovered a bicycle on the road to Damascus, the British Government set up the National Cycling Strategy in July 1996. It commits them to working towards a doubling of cycle use to 4% of all journeys by 2002 and 8% of all journeys by 2012. Cycle planners are convinced that if the British invested as much as the Germans in cycling, British figures would rise high above their current stagnation levels. Although funding has been increased, it is nowhere near enough to justify government ambitions. Britain does have two cycling phenomena

Above: Everyone rides a bike in Holland – and what wonderful bikes they are!

Below: Stefan Thonett in Cologne, Germany, earns a living from his 'Radlast' cycle delivery company, offering an environmentally-friendly service for small businesses and individuals.

that Germany does not. The first is the 6,500-mile (10,000km) Sustrans National Cycling Network, to be completed shortly after the Millennium. It will probably be more integrated and better marketed than the German network. Sustrans are involved in a multi-million pound project to change the way that Britons regard and use the bicycle, and the sheer momentum of their work will bring profound benefits to British cycling, and to touring cyclists visiting Britain from other countries. Sustrans have about 20,000 supporters (not members), and the figure is growing by about 1000 each month.

The second very British cycling phenom-

enon is the 'charity ride'. Hundreds of thousands of British citizens take part. Some of them are regular cyclists, who enjoy the rare sense of solidarity to be experienced when cycling en masse. Others are once-a-year riders. For them the indignity of cycling is only to be considered if it's for charity. And, just to make sure that the status of cycling is brought as low as possible in the process, these riders often put on fancy dress, disguise their bicycles, or at least make sure the machine is as unroadworthy as possible. Heaven forbid that they might be taken for the kind of people who might cycle during the rest of the year. Charity rides of this sort are not common in Germany. A German cyclist is more likely to pay good money for one of the many cycling holidays promoted in colour brochures by large, experienced companies – which is further proof that personal investment in cycling rises in relation to how much the community as a whole values cycling.

What about the Dutch? While larger countries have been trying to rediscover their environmental soul, the Dutch have been implementing their Masterplan Bicycle. They are no eco-angels. This plan, for the wholesale promotion of cycling, is an economic and social necessity: the Netherlands are chronically over-populated, and huge numbers of its citizens are delighted to own and use their motor cars. About 7% of all journey-kilometres are pedal-powered, and 70% involve private motoring. The promotion of public transport and cycling are simply two of the principal weapons in the fight against national gridlock and environmental decay.

Since Masterplan Bicycle is a programme which can be applied to almost any industrialised country, region or city, it is worth setting out its principal aims:

- To ensure that by the year 2010 the number of kilometres cycled is 30% higher than it was in 1986.
- That the above increase should be 50% when applied to commuter journeys
- That cycle journeys should be made considerably quicker; about 20% quicker by the year 2010. A cycle journey of up to 5 kilometres should be just as quick as it would have been if that cyclist had gone by car.
- Greater integration of rail and cycle travel, to the extent that rail use per person increases by 15%.
- All businesses with more than 50 employees must produce a transport plan which takes account of cycling.

Bicycles are often used for community policing in Britain. Here, a traditional Pashley bicycle patrols the streets in Oxford.

- 50% fewer road deaths amongst cyclists and 40% fewer injuries by the year 2010.
- A decrease in cycle theft. There are 0.9 million thefts each year, out of 15 million cycles in the Netherlands. The fear of cycle theft is regarded as a major inhibition to cycle usage.

By 1990 Masterplan Bicycle was well underway. In that year the Dutch State increased its funding for cycle paths, cycle crossings, cycle tunnels etc. by 50%. With thirteen years to go before the target date of 2010, progress towards certain targets looks slow: cycle usage has not risen in any appreciable way. The reasons are not clear. The planners cite the building of leisure facilities at too great a distance from people's homes, and one particular blow to cycle usage was the Government's decision to include free public transport within the annual grant given to all Dutch students. However, there has been huge progress in lowering cycling deaths and injuries (a 20% decrease in the last ten years) and in the integration of public transport and cycling.

Each European country tackles, or fails to tackle, its transport crisis in its own way, but a body of knowledge is growing and being shared. In other continents, such as America, the bicycle struggles to be taken seriously as a form of transport. There is a world of difference between the vast expanses of the American Continent and the densely populated states of Europe, but 'developing' countries, whose cultural agenda is set by the US, but whose cities and social structures are closer to the European model, are in danger of taking the American road to private transportation. That Europe has followed the same road for so long gives it little moral leverage, but there are at last glimmers of hope in Europe which may kindle sparks elsewhere.

The fantasy man

Amsterdam-based artist Eric Staller has come to hope for a future that is technological yet human. Among his works, which range from large-scale architecture to whimsical mini-sculpture, there is a strong pedal-powered element, closely allied to his personal philosophy.

Why I do what I do is something of a mystery to me. I was born in 1947 but I was re-born as an artist in 1970. That was when I got what I call my nature-given calling. That was when I began spontaneously to get ideas that would cause me to say to myself: "I've just got to see that!" I suppose I'm addicted to surprising myself, to exploring the unknown, producing different sensations. My ideas come from my subconscious: they come into my head during brainstorming sessions in which I daydream the impossible, the outrageous, the irrational. The idea that makes me laugh involuntarily and often over the next weeks is the one that begins to obsess me. It calls my name: "Eric, build me" until I give in. That is the only way to exorcise the fantasy.

My outlook on the world was shaped in the 1960s by the space programme and its seemingly limitless promise. School classes were interrupted for every take-off and landing. There seemed to be the expectation that every American boy could (and must!) invent a better mouse trap. The promise of a utopian world through technology was all around us. I was especially impressed by the 1964 New York Worlds Fair with pavilions called Futurama, Progressland, The MoonDome, displaying futuristic architecture by Eero Saarinen and Buckminster Fuller, dazzling multi-media theatres and a working car engine you could walk through.

From 1971-91 I lived and worked in New York, a constant inspiration with Rauchenberg, Warhol, avant garde theatre, surrealistic sound and light at night clubs. Risk-taking seemed a way of life, and life-affirming: My art was photography and sculpture: otherworldly fantasies of light, space and motion. I wanted my work to transport the viewer to a dream-like unreality, a respite from the real world. In the 80s I began to feel disillusioned by the Art World. It seemed dry and joyless. I asked myself if I wanted to go on preaching to

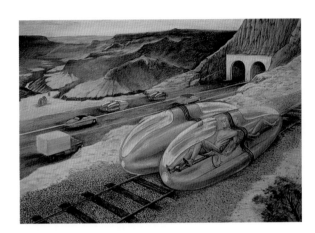

the converted. The answer came to me in 1985 with the creation of my LIGHTMOBILE, a Volkswagen Beetle covered with 1659 computerised lights. This took five months and all of my savings to build. But from the first moment I drove it out of my studio and through the streets of New York, I knew I was onto a powerful expression. This was some kind of magic wand; I could see an instantaneous surprise and delight in the faces of thousands of people.

I started to be interested in people's response as a kind of raw material for me: in a childlike way, people are touched, disarmed. I find this inspiring, and watching this collective response helps me to shape what I want to do next. Lightmobile made everyone laugh, but I then wanted to evoke another emotion. So I made BUB-BLEHEADS: four riders on a quadricycle, dressed in black, each wearing a lighted sphere on his/her head. The lights are computerised to give the illusion of the heads spinning, as if in conversation. People involuntarily gasp, hands reach for their hearts; I can read on their lips: "Oh my God! What is it?" It aggressively interrupts their private space. It's a little unsettling, other-worldly. But a second later they realise that it is harmless and rather vulnerable: something out of a dream. And then they smile; for they have been caught off-guard, goosed into enjoying a lovely sensation.

It became my goal to keep moving my art further from people's sense of reality. We are socialised out of having child-like responses; we need to quantify and explain everything. We embrace every new technology while warning of its de-humanisation. I am interested in projecting a 'nostalgic view of the future'. I create metaphors for future travel and communication that say: 'Yes, the future will be more technological AND it can be human and humorous.'

Communication is what the OCTOCYCLE is about: eight people sharing an experience, communing with one another and with the astonished passers-by. It's somewhere between art and industrial design. It's practical-ridiculous. It's a twist on other multi-person bikes. All eight riders contribute to the forward motion while sitting elbow to elbow in a two meter-diameter circle. Seven of them face each other, as if at a round table, while the eighth faces forward and steers. The feet of the riders can be seen pedalling up and down in the middle, as if mixing an invisible substance. I find it interesting to dream up a confection like this and then work with an engineer on the give-and-take process of marrying aesthetics to physics.

I am also very interested in devices for stimulating community. People are driving to and from work alone. They go to a fitness facility after work and ride a stationary bike to nowhere while talking to no-one. Yet we can have social lives, fit bodies, shared experiences, while going places, and without poisoning the air. I am now engineering and promoting human-powered trains and boats. They are designed with a blend of form and function. Like sci-fi films, they are suggestions of how the future might look. And I hope they suggest that the future just might be something to look forward to.

All images © Eric Staller

Left: 'Bubbleheads', 1987, New York City

Above left: Human-powered 'Egg-train', 1993

Above: Four-person human-powered module

Downhilling on the up

Photo courtesy 'DIRT Magazine'

Peter McGrath reviews developments in the downhill mountain biking craze

Downhill mountain bike racing is the latest craze, and MTB riders have a new rash of heroes – men and women with kevlar for skin, padded knees and elbows, and heads helmeted to avoid their owners becoming extras in a medical soap opera. Although most courses involve sections which are not downhill, downhilling (DH) often demands more nerve than stamina, and the top names can give the impression that fitness regimes are for wimps.

Downhilling has its own sub-culture. Take away the bikes, add snowboards or surfboards and the people would look just as comfortable. They're mostly the same young crowd with disposable income. Some are deadly competitors, some are there for the fun of a frenetic few minutes at the mercy of gravity, some simply to watch. And they're ready to pay for the latest equipment – and that's behind the marketing interest. But almost everyone can find a bike for careering down a hill: whether it's a one-gear hack with cowhorn handlebars or a crazed GT. Downhilling is an atavistic pleasure known to most children, but usually forgotten when they grow into adult pomposity. Most lads have tales of hammering a bike down a hillside. Some have scars to prove it. The first mountain bikers were, of course, the Marin County crew in the mid-70s. And their rides? Pure downhill.

The top machines are tuned to the rider's needs: they are fast and nearly bombproof with aluminium everything, and disc brakes. I was recently sent a pair of Shimano V-brakes for test, accompanied by grave warnings: "They're designed to give downhillers one-finger braking at speeds of 40 or 50 plus miles an hour... (64-80km/h)" was the breathless quote. Hang on, I've JUST touched 50mph down an Alpine col, in a nose-on-the-crossbar aero tuck on a naked road-bike – so how can anybody hit 50 off-road? But hyperbole is part of the DH scene.

DH bikes have become increasingly specialised, but the trickle-down of DH bike components into daily cycling life has begun. A top 1997 DH bike looks more like a trials motorbike without the engine. The front suspension forks are massive, the frame built of composites or oversize tubes, the rear suspension is often via highly-tuned linkages and oil-damped shock absorbers. V brakes, or disc brakes front and rear provide the much-need braking. Serious downhiller racers usually run a single chainring and fit tensioning devices to stop the chain being sucked between wheel or thrown off during the race.

Manufacturers are keen to have their products used, and top riders have bikes individually built, and set up for the rider and the particular descent. DH is the research and development wing of today's MTB industry. One year's secret DH debutante component is heavily reviewed and advertised in the next year's commercial mountain-bike press. The dire warnings about the effectiveness of Shimano's V-brakes doesn't stop them being fitted to mid-price MTBs that will obviously spend as much time on the road as off, yet ads in the MTB press are now headlined by items such as the wide, upswept, braced handlebars used for fine control at high speeds.

Any DH course worth its name will include jumps, drop-offs and corners that mix an adverse camber with a loose surface. The skill levels and bike control of the participants can be phenomenal, but many riders overcook it. Crashes are frequent, and DH riders wear full-face helmets, goggles, elbow pads, knee guards and reinforced gloves.

DH bikes account for only a small market share at present, media interest is disproportionate At a time when road racing is having its sponsorship troubles, down-hilling revels in sponsorship from Grundig, with America and Europe proving fertile recruiting grounds for DH worshippers. The sport is not overly male-dominated: there are some women whose DH courage and bike control can make men on the circuit speak in awed tones. But, as in the rest of life, women find it harder to turn talent into professional sponsorship contracts.

DH frames and long-travel dual crown suspension forks are fronting manufacturer's product line-ups. Unless they're mistaken, there's money down them thar hills, and the products will trickle down to shop-bought MTBs. Better full-suspension bikes and wider use of V brakes are obvious candidates. How long before disc brakes make it to mid-price bikes?

Whatever the image, the exposure, the hype, look at DH riders once they've crossed the line. Limbs screaming with lactic acid overload, chest heaving, red-faced, leaning on the bike, but grinning through the grimace. And wonder if you'd have the skill and nerve to do it yourself.

DH might be a long way from most people's Sunday potter, or the daily duel with the cars on the way to work, but it's taking taking cycle sport in a fresh new direction, just when it seemed cyclists had tried everything.

The British magazine which covers down-hilling is *Dirt*, available on newstands and by subscription. Tel 01305 251263

Cycling takes a high profile at the Earth Centre

Year by year it seems to get worse. The environment takes a kicking, the politicians wring their hands, and we all get more anxious – or pretend it's not really happening. Now, on a former colliery site in Northern England, a group of inspired and ambitious environmentalists have embarked on a project which will show the way to many. The Earth Centre, near Doncaster, aims to be a world class visitor centre, bringing the concept and process of sustainable development to life.

It's a multi-million pound development on a 400 acre (160ha) site on the River Don at Conisbrough in the Dearne Valley, to be opened in stages from 1998 and completed by 2000. The Earth Centre is a National Millennium Landmark project, with an initial £34 million ($55 million) for Stage One already provided by the lottery-funded Millennium Commission, European Regional Development funds, and English Partnerships. If all goes well there will be, by the year 2000, a number of major attractions with supporting projects and facilities set in an attractive, working landscape and gardens. The Earth Centre has had its ups and downs, but is now firmly on course, if somewhat delayed, and the first phase of development is to be completed in 1998.

Cycling will play an important role at the Earth Centre, and Open Road, publishers of Encycleopedia, have been engaged as consultants on cycling and soft-energy transport. Whereever feasible, pedal-power will be brought into the everyday operation of the Centre, and there will be opportunities for visitors to ride a wide range of cycles on a purpose built track. In addition, the Future Works attraction aims to house a large collection of future transport in the world, with possibilities for visitors to test out some of the vehicles. Both the cycling and the soft-energy transport facilities will be part of Stage One, and are therefore scheduled to open in May '98.

Other Earth Centre attractions in Stage One include the Planet Earth Gallieries, which will offer a journey into a sustainable world, setting the stage for other Earth Centre projects to explore ideas for a sustainable future. There will also be a big top covered area and a 'wilderness theatre' hosting programmes of live entertainment and special events, such as a kite festival, and a Children's Olympics. Also to be completed in 1998 are two sustainability learning centres: the Living Institute and Water Works, which will be surrounded by landscaped gardens.

Also planned is Future Works: a focus for the best ideas and practice in innovation and efficiency. The New Millennium City Show will present a model of London, aiming to present a practical, sustainable future for the city.

There are plans for an Electronic Forum to enable visitors to exchange ideas and comment on future concerns. At '21st Century Living' visitors will be able to explore a multitude of gadgets and devices found in houses of the future.

Planned for the Millennium year, and destined to be the centrepiece of the Earth Centre is the Ark, an energy-efficient glass-roofed building housing themed exhibitions. The World Park Antarctica will incorporate light and graphics, and a simulated ice cap. The Earthscope Communication Screen, fed from an open plan control room where people can participate in the vision mixing process, will broadcast environmental news from around the globe, as well as concert events. In the Arc visitors will experience the Solar Age, represented through prisms, and 'Sunny Gyms' will be a workout space in which human physical energy is compared to the energy required for household items.

Stage One of the Earth Centre's development, including the cycling and alternative transport facilities, is planned to be a viable attraction in its own right. However far the Earth Centre develops, it promises to be a physical focus for national debate about what sort of future we want. It will be presenting the environmental dabate about our future to large numbers of visitors: 600,000 are projected for 1998, rising to 750,000 in Millennium year.

We will do our best to ensure that all visitors have the chance to enjoy an exciting cycling experience at the Earth Centre, and that they come away enthused about taking up cycling in their daily lives. We hope to help the Earth Centre become a powerhouse for new ideas in cycling, and a dynamic central point for the promotion of cycling nationally, and we'll report on progress in Bike Culture Quarterly.

The art of cycling

The Golden Years

Between the years 1880 and 1900 the gods conspired to give mankind a twin delight: the Golden Years of the bicycle and of the printed illustration.

By the 1890's the high-wheeler had been superseded by the safety bicycle, enabling the less adventurous to take to the wheel. It brought freedom to millions, and artists and writers, many of them cyclists, were soon expressing this new sense of liberation in their work.

Publishers were enjoying a boom in illustrated periodicals. Improved printing technology had given illustrators the opportunity to express themselves without restriction and the publishers knew that pictures sold magazines. New, large-page formats made the pictures very popular: readers could cut them out, colour them in, frame them, and hang them on the wall.

All this meant boom time for the illustrators. As the popularity of cycling increased hundreds of delightful romantic pictures were published. Many artists and illustrators achieved national fame, and artists not associated with the illustration genre became captivated by the bicycle. In Britain, Sir John Lavery, John Quinton Pringle and Joseph Crawhall produced some wonderful evocative impressionist paintings of bicycles and their riders, reinforcing the prestige and desirability of cycling as a whole.

Right: The romance and freedom of cycling are captured by the German artist T. Gülich

Far right: This impressionist painting by Joseph Crawhall captures in a few brush strokes the movement of the woman rider. The original painting can be seen in the Burrell Collection in Glasgow, Scotland.

Above: This work by the French artist
A. de Parys shows how popular bicycle riding
and posing were to Parisians in the Bois de
Boulogne, a delightful oasis of tree-lined
lanes and cyclists' cafés

Right: The famous magazine illustrator, Lucien
Davis, captures here the joys of winter riding,
even if there is a degree of wishful thinking in
the harmony he portrays between road users

Below: The detail in this interesting work by
Scottish artist John Quinton Pringle shows
that he was more than familiar with the
machine

Ringrider

Dinger had cruised the Ring since MotorCor had built it, and they'd looked after him well. His Formula Freedom had the latest upgrades, with the spec and performance figures listed neon-bright along the side, for all to see. Food, drink, drugs and hygiene facilities were all on-board, giving three weeks of driving between refill services. By day he tuned to Radio MotorCor; for mood music and personality tips. Evenings, with the car on autodrive, he clicked onto MotorVision, and enjoyed programmes about the natural world: butterflies, polar bears, bright-plumed birds in steamy jungles.

The controls purred in his hands, giving him the best of MotorCor's FeelGood biofeedback technology. He could sense how the machine caught and amplified his whole personality, especially when his mood took him to the wildside. But on the whole he set a steady course, living his life to the rhythm of the roadside security fenceposts, which were interrupted only by MotorCor lookout towers each kilometre. The guards looked down, and waved occasionally.

Despite its higher tariff Dinger preferred the outside lane of the Ring, with vistas of the Outlands. The inside lane gave views onto the red-brick blockscape of Cityside, rising up a hundred metres away, beyond the rubble-stubble of the safety zone.

He knew little about the people who lived there. He'd often seen them moving about in front of the buildings. He'd seen them gathered together on summer evenings, eating, drinking, dancing, and chatting in small groups around a bicycle repair stand. He'd seen documentaries about them. They were as good as lawless, and cycled round with bagfuls of wild flower seed and tree seedlings, which they planted at random, yes anywhere they liked, before vanishing, back beyond the safety zone. They wore natural fibres, and ate totally unprocessed food. But their bicycles, he had been told, were their worldly joy, and they loved them with an intensity frightening to behold.

They were strange, these people, and not to be helped. It's not as if MotorCor hadn't tried. The Company had built them exciting bike paths alongside the periphery fence, and even supplied bicycles, made by the million in a purpose-built factory, and rugged enough to last a whole year, rain or shine.

On his refill stops he had heard disloyal grumbles about this well meant company initiative. The investment, it was said, had been heavy, and could have been better spent on repairing the Ring's road surface. True, he rarely saw a repair underway, and the Ring was everywhere pitted with holes as deep as a car wheel. But MotorCor had its own way of doing things. It had invested in fitting its cars with superb multi-response suspension systems, lasting as long as three months before replacement, and allowing more experienced Ring-drivers to hit speeds of up to twenty miles an hour (30km/h), but only in top of the range vehicles.

This was Dinger's world before his encounter with the grey-haired one.

The problem had really begun a week before. The computers at MotorCor Central had noticed that Dinger's average speed had been dropping of late, with no corresponding increase in his in-car consumption levels. So they'd withdrawn his credit for the high tariff lanes, reducing him to the ignominy of the Cityside lane. He was aware of the grey one's presence before he saw him riding alongside, keeping pace, carless, care-less, along the long-abandoned cyclepath. Through the blurred rust of the fencewire he saw a man of beauty and grace. He saw body and bicycle moving as one, as if bound together, lithe arms intertwined with luxurious handlebar curves. Jet-black was the bike, with quicksilver cranks.

His grey hair dancing in the wind, the old man turned his head towards him, and smiled. Deep in Dinger's cerebral cortex some great pressure valve blew free, to rocket and rage round his brain. With frenzied hands he gave maximum acceleration. The Formula Freedom was about to show its class. It lurched wildly over the pockmarked road surface, and the suspension systems thudded and screamed as they struggled to cope. His mind was a combustion chamber of emotions and the control column hummed on maximum feedback. With safety systems on override, he threw the car into one pothole and out of another. He shouted out loud as it roared into a final crater, before cartwheeling off the road and over the fence, popping wheels and spewing out a miscellany of metal and MotorCor comestibles.

Dinger lay by his car, face down, surprised by the pleasant sensation of long grass stroking his cheeks, and rustling in his ears. Then he heard the crackle of the flames, and the the clicking freewheel of a hastily dropped bicycle. He knew that the grey-haired one was leaning over him, smiling, checking he was OK. The smell of fresh earth seemed to send a shock through Dinger's brain, and he felt that warm smile again, on the back of his neck. But he knew, even before he looked up, that the grey-haired one had sped on his way. As far as either horizon the path bore no sign of man or machine.

Jim McGurn

T-Shirts

All our T-shirts are made from top of the range premium 100% cotton by Screen Stars and are available in either large or extra-large.

▼ BIKE CULTURE T-SHIRT

The simple Bike Culture T-shirt sports the BCQ logo, designead by David Eccles, reproduced as a small crest on the front and enlarged right across the back, printed black on white.

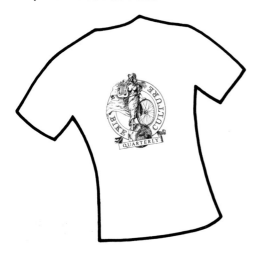

▲ BCQ 2 T-SHIRT

The BCQ 2 T-shirt also sports the BCQ logo on the front as a small crest but features the popular cover picture from BCQ No2, by David Eccles, in full colour on the back.

Owing to popular demand, we are now also offering our T-shirts in a special format for the recumbent cyclist. This format features the main image on the front as opposed to the back with the smaller logo/crest on the left sleeve.
If you would like this format please remember to tick the appropriate box on the order form.

ENCYCLEOPEDIA
▼ 96 T-SHIRT

These feature the word Encycleopedia (in black with 'cycle' picked out in red) as a small motif on the front, and a colour reproduction of the David Eccles' Encycleopedia cover design on the back.

Prices and ordering details are on pages 138/139

BICYCLE – the cycling video

We are continuing to offer this universally acclaimed video. This two hour tape is a specially edited compilation of six half-hour programmes originally broadcast in 1991:

Invention – the evolution of the modern bicycle.
Wheels of Change – Mass production and craftsmanship. The mountain bike ascendancy. Recumbents and the aerodynamics of cycling.
The Ultimate – a season with Greg LeMond, riding with the Tour de France.
The Business – How the powerbase of cycle production has shifted towards the East. The multi-billion yen racing business of Japanese Keirin.
Free Spirits – The sweetspots and obsessions of those who live by the bicycle.
Vehicle for a Small Planet – Clean air, road space and fossil fuels are being sacrificed to the motor vehicle. The argument for a mass return to the bicycle is irrefutable.

The Bicycle video costs £14.99 + postage. The sound track is in English. PAL VHS.

AUSTRALIA AND USA.
The York Films Bicycle video is available in Australia and the USA only from their agents. The retail price may differ from the above price.
Australia: *The Video Bookshelf, 25 Nelson Street, Balaclava, Victoria 3183. Tel. (03) 534 7246.*
USA: *Famous Cycling Videos Inc, 704 Hennepin Avenue, Box C1, Minneapolis, 55403. Tel. 1 800 359 3107.*

David Eccles Prints

We commissioned David Eccles, one of Britain's foremost cycling illustrators, to produce original images of 19th century cycles in the form of a limited edition set of four linocuts. Conceiving an image and printing it from a block of cork linoleum is a rare and delicate craft. A linocut has a limited capacity for printing due to the fragility of the material. David produced 75 individually numbered and signed sets of the four prints before cancelling each block.

Because both the printing and the inking are done by hand no two prints will be exactly the same.

The paper, made entirely from 100% cotton and acid-free, has been specially made by hand for this edition by Chris Bingham of Ruscombe Valley Paper. It replicates exactly paper made in the mid-to-late 1700s. For our purposes we had the making hot-pressed by the Wookey Hole Mill.

These prints are offered individually and, subject to availability, also in sets of all four prints. Each print is numbered, signed and dated by the artist.

The prints have all been window-mounted on 46cm x 41cm acid-free conservation board. For practical reasons, we cannot supply the prints ready-framed. The prints can be ordered individually or, subject to availability, as a complete co-ordinated set of four.

DURSLEY PEDERSEN TANDEM, Turn of the century Pedersens, in solo or tandem form, were an elegant and expensive alternative to conventional diamond-framed bicycles. At least one Pedersen tandem weighed an astonishing 28lb (12.7kg) and was designed to carry 24 stone (153kg).

MERGAMOBILE The 'Mergamobile' was made of wood and propelled via a pulley system operated in a treadle fashion via the pedals. The origins of the machine are unclear, and opinion varies considerably. We would welcome any new information on this mysterious machine.

ALPHA BANTAM CIRCA 1898 The Alpha Bantam was built by the Crypto Cycle Company in Clerkenwell Road, London and was one of the last in a series of attempts to maintain the popularity of direct front-drive against the ever increasing popularity of the chain-driven rear wheel drive. The Bantam sported an epicyclic hub gear in the front wheel.

BICYCLE RACING, mid 1880s High bicycles were exciting and precarious thoroughbreds. Direct drive meant that one rotation of the pedals translated into one revolution of the wheel: so wheels remained large until the gradual introduction of the smaller-wheeled safety bicycle, made possible by the happy idea of running a chain to the rear wheel.

Prices and ordering details are on pages 138/139

Bound Sets

Your chance to catch up on all BCQs so far, and to enjoy what will soon be a sought-after collector's item: the first 12 issues of Bike Culture Quarterly (Summer '94 to Spring '97) in a purpose-made maroon and gold binder. It's virtually a book in 12 parts, with over 800 adverts-free pages (590 of them in colour) of the best cycle writing around, making it, we believe, the biggest, most comprehensive cycling reference work ever compiled. It's timeless stuff – as fresh now as when it was written. You can read it as a book, or you can remove and replace each issue individually, in seconds. It's an ideal gift for any cyclist, with life-long value.

● As a non-subscriber ordering everything separately you would have to pay at least £84.50, depending on postage. We offer you the package, representing three years of our best work, including binder and postage for £45.00.

● Why? Because we believe you will like it so much that you will soon want to become a subscriber! Please bear in mind that it will not always be possible to obtain a complete set: some of the early issues had a low print run. We have sets made up, ready to send, and you will find an ordering form on page 138.

NOTES:

1 The offer includes 110 pages of the 1994/95 Encyclopedia, since BCQ3 was only ever available bound into it. This full-colour book originally sold at £15.00.

2 The above prices are for the UK only. For further countries where we have agents, prices are given on page 138. For other countries, please contact us for prices.

The smart, high quality binder is also available separately. It can hold at least 12 issues of BCQ, and has 'Bike Culture Quarterly' printed in gold on the spine.

Bike Culture Week

A unique international

cycling event in France.

Photographs by

Jason Patient

Right: All together for the camera

Below: The owner of the bike shop in Thury-Harcourt enjoyed a ride on the Rapide

Encycleopedia and Bike Culture readers get together every year for a week of cycling in France, in an international gathering of like-minded cyclists. It's based at a *gîte d'étape* in Normandy, France, in an area of very quiet and fairly flat country roads and easy-going off-road cycle routes. La *Grange d'Espins* is about 20 kilometres south of Caen, five kilometres from the delightful wooded hills of the *Suisse Normande*. It's an ancient farm, forming a secluded courtyard bordered by the remains of an 14th Century priory, all within 12 hectares of land, and very close to several ancient forests, with many well signed cycle routes through them. Good quality mountain bikes are available for hire at the *Gîte*. There are 50 beds in thirteen rooms, and unlimited camping alongside, with the usual camping facilities.

The BCQ and Encycleopedia editorial staff take part, along with cycling celebrities, such as Mike Burrows. There are simultaneous guided rides each day, one of them led by Alain Rouilliard, the owner of the *Gîte*, and smaller groups often prefer to do their own thing. A choice of shorter rides for less athletic cyclists is always on offer.

Alain and Isabel Rouilliard live on site with their children, and are keen cyclists – he often organises local cycling events. We bring along some interesting bikes, and enjoy a nice, stress-free time ourselves, alongside organising evening talks and entertainment. There are facilities for volleyball, table-tennis, seven-a-side football and horse-riding on site (book the latter in advance), with swimming, archery, canoeing, and paragliding nearby. Children are well catered for.

The cost for bed, breakfast, and one evening meal (on the evening of arrival) is £195 per person in the *Gîte*, and £145 per person camping (bring your own tent). This includes all Open Road services, and VAT. After the inclusive evening meal on the first night you can book your own packed lunches and/or evening meals once you are there. An evening meal at the *Gîte* costs 60 francs, and there is a vegetarian option.

Sorry, there can be no reduction for

Left: Talking bikes en route. John Agner from Southampton, UK, and Horst Alt from Frankfurt, Germany compare notes.

Below: BCQ and Encycleopedia's German distributors Kalle and Gaby Kalkhoff plan their homeward journey. They spent three weeks cycling back to Oldenburg on their Pedersen tandem.

Bottom: Local cycle campaigner, physio-therapist and inventor Jean-Luc Salasin brought along this sail-assisted bike – a prototype which, he admits, is more suited to beaches or parks than to the open road. In a fresh breeze, the sail certainly gave a good push!

children 14 and over, but we can offer £40 off for children over 4 years old. For children 4 and under who need a bed there is a £60 discount, and those so young that they do not need a bed can take part free of charge.

Most rooms have a shower, and a few have shower and toilet: we try to allocate them fairly according to who booked first, and will take special needs into account.

The deposit is 10% of the total (non-refundable, unless you can make an excellent case). Remember to calculate this once you have taken off your discounts for children. Open Road shareholders are entitled to an extra 5% discount. Cheques payable to Open Road Ltd. Final payment to be made by April 1998. Participants from some countries make shared travel arrangements, and details are sent to all those who book.

The dates for 1998 are beginning 24th May for six nights. For future dates, please contact us.

Booking
Please write to us with the following details: name, address, telephone number and the best time to contact you, names of all adults, names and ages of children, the total cost, and the amount of the deposit enclosed. An invoice will be sent for the remainder of the payment.

Please direct all enquiries and payments to the York office (address below). For details of how to pay from outside the UK see page 139. We can also accept credit card payments.

Open Road Ltd, The Raylor Centre, James Street, York, YO1 3DW, UK. Tel +44 1904 412200 Fax +44 1904 411155 email peter@bcqed-it.demon.co.uk

For orders of back issues and other merchandise, use this order form.

Placing your order

	USA	Mexico/Canada	+ postage	Australia/New Zealand	+ postage	Germany/Austria	+ postage	Switzerland	+ postage	UK/Rest of World	UK postage	Other European postage	Rest of World postage	Choices	Quantity	Total Price
Publications																
Encyc. 5 incl. video (Out May 98)	$ 28.00	$ 30.80	$ 4.00	—	—	DM49,-	DM8,-	SF42,-	SFr7,-	£ 16.00	£ 2.50	£ 3.50	£ 5.00			
Encyc. 5 (no video)	$ 20.00	$ 22.00	$ 4.00	—	—	DM37,-	DM8,-	SF32,-	SFr7,-	£ 12.00	£ 2.00	£ 3.00	£ 4.00			
* Encyclopedia 4 (includes video)	**	$ 19.80	$ 4.00	A$ 35.00	A$ 5.00	DM35,-	DM8,-	SF30,-	SFr7,-	£ 12.00	£ 2.50	£ 3.50	£ 5.00			
* Encyclopedia 4 (no video)	**	**	**	—	—	—	—	SF12,-	SFr7,-	£ 10.00	£ 2.00	£ 3.00	£ 4.00			
Encyclopedia 93/4	$ 9.00	$ 9.90	$ 2.50	A$ 15.00	A$ 2.50	DM14,-	DM8,-	SF12,-	SFr7,-	£ 3.50	—	£ 1.25	£ 2.00			
* Encyclopedia 94/5 (inc.BCQ3)	$ 23.00	$ 25.30	$ 3.00	A$ 25.00	A$ 3.00	DM35,-	DM8,-	SF30,-	SFr7,-	£ 6.00	—	£ 1.25	£ 2.00			
* Encyclopedia 96 (no video)	$ 18.00	$ 19.80	$ 4.00	A$ 35.00	A$ 5.00	DM30,-	DM8,-	SF26,-	SFr7,-	£ 6.00	£ 2.00	£ 2.00	£ 3.50	North America price includes video		
BCQ 1 – 12 set & binder	$118.00	$129.80	—	A$225.00	—	DM135,-	—	SF115,-	—	£ 45.00	£ 15.00	£ 15.00	£ 20.00			
* BCQ single issues (excl. BCQ3)	$ 9.50	$ 10.45	$ 2.00	A$ 10.00	A$ 1.50	DM15,-	DM4,-	SF13,-	SFr7,-	£ 6.00	£ 1.00	£ 1.50	£ 2.00	Issue(s):		
BCQ Binders (takes 12 issues)	$ 12.00	$ 13.20	$ 3.00	A$ 20.00	—	DM18,-	DM8,-	SF15,-	SFr7,-	£ 6.00	£ 1.50	£ 2.50	£ 4.00			
Subscriptions																
BCQ for 4 consec. issues (1 year)	$ 34.00	$ 37.40	—	A$ 46.00	—	DM75,-	—	SF65,-	—	£ 24.00				Start at BCQ Issue…		
BCQ for 12 consec. issues (3 years)	$102.00	$112.20	—	A$130.00	—	DM210,-	—	SF185,-	—	£ 66.00				Start at BCQ Issue…		
BCQ/E4 One Year incl. E4 video	$ 49.50	$ 54.45	—	A$ 80.00	—	DM120,-	—	SF105,-	—	£ 29.00				Start at BCQ Issue…		
BCQ/E4 One Year excl. E4 video	—	—	—	—	—	DM110,-	—	SF95,-	—	£ 27.00				Start at BCQ Issue…		
BCQ/E5 One Year incl. E5 video	$ 62.00	$ 68.20	—	—	—	DM125,-	—	SF105,-	—	£ 37.00				Start at BCQ Issue…		
BCQ/E5 One Year excl. E5 video	$ 54.00	$ 59.40	—	—	—	DM110,-	—	SF95,-	—	£ 33.00				Start at BCQ Issue…		
BCQ/E Three Years, incl. videos	$183.00	$201.30	—	—	—	DM330,-	—	SF285,-	—	£ 95.00				Start at BCQ Issue…		
BCQ/E Three years excl. videos	$160.00	$176.00	—	—	—	DM300,-	—	SF260,-	—	£ 89.00				Start at BCQ Issue…		
Open Road Art																
David Eccles limited edition print	$100.00	$110.00	$ 5.00	—	—	DM160,-	DM13,-	SF140,-	SFr11,-	£ 65.00	£ 5.00	£10.00	£20.00	Print 1/2/3/4		
David Eccles ltd.edition.(set of 4)	$350.00	$385.00	$15.00	—	—	DM550,-	DM13,-	SF480,-	SFr11,-	£220.00	£ 5.00	£10.00	£20.00			
Pedersen Poster A2	—	—	—	—	—	DM25,-	DM10,-	SF22,-	SFr9,-	—	—	—	—			
Clothing																
BCQ T-shirt B/W	$ 15.00	$ 16.50	$ 3.00	A$ 15.00	—	DM30,-	DM8,-	SF22,-	SFr7,-	£ 10.00	£ 1.00	£ 1.50	£ 2.50	XL/L; Image front / Image back		
BCQ2 T-shirt (Tortoise & Hare)	$ 22.50	$ 24.75	$ 3.00	A$ 30.00	—	DM50,-	DM8,-	SF32,-	SFr7,-	£ 15.00	£ 1.00	£ 1.50	£ 2.50	XL/L; Image front / Image back		
E96 T-shirt	$ 22.50	$ 24.75	$ 3.00	A$ 30.00	—	DM50,-	DM8,-	SF32,-	SFr7,-	£ 15.00	£ 1.00	£ 1.50	£ 2.50	XL/L; Image front / Image back		
Videos																
Video for E4	$ 8.00	$ 8.80	$ 2.50	A$ 12.00	A$ 2.00	DM15,-	DM8,-	SF13,-	SFr7,-	£ 2.00	£ 1.00	£ 2.50	£ 2.50	E4 Video/E96 Video		
Video for E5 (Available May 98)	$ 12.00	$ 13.20	$ 2.50	—	—	DM24,-	DM8,-	SF20,-	SFr7,-	£ 8.00	£ 1.00	£ 2.50	£ 2.50	Half price with book (see above)		
York Films Video	—	—	—	—	—	DM42,-	DM8,-	SF33,-	SFr7,-	£ 14.99	£ 1.00	£ 2.50	£ 2.50			

* Less subscribers' discount

Total

(For how to pay see opposite page)

* **Subscribers** are entitled to 20% off BCQ and Encyclopedia back issues where marked*, and get them post free.
Combined Encyclopedia and Bike Culture subscriptions always include the NEXT Encyclopedia to be published, unless otherwise stated. Videos are all VHS, and sent in the format usual in the country of order, unless you tell us otherwise.

Note: We have no room here to list prices for Demark and the Netherlands. We have agents in all these countries. See the page opposite for how to contact them.

If cheque enclosed please tick [ ]

CREDIT CARD DETAILS (not available in Germany)

Name Mr / Mrs / Ms

Address (if different)

Post Code

Your unique reference number (if you have one) [. . . . .]

Visa/Delta [ ]   Access/Mastercard [ ]   Eurocard [ ]

Card Number [. . .] [. . .] [. . .] [. . .]

Issue Number [.]   Expiry Date [. / .]

Switch [ ]

Switch Number [. . .]

Issue Number [.]   Valid From [. / .]   Expiry Date [. / .]

Date [. / . / .]

DELIVERY ADDRESS

Name Mr / Mrs / Ms

Address

Post Code

Telephone (daytime)

How to order

1. Make your choice from the ordering table opposite, *being sure to make the choices requested.*

2. Add up the prices. Choose the price column for your country. Remember that subscribers are entitled to 20% discount on back issues, and get them post-free. Refer to the notes under the table if in doubt.

3. Check on this page for details of where to send your order and how to pay. Note that you can usually order by telephone if you wish.

4. Finally, fill out the form with your details, and send off your order and payment. We'll get the goods to you within 28 days, but usually a lot sooner.

USA, Mexico and Canada

** To order additional copies of this book, contact The Overlook Press, 2568 Route 212, Woodstock, N.Y. 12498, U.S.A. Tel: (914) 679-6838 Fax: (914) 679-8571

Send payment and all letter correspondence regarding merchandise and back issues to:
Open Road USA, PO Box 291010, Los Angeles, CA 90029.
Tel: (213) 468 1089 **Fax:** (213) 462 4359 **email:** dylan@bikecult.com.
Credit card payments accepted. We operate a bounty program: sign up a new subscriber and we add two issues to your subscription.
California residents please add local sales tax to everything except subscriptions.

Deutschland, Österreich und die Schweiz

Alle aus Deutschland, Österreich und der Schweiz stammenden Bestellungen von einzelnen Ausgaben (BCQ oder Encyclopedia), Jahresabonnements, T-Shirts, Videos usw werden von Kalle Kalkhoff, KGB, Donnerschweerstr 45, 26123 Oldenburg, **Tel:** 0441 8850389 **Fax:** 0441 8850388 bearbeitet.
Für weitere Informationen und Preise von Einzelexemplare, rufen Sie KGB an und sprechen Sie mit Kalle.

Zahlungsmodus

Soweit Sie über ein Konto in der Bundesrepublik verfügen, senden Sie bitte mit Ihrer Bestellung einen Verrechnungs-Scheck an KGB in deutscher Währung.

Die Schweiz

Unsere neue Postcheckkontonummer für Schweizer Abonnenten ist 87-601949-5 KGB Kalle Kalkhoff. Senden Sie bitte Ihre Bestellung an KGB und den Betrag in Schweizer Währung an dieses Konto. Verwenden Sie andernfalls einen Eurocheck. Bitte denken Sie daran, 'Oldenburg' als 'Ort' anzugeben und Ihre EC-Kartennummer auf der Rückseite des Schecks zu vermerken. Euroschecks müssen ebenfalls in DM notiert werden. English versions of Bike Culture and Encycleopedia can be sent by KGB on request.

Netherlands

Subscriptions: Fietsersbond ENFB, Postbus 2828, 3500 GV Utrecht. **Tel:** 0348 417058. **Fax:** 0348 423119.
Single issues, merchandise, back numbers and supplies to shops: Luud Steenbergen, Trapperkracht, Soerabayastr. 4, 3531 EB, Utrecht, **Tel/Fax:** 030 296 1015

New Zealand

Orders are handled by:
Cycle Works PO Box 33051, Christchurch.
Tel: (03) 3386803 **Fax:** (03) 3386231 **email:** bikes@tpnet.co.nz

Australia

All Australian orders are handled by:
Ian Sims, Greenspeed, 69 Mountain Gate Drive, Ferntree Gully, VIC 3156.
Tel: (03) 9758 5541 **Fax:** (03) 9752 4115 **email:** greenshp@ozemail.com.au
Ian accepts credit cards, cheques or money orders made out to Greenspeed.

UK and Rest of the World

Please send all orders for subscriptions, back issues and merchandise to:
Open Road Ltd, P.O. Box 141, Stockport, SU2 7BY, UK.
UK only: Open Road Ltd, FREEPOST, Stockport, SK2 7Y6. *(No stamp required).*
Tel: +44 1904 412200 **Fax:** +44 1904 411155 **email:** sales@bikecult.demon.co.uk
If the automatic answering service is running, please speak slowly and clearly and make sure you include relevant card details. We accept almost all credit and debit cards. If you want us to phone you back, tell us how. We always aim to phone back within 24 hours.
All cheques and Eurocheques must be payable to Open Road Ltd. If using a Eurocheque, please send your order in Pounds Sterling, putting 'Stockport, England' as the 'Place'. Credit card payments must be made in Pounds Sterling only. When using your card by post please indicate the type of card, expiry date, registered card address, the name as it appears on the card, the card number, and the name and address for delivery. For debit cards please add issue number and 'valid from' date.
We do not accept cheques from non-UK bank accounts made out in Pounds Sterling. If you are paying in a currency other than Sterling, please ensure that you are sending enough money at the current rate of exchange.

Denmark

Carl-Georg Rasmussen, Leitra APS. Box 64, DK-2570, Ballerup, Denmark
Tel/Fax 0421 83377
A one year BCQ subscription (4 issues) costs 200DKK. A single issue costs 55DKK.

Bike Culture on the High Street

It's impossible to buy just a bicycle. You take home a machine which will become a personal friend or an expensive liability, or, more likely, something between the two. For anyone who rides regularly, a cheap bike is never exactly that. Any money saved on the day it's bought will quickly be cancelled out by repair bills and personal disruption as short-life components give up the ghost, one by one. For long periods this 'cheap' bike sits at home, until the time can be found to buy and fit a replacement part, or to take it (by car?) to the bike shop. Then the day comes when the owner decides that cycling wasn't much fun anyway: The bike was a heavy beast, and might as well stay out of sight and unrepaired: besides, it had begun to show rust...

Yet cycle technology has never been more welcoming. You can buy bikes, accessories and clothing which will do their job, give you great pleasure, and last for ages. But you are unlikely to get this in a big cut-price department store, or from a mail order catalogue. When you go to a specialist bike shop you may pay more, but you will also receive more. You are more likely to be advised by experts who are daily cyclists themselves. You will probably see a wider real choice than in a department store, especially with higher-priced bikes. You will be able to ask important questions about cycle security. You may be able to try on a range of clothing. Above all, you are less likely to be sold something which will give you long-term problems. A specialised shop will assemble and adjust your bike with care, before you take it on the road. They can offer you maintenance advice, and are more likely to give you good after-sales service. If the bike you buy is in any way unusual their deeper general experience of cycle technology will be invaluable. So going to your local bike shop can bring real personal benefits. But your decision as to how and where you spend your money plays a part in the struggle of specialised cycle shops against the powers of Mammon in the big sheds on the edge of town.

Quality specialist bike shops are essential to the fabric of a society which values cycling. This is why Encycleopedia supports such shops strongly. A good bike shop is part of the local community. We list on the following pages some of the bike shops which stock Encycleopedia. They are in many different countries, and reflect their local cycling cultures, but the simple fact that they sell such a book is a reasonable indication that they are caring shops.

It is the specialised shops who are taking an interest in the kind of bikes you see in Encycleopedia. They are often expensive to keep in stock and need considerable knowledge to explain. It also usually takes many times longer to explain and sell an unconventional cycle than it does to sell a cheap mountain bike from the Far East. Some of the shops listed will stock quite a few of the products which you see in Encycleopedia, others will stock few of them: but they all have details, specially supplied by us, the publishers, of how to source the products in Encycleopedia: not always an easy matter, given the international nature of our publication. However, a shop may decline, for very understandable reasons, to source a product for you. After all, they have no knowledge of which products we will put into Encycleopedia. They may suggest you try sourcing from a different shop. If all else fails, contact us.

A few manufacturers prefer to deal with customers directly. This is usually because their products are too specialised, or may require a degree of custom building, or perhaps, being big and bulky, they take up too much precious floor space in the average shop. However, you or the manufacturer may prefer to have the machine delivered to your local bike shop for assembly, final fitting and after sales service.

We hope you will support the cycle shops listed over the following pages, or any local bike shop which makes an effort.

A good shop will help you avoid expensive mistakes

Encycleopedia Shops

AUSTRALIA

Canberra
Canberra Cycles
70 Newcastle Str. Fyshwick, ACT 2609
Tel +61 6 280 4984 Fax+61 6 239 1257
Mo-Fr 8.00-18.00 Sa 8.00-16.00 Su 10.00-15.00

Mitcham
Cycle Science Mitcham
478 Whitehorse Road Mitcham, VIC 3132
Tel +61 3 9874 8033 Fax +61 3 9874 8442
Email freedhpv@connexus.apana.org.au
Mo-Th 9.00-18.00 Fr 9.00-21.00 Sa 9.00-17.00
A wide range of accessories and bicycles including recumbents for sale or hire. We custom build in steel or aluminium.

Perth
Quantum
64 Farmer Street, North Perth, WA 6006
Tel +61 9 443 3407 Fax +61 9 443 8687
Mo-Fr 9.00-18.00, Sa 9.00-12.00

Victoria
Greenspeed
69 Mountain Gare, Drive Ferntree Gully,VIC 3156
Tel +61 3 9758 5541 Fax +61 3 9752 4115
Email greenshp@ozemail.com.au
Website http://www.ihpva.org/com/Greenspeed/

AUSTRIA

Baden
B.I.E.R Fahrrad-Studio
Jägerhausgasse 20, 2500 Baden
Tel +43 2252 47690 Fax +43 2252 47690
Email ambrosch@ping.at Website http://ourworld.compuserve.com/homepages/fahrradstudio/
Tu-Th 10.00-12.00 & 15.00-18.00 Sa 10.00-12.00 Recumbents trailers, city bikes, MTBs and good accessories.

BELGIUM

Ghent
De Ligfiets
Lange Violettestraat 217, B 9000 Ghent
Tel/Fax +32 9 223 4496
The Belgian recumbent specialists. Hire and sale of M5, Challenge, Flevobike, Windcheetah, etc. With more than 8 years of daily recumbent use, we know what we're talking about.

CANADA

Victoria
Fairfield Bicycle Shop
1275 Oscar St., Victoria, BC V8V 2X6
Tel +1 250 381 2453 or 604 385 8978
Fax +1 250 384 2453
Practical bikes for the real world. Commuters' oasis in an MTB desert. Frame building, cycle repair courses, cycling coalition work.

Vancouver
Reckless: the bike store
1810 Fir St (at 2nd ave), Vancouver, BC V6J 3B1
Tel +1 604 731 2420 Fax +1 604 266 9090
Email rektek@intouch.bc.ca
Quality rentals, guided or independent tours, full, friendly service and repairs. We speak French, Italian, Spanish, Japanese, German & Cantonese. Free air and free oil any time!

DENMARK

Copenhagen
Christiania Cykler
Oster Port Refshalevej 2, 1432 Copenhagen K
Tel +45 32 954520 Fax +45 31 544593
Mo-Fr 10.00-17.30 A highly professional, enthusiastic shop within the famous Christiania commune, yet attracting customers from all over Copenhagen. Specialises in Pedersens and MTBs.

FRANCE

Paris
Bicloune (Le Comptoir du Cycle)
7 Rue Froment, 75011 Paris
Tel +33 148 054775 Fax +33 148 054770
Specialists in international bikes and parts, particularly Dutch, eg Gazelle, Batavus. Also Schwinn and Scott. Antiques department: complete bicycles, spares, catalogues and postcards.

GERMANY

Bad Bevensen
Fahrradhaus
Medingerstr. 20, 29549 Bad Bevenson
Tel +49 5821 1305 Fax +49 5821 41353
Mo-Fr 8.30-18.00 Sa 9.00-13.00 We are amusing, honest, committed, friendly, prepared, competent, critical, brave, naive, self-exploiting, conscientious, tolerant, but above all cyclists!

Bad Endorf
Muskelbetriebene Fahrzeuge (MBF)
Poststr. 1, 83093 Bad Endorf, Tel 08053 2374
Fax 08053 2397 Mobile 0172 6014786
HPVs for the open-minded. Test-rides and hire. TWIKE, recumbents, Pedersens, high bikes, folding bikes, transporter bikes, trailers,etc.

Bamberg
Mück's Radladen
Schrottenberggasse 2, 96049 Bamberg
Tel +49 951 578 53 Fax +49 951 57809
Mo-Fr 10.00-18.30 Sa 10.00-14.00. In the old-town. Top class city bikes, MTBs, recumbents, Pedersens. Our business is built around our customers' wishes and needs.

Bergisch Gladbach (VSF)
Veloladen-Liegeräder
Dolmanstr. 20, 51427 Bergisch Gladbach
Tel +49 2204 61075 Fax +49 2204 61076
Mo-Fr 12.00-18.30 Th 12.00-20.00 Sa 10.00-14.00 A huge selection, with know-how, and objective advice. Ortwin Kürten & Klaus Schröder. Members of the VSF & German HPV Club.

Berlin
Ostrad (VSF)
Winsstr. 48, 10405 Berlin
Tel +49 30 44341393 Fax +49 30 44341394
Email OstradGmbH@aol.com
Mo-Fr 10.00-18.30 Th 12.00-20.00 Sa10.00-13.30 Highly qualified staff. Accessories, recumbents for sale and hire, good advice. Planning recumbent weekend tours. See page 76.

Bonn
Fahrradladen in der Südstadt
Ermekeilstr. 7, 53113 Bonn
Tel +49 228 264899
Mo-Sa 10.00-13.00 Mo-Tu & Th-Fr 15.00-18.00 New and used cycles, parts and accessories. Lots of competent advice, and a friendly smile.

Cologne
Zwei plus Zwei (VSF)
Bismarkstr. 56-62, 50672 Köln
Tel +49 221 951 4700 Fax +49 221 951 7020
Mo-Fr 10.00-18.00 Sa 10.00-15.00 Apr-Sep
Mo-We 10.00-18.00 Th-Fr 10.00-20.00
Sat 10.00-16.00 200 sq/m of special cycles. Specialises in trailers, folding bikes and scooters.

Ditzingen Stuttgart
Pedalkraft F. Eberhardt Spezialräder
Hirschlanderstr. 2, 71254 Ditzingen
Tel 07156 8369 Fax 07156 34034
Mo-Fr 9.00-13.00 & 15.00-18.30 Folding-bikes and recumbents: Brompton, Birdy, Bernds, Moulton, Galaxe, Montague folding tandems, Radius, Bevo.

Duisburg (VSF)
Radwerk
Oberstr. 42, 47051 Duisberg
Tel +49 203 24032 Fax +49 203 288116
Open daily until 20.00 Service, recumbents, tandems, trailers and everything needed for cycling.

Düsseldorf
Cycle Service
Oberbilker Allee 57b, 40223 Düsseldorf
Tel +49 211 340399 Fax +49 211 3180250
Mobile 0172 219 6291
Mo-Fr 10.00-20.00 Sa 10.00-16.00
Recumbents, touring bikes, MTBs, hire bikes, and specialised bikes of all kinds.

Erlangen
Freilauf GmbH (VSF)
Lazarettstr. 4, 91054 Erlangen
Tel 09131 202220 Fax 09131 201710
Mo-Fr 10.00-19.00 Sa 10.00-16.00 A fascinating selection of child trailers, tandems, folding bikes, recumbents and Pedersens.

Frankfurt-am-Main
Die Fahrradscheune-Spezialräder
Alt Harheim. 27, 60437 Frankfurt-am-Main
Tel +49 6101 48958 Fax +49 6101 48958
Frankfurt's special cycling shop! Everyone from beginners to idependent cyclists will find everything they need!

Per Pedale GmbH (VSF)
Leipzigerstr. 4, 60487 Frankfurt-am-Main
Tel +49 69 707 23 63 Fax +49 69 772084
Mo 10.00-18.30 Sa 9.00-13.30

Radschlag (VSF)
Hallgartenstr. 56, 60389 Frankfurt-am-Main
Tel +49 69 452064 Fax +49 69 453284
Tu-Fr 11.00-18.30 Th 11.00-20.00 Sa 9.30-13.30 The internationally-minded cycle shop in cosmopolitan Frankfurt – English, French, and Turkish spoken. Trailers, folding bikes, tandems and recumbents.

Frechen Königsdorf
Lowrider
Starenweg 3, 50226 Frechen Königsdorf
Tel +49 2234 967131 Fax +49 2234 967132
Mo-Fr 10.00-13.00 & 14.00-18.00
Sa 10.00-14.00, also by appointment
Specialises in racing, city, touring, recumbents, tandems, trailers, transporters, Servicing, hire, accessories, used recumbents.

Freiburg/Br.
Radhaus (VSF)
Münchhofstr. 4, 79106 Freiburg
Tel +49 761 280 832 Fax +49 761 280 838
Mo-Fr 9.00-13.00&15.00-18.30 Sa 10.00-14.00 City, touring bikes, recumbents,trailers, Birdy, Friday, Brompton, Galaxe, Pedersen, Radius.

Göttingen-Weende
Radweise Fahrräder GmbH
Breite Str. 18, 37077 Göttingen Weende
Tel +49 551 34533 Fax +49 551 34533
Mo-Fr 9.30-13.00 15.00-18.00 Useful, unique bikes for everybody. All three proprietors manage the shop, but also work as a team. If you have any questions, we'll answer them!

Germersheim
Haasies Radschlag (VSF)
Marktstr. 22, 76726 Germersheim
Tel +49 7274 4863 Fax +49 7274 779360
Mo-Fr 10.00-12.30 14.30-19.00 Sa 9.00-13.00 Closed Wednesday mornings. Pedersen book publisher, organises the 'alternative cycling fair' in Southern Germany, large selection of special bikes and trailers - test-rides available.

Halle/Saale
Fahrradies (VSF)
Windthortstr. 20, 06114 Halle/Saale
Tel +49 345 522 6756 Fax +49 345 283 6865
Mo-Fr 10.00-12.00 13.00-19.00 Sa 10.00-15.00 A lovely shop in a historic town, and well worth a visit! Featured in BCQ.

Hamburg
Pro Velo (VSF)
Reetwerder 7, 21029 Hamburg
Tel +49 40 721 3109 Fax +49 40 721 2988
Oct-Feb Tu-Fr 10.00-18.00, Mar-Sep Tu-Fr 10.00-20.00 Sa 10-16. Advice, service, hiring, city, touring, racing load carrying, tandems, recumbents, folders, trikes, trailers, MTBs, BMX, etc.

Radhaus im Werkhof GmbH (VSF)
Gaußstr. 19, 22765 Hamburg
Tel +49 40 393992 Fax +49 40 3902302
Tu-Fr 10.00-13.00 & 15.00-18.00 Sa 10.00-18.00 Self-help workshop. Recycling and ecological repairs. City, touring, children's bikes, recumbents, tandems, trailers.

The New Cyclist
Grindelberg 45, 20144 Hamburg
Tel +49 40 422 0658 Fax +49 40 422 0659
Mo-Fr 10.00-19.00 Sa 10.00-13.00 Proprietor: Michael Schäfer. Frame builder. Exclusive custom-built tourers and MTBs., Folders, recumbents. English frames a speciality.

Hannover
Räderwerk GmbH (VSF)
Calenbergerstr. 50, 30169 Hannover
Tel +49 511 717174 Fax +49 511 715151
Mo Tu Th Fr 10.00-18.00 We 14.00-18.00
Sa 10.00-13.00
'Museum of the Modern Bike' 30 recumbents, 10 trikes, 10 folding bikes, load carriers, child trailers, cycles for the disabled.

Heilbronn
Fahrradhaus Bender GmbH
Holzstr. 1/1 + 6, 74072 Heilbronn
Tel +49 7131 96150 Fax +49 7131 627939
Mo-Fr 9.00-12.30 14.00-18.00 Sa 9.00-12.30 We offer: Brompton, Radius, Leitra, Hoening, Pedersen, Schlumpf, Schmidt-Dynamo, etc. We also have a 500m² show space.

Hüllhorst
Radhaus
Kurzestr. 9, 32609 Hüllhorst
Tel +49 5744 5454 Fax +49 5744 5469
Mo-Fr 15.00-19.00 Sa 10.00-13.00 Specialised bikes for hire: AnthroTech, Birdy, Brompton, Pedersen, Radius, Windcheetah.

Kerpen
Rückenwind, Fa. Fritsch
Friedensring 35, 50171
Tel +49 2237 922 456
Fax +49 2237 922 458

Lauda an der Tauber
Forum Fahrrad Zukunft (VSF)
Rathausstr. 33, 97912 Lauda an der Tauber
Tel +49 9343 65400 Fax +49 9343 65407
Child-trailers, recumbents, velomobiles and more!

Lübeck
Sattelfest GmbH (VSF)
Kanalstr. 70, 23552 Lübeck
Tel +49 451 704687 Fax +49 451 7063742
Mo-Fr 9.00-18.00 Sa 9.00-14.00 Town bikes, tourers, racers, folders, recumbents, trailers, clothing. Tandem and recumbent hire.

Mainz
Fahrrad-Laden Berens & Reus GmbH (VSF)
Albinistr. 15, 55116 Mainz
Tel +49 6131 225013 Fax 06131 230017
Tu-Fr 10.00-13.00 & 14.30-18.30 Sa 10.00-14.00 Closed on Mondays. A full selection! Also Brompton, Birdy and Bernds folding bikes.

Münster
Drahtesel
Servatiiplatz 7, 48413 Münster
Tel +49 251 511228 Fax +49 251 56252
Mo-Fr 10.00-13.30 & 14.30-19.00
Sa 10.00-15.00 Closed on Wednesday mornings. Tandems, Koga-Miyata, Villiger, Trek, Cannondale, Giant and own makes. Shimano service centre.

Nürnberg
Velo (am Marientunnel) (VSF)
Köhnstr. 38, 90478 Nürnberg
Tel +49 911 473611 Fax +49 911 467707
Mo-Fr 10.00-18.00 Sa 10.00-18.00 Closed Wednesday. Cycling culture and service! Robust quality city and touring, child and transport trailers, folders. MTB/full-suspension specialists

Offenbach
H.+D. Meyer OHG
Bahnhofstr. 18, 63067 Offenbach Tel +49 69 815832 Fax +49 69 889977 Email sow.@sn-icht
Tu-Fr 10.00-13.00, 15.00-18.30 Sa 10.00-14.00 Moulton, Pedersen, folders, tandems, no rubbish.

Oldenburg
Die Speiche GmbH (VSF)
Donnerschweerstr. 45, 26123 Oldenburg
Tel +49 441 84123 Fax +49 441 83471
Mo-Fr 9.30-13.00 14.00-18.00, Sa 9.30-13.30 Cycles, trailers, accessories. Renowned quality service. Bike loans, self-help workshop, courier-service next door.

KGB
Donnerschweerstr. 45, 26123 Oldenburg
Tel +49 441 885 03 89 Fax +49 441 885 03 88
Mo-Fr 10.00-13.00&14.00-17.00 Largest Pedersen, Galaxe und high bicycle exhibition in Germany. Distribution centre for Bike Culture Quarterly and Encycleopedia. Not really a cycle shop, but worth a visit!

Regensburg
Fahr Rad Laden A.C.H.T. GmbH (VSF)
Furtmayrstr. 12, 93053 Regensburg
Tel +49 941 7000365 Fax +49 941 7000546
Mo-Fr 10.00-18.00, Sa 10.00-14.00 Pedersens, recumbents, transport and disability cycles.

Stuttgart
Radladen Doppelaxel GmbH (VSF)
Lerchenstr 40, 70176 Stuttgart
Tel +49 711 226 1515 Fax 0711 226 1984
Tu-Fr 10.00-18.00, Sa 9.00-14.00
Many recumbents, city bikes, Bromptons, Pedersens, recumbents, tourers, accessories.

Tann
Spezial-Fahrräder Josef Hofer
Simbacherstr. 16, 84367 Tann
Tel +49 8572 1461 Fax +49 8572 1461
Sa 9.00-16.00 Appointments taken. Sale and hire of recumbents, folders, transporters, child trailers trailers, etc.

Trebur
Fahrrad-Claus (VSF)
Astheimerstr. 58, 65468 Trebur
Tel +49 6147 7915 Fax +49 6147 1329
Mo Tu Th Fr 9.00-12.30 & 14.30-18.00
From children's bikes to touring bikes: recumbents, folding bikes, bike hire, trailers. Test rides available. Special needs? Ask!

Troisdorf
VamBike (VSF)
Alte Poststr. 21, 53840 Troisdorf
Tel +49 2241 78645 Fax +49 2241 83357
Email Liegerad@aol.com
Mo-Fr 10.00-13.00 13.30-18.30 außer Mi Sa 10.00-14.00. High quality cycle technology for that special pedalling experience. Recumbent specialists.

Uelzen
Die Speichenstimmer (VSF)
Sternplatz 5, 29525 Uelzen
Tel +49 581 2023 Fax +49 581 2024 A full selection: touring bikes, recumbents, MTBs, accessories.

Weil der Stadt
Velotraum
Herrenbergerstr., 72163 Weil der Stadt
Tel +49 7033 9990 Fax +49 7033 9920
Closed on Mondays Tu-Fr 10.00-13.00 & 14.00-19.00 Sa 10.00-14.00 Nomen est Omen. A full selection – own design of 26' touring bike, Santana tandems, cycles made to measure, folders, recumbents.

IRELAND

Dublin
Square Wheel Cycleworks
Temple Lane South, (Off Dame Street), Dublin 2
Tel +353 16790838 Fax +353 16774234
Email A centre of cycle culture, with a full repair and bike parking service. Associated café.

NETHERLANDS

Amersfoort
Bike Shop Amersfoort
Leusderweg 92-94, 3817 KC Amersfoort
Tel +31 4651321 Fax +31 4651323
Recumbents, scooters, ATB's, hybrids, tandems, trailers, ATBs. Both utility and sport-oriented cycleshop.

Amsterdam
"Het Mannetje" in Transport
Quellijnstraat 48, 1072 XT Amsterdam
Tel +31 20 679 2139 Fax +31 20 679 2139
Transporter bikes, transporter tandems and tricycles. Specialist in the transport of two or more children on one bike. Motto: 'Freight under your own steam' (vracht op eigen kracht). A machine for every load up to 250kg.

Tromm Tweewielers
Europaplein 45 t/o RAI, 1078 GV Amsterdam
Tel +31 20 6642099
Specialist in folding bikes (35 models) and mountain bikes. Importer of quality English folding bikes. Trailers and scooters.

Breda
Schietekat Tweewielers
Korte Boschstraat 1-3, 4811 ES Breda
Tel+31 76 521 2830 Fax +31 76 521 2830
Tandems, ATBs, touring bikes, recumbents, trailers, folding bikes, Pedersen. Promotion of new products, such as scooters. Hire possible.

Eindhoven
De Liggende Hollander
Tourslaan 33 en 41, 5627 KW Eindhoven
Tel +31 40 242 4368 Fax +31 40 242 4368
Sale and hire of recumbents, trailers and folding bikes. Open days for potential customers. Organises recumbent cycling holidays.

Den Haag
Kemper
Piet Heinstraat 42, 2518 CJ Den Haag
Tel +3170 345 9696

Folding bike and recumbent specialist, trailers and tandems. Also hire of recumbent and folding bikes. Accompanied try-out touring runs for those interested in recumbents.

Haarlem
Optima Cycles
Gedempte Raamgracht 28A zw, 2011 WJ Haarlem Tel +31 534 1502 Fax +31 23 534 1502
Email Optima28@worldaccess.nl
Design, building, sale and hire of recumbents and parts. Folding bikes, transporter bikes and necessary spare parts. Sale and hire of trailers. Pedersen and Bike Friday (official dealer).

Rotterdam
Bikers' Best
Noordsingel 3, 3035 EG Rotterdam
Tel +31 10 4662916
Widely competent cycle shop with everything for racing, ATB and hybrid cycles, BMX/freestyle, cruisers, recumbents, scooters, trailers, clothing. Sale and repairs, try-out and trade-ins possible.

Utrecht
Trapperkracht
Soerabayastraat 4, 3531 EB Utrecht
Tel +3120 296 1015 Fax 030 296 1015
Sale and hire of products for cycling with children: Baby Bike, trailers, trailerbikes and tandems. Sale and hire of luggage trailers. Specialist in heavy transport using pedal power. Tricycles, and consultant for disabled cyclists. Back copies of BCQ and Encycleopedia.

Utrecht
Wim Kok Fietsplezier
Nachtegaalstraat 51, 3581 AD Utrecht
Tel +31 30 2315780 Fax 030 2316675
All-round excellent cycle shop for touring, race, ATB, hybrids, tandems, scooters. Folding bike and trailer specialist. Many unusual lines, clothing, helmets, etc.

Winschoten
Maas Fietsen
Blijhamsterstraat 22, 9671 AW Winschoten
Tel +31 597 412336, Fax +31 597 414 824.
Versatile cycle shop: ATB, racing, recumbents, tandems, trailers. Large collection of clothing, lightweight panniers, and accessories. Hire of many different cycles possible.

NORWAY

Randaberg (Stavanger)
Felgen Sykkel
Randabergveien 372, 4070 Randaberg
Tel/Fax +47 514 19477
An enthusiastic, friendly shop, always willing to help the touring cyclist. Established first in Randaberg, 1991. *Felgen Sykkel* opened a 2nd shop in 1993 at Kongsgd 24, Stavanger
Tel +47 514 51896190

SWITZERLAND

Langenthal
Velorama
Spitalgasse 3, 4900 Langenthal
Tel +41 63 922 9650
Mo We Th Fr 9.00-18.30 Sa 8.00-16.00 Special bicycles and custome work. Tourers, recumbents and town bikes. Accessories and clothing.

Solothurn
Velo-Werkstatt
Baselstr. 47A, 4500 Solothurn
Tel +41 32 623 4676 Fax +41 32 623 4676
Tu-Fr 9.00-12.15 u. 13.30-18.30 Sa 9.00-12.15 & 13.30-16.00 To describe our shop in 20 words is impossible. Imagine it for yourself instead.

UNITED KINGDOM

Bath
Avon Valley Cyclery
Rear of Bath Spa Train Station, Bath, Avon BA1 1SX Tel +44 1225 442442 Fax +44 1225 446267
Mo-Su 9.00-18.00 We sell loads of folders, practical road bikes and the odd recumbent. We go out of our way to help serious customers.

John's Bikes
80-84 Walcot Street, Bath, Avon BA1 5BD
Tel +44 1225 334633 Fax +44 1225 480132
Mo-Su 9.00-17.30 Specialists in touring cycling since 1972. Shimano service centre. Main stockists for Marin and Trek. Bike hire available April through September.

Birmingham
Feet First
170 Widney Manor Road, Solihull, W Midlands
Tel +44 121 704 4412 Fax +44 121 233 9928
Email garyh@compuserve.com or gary7@dial.pipex.com
Hrs 6 days per week – please phone first. Specialist offering demonstrations, hire and sales of a wide range of UK and European recumbents, folding bikes and special needs.

On Your Bike
10 Priory Queensway, Birmingham B4 6BS
Tel +44 121 627 1590
Mon-Fri 10.00-18.00 Sat 9.30-18.00 Situated in the centre of the city and staffed by enthusiastic knowledgeable staff, the store is a mecca for cyclists in the Midlands.

Bristol
Mud Dock Cycleworks and Café
40 The Grove, Bristol BS1 4RB.
Tel +44 117 9292151 Fax +44 117 9292171
Email mud_dock@dial.pipex.com
Shop Tu-Sa 8.30-6.30 Café Tue-Sat 8.30-21.00 Sun 10.00-17.00 Europe's first totally integrated bar/restaurant and bike shop, overlooking Bristol's scenic dockside. Mediterranean food, American bikes, English beer! Unique.

Cambridge
Ben Hayward Cycles
69 Trumpington Street, Cambridge CB2 1RJ.
Tel 01223 352294 (workshop 301118)
Fax +44 1223 573989
Email robturner@dial.pipex.com
Mon-Sat 8.30-17.30 A friendly, expert, well-stocked, all-rounder of a shop, covering all aspects of cycling for leisure, exercise, sport and transport.

Cambridgeshire (nr. Ely)
D. Tek HPVs
Main Street, Little Thetford, Nr. Ely, Cambridgeshire CB6 1BR
Tel +44 1353 648177 Fax 01353 648777
BT One Number 07071 CYCLES
March-Oct. 7 days a week 9.30 to 17.00 Winter Mo-Fr 10-4. Bookings essential, other hours by arrangement. Outstanding range of recumbents for hire or sale. Unique 'one-stop trailer shop'. Solutions for the disabled 'We won't say 'can't!'

Chester (Cheshire)
The Bike Factory
153-161 Boughton, Chester, CH3 5BH
Tel +44 1244 317893 Fax +44 1244 317916
Also: Davies Bros. Cycles, 262 Cuppin St., Chester. Both shops open Mo-Sat 9.30-17.30 Su 10.00-4.00 Th 9.30-18.00 Pashley, Dawes (including Dawes recumbent), Brompton, MTBs, child-carrying attachments. Own hand-built frames. Davies Bros Cycles on the same site since 1925.

Cornwall (Wadebridge)
Bridge Bike Hire
Camel Trail, Eddystone Road, Wadebridge, Cornwall PL27 7AL
Tel +44 1208 815715 Fax +44 1208 814407
364 days a year 9.00-17.00 A unique opportunity to experience new and innovative products at our hire shop on the scenic Camel Trail in Cornwall.

Dorset (Dorchester)
Dorchester Cycles
31Gt Western Road, Dorchester, Dorset DT1 1UF
Tel +44 1305 268787 Fax +44 1304 268784
Mo-Sa 9.00-17.30 Tourers, tandems, unicycles, folders, hybrids & ATBs plus servicing and repairs. Enormous selection of accessories, clothing and spare parts. Cycle hire always available.

East Sussex (Forest Row)
FutureCycles
Friends Yard, London Road, Forest Row, Sussex RH18 5EE
Tel +44 1342 822 847 Fax 01342 826 726
Email enc@futurecycles.prestel.co.uk
Website http://there.is/futurecycles
Mo-Sa 9.30-17.30 Specialising in recumbents, manufacturers of the Streetglider, we offer a complete range of conventional bikes including folders. Traffic-free test ride area in rural location.

Edinburgh
Bike Trax
13 Lochrin Place, Edinburgh EH3 9QX
Tel +44 131 228 6633 Fax +44 131 228 6333
Email 101520,2274@compuserve.com
Mo 10-17.30 A new shop aimed at the leisure and touring cyclist (not racers). Stocking hybrids, tourers, budget mountain bikes, trailers, kids seats, kiddy trailers, and a full repair service.

Glasgow
Gear of Glasgow
19 Gibson Street, Hillhead, Glasgow G12 8NU
Tel/Fax +44 141 339 1179
Mo-Sa 10.00-18.00 Closed Sun We specialise in mountain bikes and recumbents, now a Shimano Service centre, we have started mountain bike and recumbent tours.

Griffon Alternative Cycles
52 Caldercuilt Road, Glasgow G20 0AL.
Tel +44 141 946 3739
A small independent framebuilder and recumbent dealer, we will import any cycle or part on demand, and will build anything unusual.

Guernsey
Ian Brown Cycle Shop
Route Militaire, Saint Sampsons, Guernsey, Channel Isles GY2 4DZ
Tel +44 1481 41308 Fax +44 1481 41309
Mo-Sa 9.00-17.30 Specialised cycle dealer, run by cyclists, not just bicycles, but trailers, trikes, and trailerbikes. No VAT and no disappointed customers.

Kent (Rochester)
Geoff Wiles Cycles
45-47 Caxton Road, Strood, Rochester, Kent ME2 2BU
Tel +44 1634 722586 Fax +44 1634 727416
A friendly shop with a wide range of cycles. Also made-to-measure, and a knowledgeable custom service for the disabled. See also page 117.

Kielder (Northumberland)
Kielder Bikes
Castle Hill, Kielder. Tel +44 1434 250392
Apr-Sep: 10.00-18.00 Otherwise by appointment. Hire bikes, cycle sales, parts, repair. Rescue service for touring cyclists. Scenic situation by castle. Owner Ken Bone lives on site.

Lancaster
Northwest HPV
32 St. George's Quay, Lancaster LA1 1RD
Tel +44 1524 849 083
Open any day of the year by appointment. Peter Cox offers recumbents, folders, Moultons, trailers for sale or hire. Mobile repairs service, mail order parts finding service.

Lincolnshire (Peterborough)
Terry Wright Cycles
39/45 Bridge Street, Deeping St James, Peterborough PE6 8HA
Tel +44 1778 344051 Fax +44 1778 347111
Mo-Th 8.45-17.45 Fri 8.45-7 Sat 8.45-5 Our objective is to promote cycling as the number one health and leisure activity. Professional staff enthuse and inform, whilst our extensive stock caters for every need.

Liverpool
Liverpool Cycle Centre
9-13 Berry St., Liverpool L1 9DF
Tel/Fax +44 151 708 8819
Mo-Fr 10.00-6.00 Providing a helpful service to everyone from the first-time buyer to the seasoned professional, regardless of gender.

London
Freewheel
275 West End Lane, West Hampstead, London NW6 1QS
Tel +44 171 435 3725 Fax +44 171 794 4484
Mo-Sa 9.00-18.00 Th 9.00-19.00 Sundays Easter-Christmas. Wether bikes, accessories or clothing, Freewheel is North London's premier bike shop for friendly and personal service on all the best brands.

On Your Bike
52/54 Tooley Street, London Bridge, London SE1 2SZ
Tel +44 171 378 6669 Fax +44 171 3577600
Mo-Fr 9.00-18.00 Sat 9.30-17.30 Su 11-4
Since 1983, OYB have catered for the city cyclist, also keeping the latest components and clothing in stock for the avid mountainbiker and enthusiast.

London Recumbents
Rangers Yard, Dulwich Park, College Road, Burbage Road, London SE21 7BQ
Tel +44 181 299 6636 or +44171 635 9761
The recumbent test centre. Large range of recumbents to hire or buy. Bikes for people with special needs and family cycling.

Freewheel
53/55 Pimlico Road, London SW1W 8NE
Tel +44 171 730 6668 Fax +44 171 730 3783
Mon-Sat 9.00-18.00 From folders to full suspension, Freewheel Chelsea squeezes an amazing range of bikes, accessories and clothing in its intimate friendly shop.

Phoenix Cycles
59a Battersea Bridge Road, London SW11 3AU
Tel +44 171 7382766 Fax +44 171 7382766
Tu-Fr 10.00-18.30 Sat 10-5. The specialists in folding bikes. We stock Birdy, Brompton, Fold-it, Micro & Strutt. Friendly efficient service in central London.

Brixton Cycles
435-437 Coldharbour Lane, Brixton, London SW9 8LN
Tel +44 171 733 6055 Fax +44 171 733 5595
Email brixcyke@dirc on.co.uk
Mo-Sa 9.00-18.00 Th 9.00-17.00 closed for lunch every day 2.30-3.15 Sale and repair of all types of bicycle. Hub gears, commuter support, advice, trailers. London's only bicycle co-op.

Bicycle Workshop
27 All Saints Road, Westbourne Park, London W11 1HE Tel +44 171 229 4850
Tu-Sa 10.00-18.00 Closed 14.00-15.00
Specialises in repairs, including jobs many shops don't like. Sells spares and accessories. Has a strong base in the local community and a wider catchment area.

Cyclecare-Olympia
30 Blythe Road, London W14 0HA
Tel +44 171 6029757 Fax +44 171 6029757
Rent-try before you buy: Brompton, Slipstream, Pendle, Tube Rider, Yak. Advice on and selection of child seats & survival tools. Repairs. Wheelbuilding. Export.

Stuart Bikes
309/311 Horn Lane, London W3 0BU
Tel +44 181 993 3484 Fax +44 181 993 1891
Mo-Sa 9.30-18.00 Sun 11.00-16.00 Closed Wedenesday. Sister company to Bicycling Books specialising in cycling books, videos, jewellery novelties and also sells cycles, helmets, clothing and shoes.

Bikefix/Bike Trader
48 Lambs Conduit Street, London WC1N 3LJ
Tel +44 171 405 1218 Fax +44 171 405 4639
Email bikefix@dircon.co.uk
Mo-Fr 8.30-19.00 Sa 10.00-16.00
A complete service and sales centre where you can hire or buy many specialist products including recumbents, trailers, and folding bicycles.

Manchester
Bicycle Doctor
68-70 Dickenson Road, Rusholme, Manchester M14 5HF
Tel +44 161 2241303 Fax +44 161 2573102
Mo-Fr 10.00-18.00 Sa 10.00-17.30 Popular established workers' coop run by an enthusiastic and motivated team. Showrooms and workshop recently expanded, customer service our priority!

Somerset (Bridgwater)
St John Street Cycles
91/93 St John Street, Bridgwater, Somerset TA65HX
Tel +44 1278 423632 Fax +44 1278 431107
Email sjscycles@dial.pipex.com
Website http://www.sjscycles.com
Hrs Mon-Sat 9-6 Sun 10-4 Probably Europe's largest retail supplier of tandems (see our Voyager Childback on p. 17) and audax bikes. Free UK delivery. 30 keen staff.

Surrey (Dorking)
Action Packs
The Booking Hall, Boxhill Station, Westhumble, Surrey RH5 6BT
Tel +44 1306 886944 Fax +44 1306 886944
Th-Mo 9.30-17.30 We 9.30-13.00 Cycle hire, sales, service and accessories. Accessible from London Victoria & M25. Based in the Surrey Hills on A24 near Dorking.

Warwickshire (Stratford-upon-Avon)
Union Street Cycles
6a Union Street, Stratford-upon-Avon, Warwickshire CV37 6QT
Tel/Fax +44 1789 297214
9.00-17.30 Wide range of Pashley hand-built specialist cycles, creatively displayed with lifestyle imagery (incl. a beach!) and accessories. Covers leisure and utility cycling.

Worcestershire (Pershore)
Websters
71 High Street, Pershore, Worcestershire WR10 1EU
Tel +44 1386 561484 Fax +44 1386 561484
Tu-Sa 9.00-17.30 Closed on Monday Small shop but BIG on service, sales, repairs, parts, clothing. Touring advice & emergency aid. Discounts to Club, YHA, CTC etc.

York
Cycle Heaven
5 Bishopthorpe Road, York YO2 1NA
Tel +44 1904 636578
Mo-Sa 9.00-18.00 Specialists in alternative transport, Cycle Heaven are dedicated to the renaissance of mass utility cycling. Cycle Heaven is also a Shimano Service Centre.

York Cycleworks
14-16 Lawrence Street, York YO1 3BN
Tel 01904 626 664 Fax 01904 612 356
Hrs Mon-Sat 9-6 York Cycleworks is a worker co-operative. We actively encourage all kinds of cyclists and stock an eclectic cornucopia of cycles.

USA

Alaska
The Bicycle Shop
1035 W Northern Lights Blvd., Anchorage, AK 99503-2409
Tel +1 907 272 5219 Fax +1 907 272 8542
An Anchorage institution, the Bicycle Shop has had the same owner since 1964 and is proud to be a family shop and one of Alaska's original Schwinn dealers.

Arizona
Bike Emporium
8433 E. Mc Donald Drive, Scottsdale, AZ 85250-6334. Tel +1 602 991 5430

Fair Wheel Bicycle
1110 East 6th Street, Tucson, AZ 85719
Tel +1 520 884 9018 Fax +1 520 884 0063

Mountain Sports
1800 South Milton St E. 100, Flagstaff, AZ 86001. Tel 520 779 5156
Toll Free 800 286 5156 Fax 520 774 5509
Email mountain@infomagic.com
Website http://www.mountainsport.com
A speciality outdoor retailer with a big interest in alternative transport. We well mainly mountain bikes and commuter vehicles of all types.

Racer's Edge Bicycles
2623 No. Campbell, Tucson, AZ 85719
Tel +1 520-795-BIKE Fax +1 520 795 1512
Email edge@racersedge.com
Website http://www.racersedge.com

California
American Cyclery
510 Frederick St., San Francisco, CA 94117
Tel +1 415 564 2304 Fax +1 415 664 6653
Email biketrdr@crl.com
Website http://www.bicycletrader.com
An historic landmark of San Francisco and West Coast Cycling, specializing in custom, classic and high quality commuting bikes, and offering a unique array of European and American bicycles.

Aquarian Bicycles
486 Washington St., Monterey, CA 93940
Tel +1 408 375 2144 Fax +1 408 375 2843
Voted the best bike shop eight years in a row by the county paper, Aquarian specializes in mid- to high-end bicycles, recumbents and tender loving care.

Cupertino Bike shop
10493 So. De Anza Blvd., Cupertino, CA 95014
Tel +1 408 255 2217 Fax +1 408 255 5382
Email sprocket@cupertinobike.com
Website http://www.cupertinobike.com
In 44 years we've created a positive enviroment for all cycling enthusiasts, focusing on all aspects of road, tandem and mountain biking.

Cycle Dynamics
5670 Dempsey Pl., Santa Rosa, CA 95403
Tel +1 707 545 2453 Fax +1 707 545 2453
Email cdynamics@gnn.com

Open Air Bicycles
437 W. Channel Islands Blvd., Port Hueneme, CA 93041
Tel +1 805 985 5045 Fax +1 805 984 7123 A local store dedicated to keeping cycling fun and carefree on the beautiful south central coast of California.

Pacific Coast Cycles
2801 Roosevelt, Carlsbad, CA 92008
Tel +1 619 729 7671
Road, mountain, classic-to-modern, certified wheel building (special purpose and problem solving), ATB experts, knowledge and parts for older bikes, sealed bearings, mountain bike drop bars.

Palo Alto Bicycles
171 University Ave., Palo Alto, CA 94301
Tel +1 415 328 7411 Fax +1 415 328 0323
Email paloalto@pacbell.net
Family owned and operated since 1930. Located in California's bicycle friendly Silicon Valley. Friendly knowledgeable staff, quality selection and expert service.

People Movers
980 North Main St., Orange, CA 92667.
Tel 714 633 3663 Fax 714 633 7890
Email peplemovrs@aol.com
People Movers has been open for five years and regularly adds new and unusual products to their line to meet the unique requirements of their recumbent customers.

Sunshine Bicycle Center
737 Center Blvd, Fairfax, CA 94930.
Tel 415 459 3334 Fax 415 459 3708
For 26 years, Sunshine's formula for success is service supplied by a helpful, knowledgeable staff, and a no B. S. attitude.

The Chain Gang Bike Shop
1180 Industrial Street #A, Redding, CA 96002
Tel +1 916 223 3400 Fax +1 916 223 3783
Instrumental in making bicycling a part of its community's history and a recent convert to and advocate of recumbent bicycles.

The Missing Link Bicycle Co-op
1988 Shattuck Ave., Berkeley, CA 94704
Tel +1 510 843 7471 Fax +1 510 848 5322
Set up as workers' co-op. Radical ideas for promoting pedal power. Free repair classes, facilities for doing your own repairs.

The Rest Stop
3230 Folsom Blvd., Sacramento, CA 95816.
Tel 916 453 1870 Fax 916 453 1005
Email pinkdog@bbs.macnexus.org
Hard-to-find accessories and unusual items. Oriented to customer convenience, community involvement, bicycle event and information center.

Wheelsmith
201 Hamilton Ave., Palo Alto, CA 94301
Tel +1 415 324 1919 ext 12 Fax +1 415 324 2247
Email ric@wheelsmith.com
Website http://www.wheelsmith.com
Founded by Eric and Jon Hjertberg, Wheelsmith is a different kind of bicycle business. 'Store, workshop, museum' is still our motto 22 years later.

Colorado
American Cyclery
2140 S. Albion, Denver, CO 80222
Tel +1 303 756 1023 Toll Free 888 236 1941
Started in 1959, everyone in Denver knows Pat, the owner: mountain bikes, road bikes, family-oriented shop. Sales, service.

AngleTech Cyclery
318 No. Hwy 67, P O B 1893 Woodland Park, CO 80863. Tel +1 719 687 7475
Toll Free 800 793 3038 Fax +1 719 687 7475
Email anglezoom@aol.com
Website http://www.bikeroute.com/AngleTech
An alternative cyclist's dream. A full line of recumbents, folding bikes and cycles for special needs. Two hours browse time recommended.

Louisville Cyclery
1032 South Boulder Road, Louisville, CO 80027
Tel +1 303 665 6343 Email loucyclery@aol.com
A full-service shop with a heavy emphasis on road bikes and products. Custom bikes, fits and wheels. Owner-operated since 1980.

The Alpha Bicycle Co
6838 So. Yosemite, Englewood, CO 80112
Tel +1 303 220 9799 Fax +1 303 220 9799
Email elleny@alphabicycle.com
Websitehttp:// www.alphabicycle.com

Florida
Fools Crow Cycles & Tours
1046 Commercial Dr., Tallahassee, FL 32310
Tel +1 904 224 4767 Email edde@freenet.tlh.fl.us
Website http://www.bikeroute.com/FoolsCrow HPV.htm
A user-friendly shop specilizing in recumbents and cool bikes the other guys don't carry.

Lakeshore Schwinn
2108 Blanding Blvd., Jacksonville, FL 32210
Tel+1 904 388 0612 Fax +1 904 384 7945
An old-style family bike shop. We want to sell you what you want, not what we think you need. If we don't have it, we'll get it.

Georgia
Free Flite
2800 Canton Rd., Marietta, GA 30066
Tel +1 770 422 5237 Fax 770 422 5237
Email freflite@mindspring.com
Operating since 1978, Free Flite has grown to become the area's premier bicycle shop. Dedicated to cycling enthusiasts at your service.

Hawaii
Island Triathlon & Bike
569 Kapahulu Ave., Honolulu, HI 96815
Tel +1 808 737 7433 Sales +1 808 732 7227
Fax +1 808 737 2399 Email itb@aloha.net
Website http://haleakala.aloha.net/~itb/
A multisport shop staffed by experienced, knowledgeable athletes and sales professionals, serving beginners and pros alike!

Illinois
Rapid Transit
1900 West No. Ave., Chicago, IL 60622
Tel +1 773 227 2288 Fax +1 773 227 2328
Bikes for the year-round urban cyclist. Run by commuter cyclists. Also recumbents (including the ATP Vision) available for test rides.

Maine
Back Bay Bicycle, Inc
333 Forest Ave., Portland, ME 04101
Tel +1 207 773 6906 Fax +1 207 773 5404

Maryland
Mt Airy Bicycle
4540 Old National Pike (Md 144@Md 27), Mt Airy, MD 21771 Tel +1 410 795 2929
Email abikie@aol.com
Website http://www. bike123.com
Earth's most interesting collection. Virtual museum. All for sale. Vintage/modern. 100 tandems. 50 Recumbents. Rentals. Trades. Long test rides.

College Park Bicycle
4360 Knox Rd, College Park, MD 20740
Tel +1 301 864 2211Email abikie@aol.com
Website http://www.bike123.com
Over 800 used bikes for sale, rapid frame repair, same-day wheel building and six types of trailers. Extensive hire service includes recumbents, tandems and folders.

Massachusets
Lincoln Guide Service
152 Lincoln Rd., Lincoln, MA 01773-0100
Tel +1 617 259 1111 Fax +1 617 259 1722
Everything for the self-propelled: bikes, cross country skis, snow shoes and in-line skates. Ryan and Lightning recumbents. Cycle repair classes.

Michigan
Recumbent Sea
1334 Logan S E, Grand Rapids, MI 49506
Tel +1 616 454 3260 or +1 616 877 2050
Fax 616 454 4718 Email bikewalla@juno.com
Specializing in affordable recumbents, special needs and other unusual bikes. We are a seasonal shop so call for an appointment.

Minnesota
Calhoun Cycle
1622 West Lake St., Minneapolis, MN 55408.
Tel 612 827 8231

Freewheel Bicycle Co - op
1812 South Sixth St., Minneapolis, MN 55454
Tel +1 612 339 2219 Fax +1 612 339 8268
Email freewheel@freewheelbicycle.com
Website http://www.freewheelbicycle.com.
Centrally located within Minnesota's twin cities, we sell new bikes, service any brand, and offer a do-it-yourself workshop for our customers. Repair classes and a thorough parts, accessories and small parts selection.

Sunset Cycle
10136 Sunset Ave, Circle Pines, MN 55014
Tel +1 612 786 3205
Sales and service of all bikes including recumbents, hybrids, road bikes, antique bikes. Repainting and repairing. Community education classes in bike repair. Family-run shop.

New Jersey
North East Recumbents
9 Wayland Dr., Verona, NJ 07044
Tel +1 201 239 8968
Over a dozen different recumbents for sale and rent. Good advice for novices, excellent service and facilities, custom modifications.

Oregon
Citybikes Workers' Cooperative
734 S E Ankeny, Portland, OR 97214
Tel +1 503 239 6951 or +1 503 239 0553 A worker-owned cooperative aimed at making bike-riding and commuting easily accessible. Specializing in 3-speeds, trailers and upright commuter bikes.

Eugene Bicycle Works / C A T
455 West 1st Ave, Eugene, OR 97401
Tel +1 541 683 3397 Fax 541 686 1015
Email cat@efn.org
The CAT believes that bicycles are essential tools for modern civilization and builds, sells and rents utilitarian bicycles, cargo bikes, heavy-duty work trailers, recumbents and adult tricycles.

Philadelphia
Jay's Pedal Power Bikes
512 E. Girard Ave., Philadelphia, PA 19125
Tel +1 215 425 5111 Fax +1 215 426 2653
Jay's is a professional shop with 20 years experience and a large selection of components and small parts. Electric bikes coming soon.

Tennesee
Mt. Moriah Bicycle Co, Inc.
5715 Mt. Moriah, Memphis, TN 38115
Tel +1 901 795 4343 Fax +1 901 795 4310
Email amagliani@aol.com
Oldest continuous Schwinn dealership in the world. Triathlon and other high-end cycles. Many 'alternative' bikes, including recumbents and portables.

Texas
Freewheeling Bicycles
2401 San Gabriel, Austin TX 78705
Tel +1 512 477 6846 Fax +1 512 478 3733
A caring, professional service, and a fine choice of cycles and accessories. Good advice for novices.

Utah
Avalon Recumbents
465 So. 1250 East Pleasant Grove, UT 84062
Tel +1 801 785 2994 Fax +1 801 785 2994
Specializing in recumbents and hard-to-find bikes, handcycles, special needs bikes and trikes, trailers and folding bikes. Bikes for hire, too.

Washington
Elliott Bay Bicycles
2116 Western Ave., Seattle, WA 98121
Tel +1 206 441 8144 Fax +1206 441 1815
Home of the Davidson line of handbuilt bicycles. A wealth of experience in racing, international touring and custom design.

The Bikesmith
2309 No. 45th, Seattle, WA 98103
Tel 206 632 3102
Speciality: whatever no one else does. Bike and parts – vintage to modern, new, used and reconditioned. Custom jobs welcomed.

Washington DC
City Bikes
2501 Champlain St. N W, Washington, DC 20009 Tel +1 202 265 1564 Fax 202 462 7020
Website http://www.surewould.com/citybikes
Supports bicycling as THE transportation alternative. Bikes, gear, parking, etc. Everything you need to ride. Declare your auto-nomy – ride a bike!

Wisconsin
Yellow Jersey
419 State St., Madison, WI 53703.
Tel +1 608 257 4737 Office +1 608 257 4818
Fax +1 608 257 5161
Email yellowje@execpc.com Website http://www.execpc.com/yellowje
Full service since 1971. Machining, frame service, eclectic bits, custom fabrication/modification. Real touring bikes, internal gearboxes, roadsters, Dynohubs, too!

Wyoming
Dr. Spokes Cyclery & Museum
240 South Center, Casper, WY 82601-2524
Tel +1 307 265 7740 Fax +1 307 265 7740
Buy-Sell-Trade antique bicycles, tricycles, pedal cars, related advertising samples and curios. We do restoration and plating, too.

Manufacturers Details

A. Winther A/S Dolphin and Donkey trailers
Denmark Rygesmindevej 2, DK 8653 Them
T: +45 8684 7288 F: +45 8684 8528.
Germany Utopia Fahrradmanufaktur, Eschberger Weg 1, 66121 Saarbrücken
T: +49 681 516506 F: +49 681 815 098.
Holland Van Meurs & Co., Postbus 122, 4130 EC Vianen T: +31 34 73 51 855
F: +31 34 73 51 334. *Norway* Sport-Casa A/S, Postboks 377, 1801 Askim T: +47 69 88 89 10
F: +47 69 88 52 44. *Switzerland* Vitelli Velo-Bedarf AG, Dornacherstr. 101, 4053 Basel
T: +41 61 361 7070 F: +41 61 361 5770.

A.S. Engineering S-327
U.K A.S Engineering c/o TNT Mailfast, MOW/MOW/10012/14, PO Box 66, Hounslow TW5 9RT. T/F: +7 095 430 3897.
Email: ykpro@aha.rv
Russia (TNT is better) Akad. Anokhin Street, 12-363, Moscow T/F: +7 095 430 3897.
Canada Bob Simons, B.S. Amphicycles, 208 Walker's Hook Road, Saltspring Island, B.C. V8K 1P5 F: +1 604 537 4221.
Holland Benelux Germany Mark Salman, Salman's Technical Services, Preangerstraat 52 ZWART, 2022 RT Haarlem, Holland
T/F: +31 23 538 7015.

Airoshield AIRO-Shield
USA 1973 North Nellis Blvd., Suite 121, Las Vegas, Nevada 89115-3654
T: +1 702 382 7288 F: +1 702 382 7288
Email: Tom@ttinet.com
Website http://www.ttinet.com/tom

Alligt Ligfietsen Classic
Netherlands Postbus 6494, 5600HL Eindhoven
T: +31 40251 5728 F: +31 40251 5728.

AnthroTech Leichtfahrzeugtechnik GmbH i.G. AnthroTech
Germany Rothenbergstr. 7, 90542 Eckental-Frohnhof
T: +49 9126 288 644 F: +49 9126 288 321.

ARES Group Karbyk
Italy Via Guglielmo Marconi no. 18, 33010 Reana del Rojale (UD) T: +39 330 545 091
F: +39 432 857 504.

Arved Klütz Quantum
Germany Steinstr. 5, 25364 Hornerkirchen
T: +49 4121 483898 F: +49 4121 483899.

Batavus Relaxx
Netherlands Industrieweg 4, 8444 AR Heerenveen T: +31 513 63 8999
F: +31 513 63 8262 Email: info@batavus.com
Website http://www.batavus.com

Berkut Berkut B-317
Russia Department of 'Outlook Ltd', adm. Marakov Street 45-91, Moscow 125 212
T: +7 095 452 33 98 F: +7 095 452 33 98.
Germany, Holland, Belgium, Luxembourg, France, UK & Eire, Denmark, Italy, Norway, Sweden, Finland contact Manfred Klauda, Westenriederstr. 26, 80331 Munich, Germany
T: +49 171 370 4970 or +49 89 290 4121
F: +49 89 333 955.

Bernds zeitgemäße Mobilität Bernds Faltrad
Germany Wittekind Str. 16, 32758 Detmold
T: +49 5231 17777 F: +49 5231 17778.

Bicycles by Haluzak Traverse
USA Bicycles by Haluzak, 2166 Burbank Avenue, Santa Rosa, California 95407
T: +1 707 544 6243
Email: recumbent2@aol.com

Bike Hod All Terrain Trailers Bike Hod
UK PO Box 2607, Lewes, Sussex BN7 1DH T: +44 1273 480 479 F: +44 1273 480 479.
Germany Voss Spezialrad GmbH, Tulpenweg 2, D-25524 Itzehoe T: +49 4821 78023
F: +49 4821 79693.

BikeE BikeE
USA 5460 SW Philomath Blvd, Corvallis, OR 97333-1039 T: +1 541 753 9747
F: +1 541 753 8004 Email: BikeEvol@aol.com

Bjällby Recumbents Easy & Tough
Denmark Stationwej 10A, DK-3520 Farum
T: +45 4295 6005 (home)
F: +45 43 62 87 83 (work).

BOB Trailers YAK trailer
USA 3641 Sacramento Dr. #3, San Luis Obispo, CA 93401 T: +1 805 541 2554
F: +1 805 543 8464 Email: bobinc@callamer.com
Website http://www.callamer.com/bobinc
Australia St. Kilda Cycles T: +61 3 534 3074
F: +61 3 534 3045. *Austria* Funbike
T: +43 662 854 1010 F: +43 662 854 1055.

Canada Bell Sports Canada, Inc., Cycletech Division, 700 Chemin Bernard, C.P. 11,000, Granby, Quebec. J2G 9H7 *Denmark* A. Winther A/S T: +45 86 84 72 88 F: +45 86 84 8528.
Germany Sport Import GmbH T: +49 44 05 92 800 F: +49 44 05 92 8049; Zwei + Zwei, Köln
T: +49 221 95 14 70 0 F: +49 221 95 14 70 20.
Benelux Singing Rock, *Belgium* T: +32 50 827 101
F: +32 50 827 089. *New Zealand* Cycle Works
T: +64 3 338 68 03 F: +64 3 338 62 31
Email: bikes@tpnet.co.nz *Norway* DBS Racing Depot T: +47 51 68 62 60 (64 for Svein)
F: +47 51 68 62 62 *Switzerland* MTB Cycletech
T: +41 31 972 5572 F: +41 31 972 3566
Email: mtb-cycletech@ping.ch *UK & Eire* Neatwork T: +44 1890 883 456
F: +44 1890 882 709. *USA* GT/Riteway, CA
T: 800 869 9866 x 7172 F: +1 714 513 7114;
Salsa Cycles, CA T: +1 707 762 8191
F: +1 707 762 6847; RANS Recumbents, KS
T: +1 913 625 6346 F: +1 913 625 2795.

Boulder Bikes Paris-Roubaix
USA PO Box 1400, Lyons, CO 80540
T: +1 303 823 5021 F: +1 303 823 5025
Email: rkd_llc@indra.com
Website http://cyclery.com/boulder_bikes/

Bromakin Wheelchairs Bromakin Trice
UK 12 Prince William Road, Belton Park, Loughborough, Leicestershire, LE11 5GU
T: +44 1509 217 569 F: +44 1509 233 954
Email: peter@bromakin.co.uk

Brompton Bicycle Ltd Brompton
UK 2 Bollo Lane, Chiswick Park, London W4 5NV T: +44 181 742 8251 F: +44 181 742 8353.
Denmark Preben Pedersen, Sminge Cykler, Sortenborgvej 7, DK-8600 Silkeborg
T: 8680 0411 F: 8682 8622. *Germany* Voss Spezial-Rad GmbH, D-25524 Itzehoe-Ebendorf, Tulpenweg 2 T: +49 4821 78023
F: +49 4821 41014. *USA* CM Wasson Co, 423 Chaucer St., Palo Alto, CA 94301-2202
T: 415 321 0808 F: 415 321 8375.

Burley Design Cooperative Piccolo
USA 4020 Stewart Road, Eugene, OR 97402
T: +1 541 687 1644 F: +1 541 687 0436
Email: burleybike@burley.com
Website: http://www.Burley.com *Australia* Togo Products Pty, Ltd. T: +61 3 9592 0882.
Denmark DCF, Copenhagen T: +45 33 32 0121.
Germany Centurion Renner KG, Magstadt
T: +49 7159 9459 30. *Holland* Better Bikes Holland, Utrecht T: +31 302 315 780. *Finland* Mt-bike, Joensun T: +358 73 224 891 or Velosport ky, Helsinki T: + 358 9 757 1377.
Norway G-Sport Futura, Kristiansund
T: +47 7167 1792 or Sykkeldelisk
T: +47 2241 5080. *Switzerland* Haso's Velo-Laden T: +41 1937 4330. *UK & Eire* UK Trailer T: +44 1208 815 715. *USA* Call Burley 1 800 311 5294 for details of Burley dealers nationwide.

Carradice of Nelson Ltd Carradice Bags
UK Westmoreland Works, St Mary's Street, Nelson, BB9 7BA T: +44 1282 615 886
F: +44 1282 602 329 *Germany* Rasko
T: +49 241 533 006 F: +49 241 557 350
Switzerland Vitelli Velo-Bedarf
T: +41 613 617 070 F: +41 613 615 770. *USA* Rivendell T: +1 510 933 7304
F: +1 510 933 7305.

Christiania Bikes HTL Box Transporter
Denmark Dammegardsvej 22, 3782 Klemensker
T: +45 56 966700 F: +45 56 966708.
Email: CSB@post3.tele.dk *Germany* Christiania Bikes, Köpernicker Str 8b, 10997 Berlin 36
T: +49 30 618 8015 F: +49 30 611 3697;
Räderwerk, Calenberger Str. 50, 30169 Hannover
T: +49 511 717174 F: +49 511 715 151; Zwei plus Zwei: Bismarkstr. 56-62, 50672 Köln
T: +49 221 9514700 F: +49 221 95147020.
Netherland Christiania Bikes, Christiania Import, Boslaan 10, 7875 AR Exloo T/F: +31 591 549539.

Citytramp TransportRoller GmbH Citytramp
Germany Teckstr. 37, 71116 Gärtringen
T: +49 7034 266 61 F: +49 7034 266 61
Email: 0203664323-0001@t-online.de

Condor Cycles Condor Cycles
UK 144-148 Gray's Inn Road, London WC1X 8AX T: +44 171 837 7641
F: +44 171 837 5560.

Cool Breeze UK Ltd Prone Low Profile
UK 194 Upper Street, Islington, London N1 1RQ
T: +44 171 704 9273 F: +44 171 354 9641.

Cresswell Cycles Foldit & Micro U+2
UK 342 Cherrywood Road, Bordesley Green, Birmingham, B9 4UU T: +44 121 772 2512
F: +44 121 773 9548.

Crystal Engineering Trice
Unit 1A Jubilee Wharf, Commercial Road, Penryn, Cornwall TR10 8AQ
T: +44 1326 378 848 F: +44 1326 378 848
Email: tricehpv@globalnet.co.u *Denmark* FLINT'S, Pilestraede 8b, 1112 København K
T: +45 3313 2328 F: +45 3313 2329
Email: npfd@inet.uni-c.dk *Germany* Klaus Schröder, Veloladen, Dolmanstr. 20, 51427 Bergisch Gladbach T: +49 2204 61075
F: +49 2204 61076. *Netherlands* Drs Kees van Breukelen, Double Performance, Antwerpsweg 13, 2803 Gouda T: +31 182 573 833
F: +31 182 573 833. *USA* Angletech, 318 N. Highway 67, P.O. Box 1893, Woodland Park, Colorado 80866-1893 T: +1 719 687 7475
Email: anglezoom@aol.com Call Kelvin Clark.
Norway Mr. Karstein Brunvatne, Skilso, N4818 Farvik, Norway T: +47 370 86 029. *Switzerland* Mr. David Picken, Frankenhoeheweg 5, 3012 Bern T: + 41 31 302 51 60. *USA* Fools Crow Cycles, 1046 Commercial Drive, Tallahassee, Florida 32310 T: +1 904 224 4767.
Email: edde@freenet.tlh.fl.us or People Movers, 980 N. Main St Orange, California 92867
T: +1 714 633 3663
Email: PepleMovrs@aol.com.

Culty Culty
Germany Thomas Poreski, Herderstr. 11, 72762 Reutlingen T: +49 177 2777 592
F: +49 7121 231 51. *UK & Eire* John Prince, Severn Mill, The Strand, Westbury-on-Severn, Glos. GL14 1PG T: +44 1452 760231
T/F: +44 1452 760368.

Design Management AS Bicycle Lift
Norway Teknostallen (Trondheim Innovation Centre), Prof Brochs gt. 6, N-7030 Trondheim
T: +47 7354 0266 F: +47 7394 3861

Design Mobility Swift Folder
USA PO Box 1005, Eugene, Oregon 97440, USA T: +1 503 343 5568 F: +1 503 683 3397
Email: cat@efn.org *USA* Eugene Bike Works (Oregon) +1 541-683-3397 or Precision Bike Works (New York) +1 212-242-7377 or The Hub (New York) +1 212-254-8844
Email: enquiries to cat@efn.org are to Human Powered Machines in Eugene, Oregon.

EGS Synchro-Shift
France Z.I. Nord, BP 476, 86106 Châtellerault
T: +33 549 21 42 42 F: +33 549 85 3542.
Australia Narrow Margin, 39 Harris St, Paddington, NSW 202. *Germany* Sport Import, 26188 Edewecht *Benelux* Codagex, Meistraat 3, B-2480 Dessel.

Eric Staller Octos
Netherlands Herengracht 100, 1015 BS Amsterdam T: +31 20 624 9198
F: +31 20 624 9198 Email: urbanufo@euronet.nl

Everton Smith A/S Transporter and Long John
Denmark Gl. Grandvej 4, 5580 Nr. Åby
T: +45 64 28 11 22 F: +45 64 28 1144.

Extreme Engineering Ltd. Rubicon
UK 14 Fairways, Toft, Bourne, Lincolnshire PE10 0BS T: +44 177 859 0339 F: +44 177 859 0339.
Email: RAYWATEXTREMEENG@msn.com *USA* People Movers, 980 No. Main St., Orange, CA 92667 T: +1 714 633 3663 F: +1 714 663 7890.

Fahrrad-Manufaktur C-140 Tourer
Germany Zum Panrepel 24, 28307 Bremen
T: +49 421 43857 0 F: +49 421 43857 99.

Fast New Pedal Power Ltd Fastnet
UK 24 Old Mill Road, Portishead, Bristol, BS20 9BX T: +44 1934 820 308 F: +44 1275 818288.

Firma Egon Rahe Eleganz
Germany Adenauerstr. 8, 33428 Marienfeld
T: +49 5247 800 44 F: +49 5247 80044.

Firma Marec Hase Lepus
Germany Karl-Friedrich-Str. 88, 44795 Bochum
T: +49 234 946 9050 F: +49 234 946 9099.

Flevobike Alleweder
Netherlands De Morinel 55, 8251 HT Dronten
T: +31 321 312 027 F: +31 321 319 350
Email: flevobike@pi.net

Florian Schlumpf Spezialmaschinenbau Mountain Drive
Switzerland Dorfstr. 10, CH-7324 Vilters
T: +41 8172 38009 F: +41 8172 38364
Email: schlumpf_ing@bluewin.ch

Geoff Wiles Cycles 'W' Performance Products Hubs
UK 45-47 Cuxton Road (A228), Strood, Rochester upon Medway, Kent ME2 2BU
T: +44 634 722586 F: +44 1634 727 416.

Giant Giant MCR/TCR
Contact your nearest dealer, or try the agents below. *Australia* Giant Bicycle Co. Pty Ltd.
T: +61 395 321 899 F: +61 395 320960.
Canada Giant Bicycle Canada Inc.
T: +1 604 251 2453 F: +1 604 251 2473.
Europe Giant Europe BV, Pascallaan 66, 8218 NL Lelystad, Netherlands T: +31 320 296296
F: +31 320 296200. *New Zealand* Giant in New Zealand, Cycletech New Zealand
T: +64 429 88367 F: +64 429 73102.
Japan Giant Co. Ltd, T: +81 45 505 0111
F: 506 6501. *Taiwan* Giant Inc., No. 19 Shun Farn Road, 43712 Tachia, Taichung Hsien, Taiwan ROC. T: +886 4 681 4771
F: +886 4 681 5344. *USA* Giant USA, 475 Apra Street, Rancho Dominiquez, CA 90220 T: +1 310 223 0212
F: +1 310 609 3906.

Greenspeed Tandem Touring Trike
Australia 69 Mountain Gate Drive, Ferntree Gully, Vic 3156 T: +61 39758 5541
F: +61 39752 4115
Email: greenshp@ozemail.com.au
Website: http://www.ihpva.org/com/Greenspeed/

Highpath Engineering Eggrings
UK Cornant, Cribyn, Llanbedr PS, Ceredigion, SA48 7QW T: +44 1570 470035
F: +44 1570 470035. *Switzerland* Bikewan Imports, Lettenstr. 12, 9008 St Gallen
T: +41 71 244 6601 F: +44 71 244 6602.

HP Velotechnik Wavey and Streamer
Germany Goethestr. 5, 65830 Kriftel
T: +49 61 92 41010 F: +49 6192 910218.

Human Powered Machines Lightweight Long Haul
USA PO Box 1005, Eugene, Oregon 97440
T: +1 503 343 5568 F: +1 503 683 3397
Email: cat@efn.org
Website http://www.efn.org/~cat *Also try* Eugene Bike Works (Oregon) +1 541 683 3397.

Ibis Bow-Ti
USA PO Box 275, Sebastopol, CA 95473
T: +1 707 829 5615 F: +1 707 829 5687
Email: Chucklbis@aol.com
Website www.ibiscycles.com

Jesper Sølling Cykelproduktion Pedersen of Copenhagen
Denmark Hovdigevej 4, Holme 8400 Ebeltoft
T: +45 863 46190 F: +45 863 46191.
Germany KGB, Donnerschweerstr. 45, Oldenburg 26123 T: +49 441 885 0389
F: +49 441 885 0388. *Netherlands* Bart Rensink, Commelinstraat 162, 1093 VD, Amsterdam T: +31 20 663 3918
F: +31 20 663 1173. *Switzerland* Bikes: KGB (see Germany). Frames: Velolaboratorium, Schmelzbergstr. 40, 8044, Zürich
T: +41 01 251 4707 F: +41 01 251 4762.
UK & Eire The Seat of the Pants Company, PO Box 5, Sale, Cheshire MK33 4AP
T: +44 161 928 5575 F: +44 161 928 5585.

Joe Breeze Cycles Breezer Twister
Contact national distributors below for details of your nearest stockist *Italy* Panimpex
T: +39 6 3036 0417 F: +39 6 3036 0417.
Canada Cyber Sport T: +1 604 325 2033
F: +1 604 325 2023 E-Mail: philhead@axionet.com
Japan Norton Bicycle Ind. Co. Ltd.
T: +81 03 3626 7912 F: +81 03 3829 2994.
Germany Bike Action GmbH
T: +49 6071 92340 F: +49 6071 81605
Belgium NGB T: +32 02 332 1565
F: +32 02 332 1549. *Taiwan* J Bicycle Studio
T: +886 04 326 4150 F: +886 04 326 4150.
Norway Mega Cycles T: +47 67 53 06 10
F: +47 67 58 20 12. *Switzerland* Frame of Mind
T: +41 81 947 5303 F: +41 81 947 5120.
UK CANAM Cycle Ltd. T: +44 113 2711923
F: +44 113 2712598. *Ireland* CANAM Cycle Ltd.
T: +44 1846 605255 F: +44 1846 605 229.
USA-West The Merry Sales Company, CA,
T: +1 415 871 8870 F: +1 415 589 1222.
USA East Quality Bike Products, MN
T: +1 612 941 9391 F: +1 612 941 9799.
Other countries InterJet, 2-7-38 Nishimiyahara, Yodogawa-Ku, Osaka 532, Japan
T: +81 06 393 3611 F: +81 06 393 3822.

Kemper Fahrradtechnik Classic Pedersen
Germany Rheinweg 70A, 41812 Erkelinz Grambusch T/F: +49 2431 77017.
Branch office in Germany: Kemper, Phillipp-Reis-Str. 11, 40215 Düsseldorf
T: +49 211 343 371 F: +49 211 343 371.
Netherlands Het mannetje, Quellijnstraat 48, 1072 XT, Amsterdam T: +31 20 6792 139
F: +31 20 676 1828.

Kingcycle Kingcycle
UK Lane End Road, Sands, High Wycombe, Bucks, HP12 4JQ T: +44 1494 524004. F: +44 1494 437 591 *Germany* Vambike, Alte Poststr. 21, 53840 Troisdorf
T: +49 2241 78645 F: +49 2241 83357.

Koga BV Emotion GlobeTraveller
Netherlands Postbus 167, 8440 AD Heerenveen T: +31 5136 30111 F: +31 513 633289
Email: info@koga.com Website: www.koga.com

Kool Stop International Inc.
Kool-Mule Brake Blocks Original Trailer and Kool-Stride Tire Chains and Tire Cleats
USA Try your local bike shop. In cases of difficulty, see below KOOL-STOP International, 1061 S. Cypress Street, La Habra, CA 90632 T: +1 714 738 4971 F: +1 714 992 6191. *Netherlands* Third Wave Carriers bv, Zuidermolenweg 20, 1069 CG Amsterdam T: +31 2 06107 033 F: +31 2 06107099.

Kunst&Leder Leather Accessories
Germany Esbacher Str. 2, 91746 Weidenbach T: +49 982 69446. *Alternative address* Workshop and 'Allerhand' Kunst&Leder Gallery Turnitzstr. 29, 91522 Ausbach
T: +49 981 95767, Mon-Fri 1200-1800.

Leitra APS Leitra
Denmark Box 64, 2750 Ballerup
T: +45 42 18 33 77 F: +45 42 18 33 77. *Germany* Velopedes, Neustadt 7, 24939 Flensburg T: +49 461 46699 or FORUM Michael Malich, PO Box 1234 am Rathaus 97912 Lauda/Taubertal T: +49 9343 65400 or ULTRA-RAD, Angerstr. 7, 37073 Göttingen. T/F: +49 551 484 113 or Tobias Enke Fahrradvertrieb, Westerfeldstr. 164, 33613 Bielefeld T: +49 171 364 2877.

Linear Manufacturing Inc Linear Tandem
USA RR1, Box 173, Guttenberg, Iowa 52052 T: +1 319 252 1637 F: +1 319 252 3305. *Canada* Hi Trans Technologies.
T: +1 905 850 9635 F: +1 905 851 5938. *Germany* Voss Spezial-Rad GmbH, Tulpenweg 2, 25524 Itzehoe-Edendorf T: +49 4821 41409 F: +49 4821 41014. *UK & Eire* Neatwork, Guards Road, Coldstream, Berwickshire TD12 4NW T: +44 1890 833 456 F: +44 1890 882 709.

Lyonsport Adjustable Stem
USA 1175 Plumtree Lane, Grants Pass, OR 97526 T: +1 541 476 7092
Email: lyonsport@aol.com

Main Street Pedicabs Pedi-Cab
USA 3003 Arapahoe Street, Suite 222, Denver, Colorado 80205 T: +1 303 604 2330
F: +1 303 604 2404 Email: pedicab@usa.net
Website: http://www.pedicab.com

Merlin Metalworks
Merlin Road bike with S and S Coupling
USA 40 Smith Place, Cambridge, MA 02138 T: +1 617 661 6688 F: +1 617 661 6673
Email: dfox@merlinbike.com
Website: http://merlinbike.com *Germany, Denmark, Benelux and Switzerland* Merlin Titanium s.a.r.l., Rue de Commerce, 1854 Leysin, Switzerland T/F: +41 25 34 38 00.

Montara Mountain Bike MP200 Pedals
USA 61 Clarendon Road, Pacifica, CA 94044 T: +1 415 359 1326 Email: mtb@montaramtb.com Website: www.montaramtb.com

Nightsun Performance Lighting Nightsun XC
USA 995 South Fair Oaks Drive, Pasadena, CA 91105 T: +1 818 799 5074 F: +1 818 799 0923.

Ostrad GmbH Ostrad Adagio
Germany Winsstr. 48, 10405 Berlin
T: +49 30 443 413 93 F: +49 30 443 413 94
Email: OstradGmbH@aol.com *UK shops* Gear of Glasgow, 19 Gibson St., Hillhead, Glasgow G12 8NU T/F: +44 141 3391 179 or Bikefix, 48 Lambs Conduit Street, London WC1
T: +44 171 405 1218.

Pamir Engineering Pamir Tools
USA PO Box 323 Fairview, PA
T: +1 814 474 2228 F: +1 814 474 2228
Email: pamireng@aol.com
Website: http://members.aol.com/pamireng

Paris Maderna GmbH TranSport
Austria Zeltgasse 12, A-1080 Wien
T: +43 1403 0158 F: +43 1403 01584.

Pashley
Land Rover APB, Tube Rider / Paramount, Courier
UK Mason's Road, Stratford-upon-Avon, Warwickshire, CV37 9NL T: +44 1789 292 263 F: +44 1789 414 201.

Peter Busse Sicherheitstechnik
Pitlock Security System
Germany Liegnitzer Str. 15, 10999 Berlin
T: +49 30 611 2092 F: +49 30 611 2093.

Spain Hans Bloem, Marcos Zapata, 13-1oC, 29017 Malaga T/F: +34 5 2200868. *France* Pegase Evolution, 127 bis. Avenue Pasteur, 33270 Floirac/Bordeaux
T/F: +33 556404953. *Netherlands* BIKE Park, Zuiderstate, Badweg 2, 8934 AA Leeuwarden T: +31 58 288 2131 F: +31 58 288 4241. *Switzerland* FAMO AG, Pilatusstr. 53, 6003 Luzern T: +41 412 400 070 F: +41 41 240 0071.

PIVOT-Liegeräder Harpoon
Germany Ahornstr. 15, 88069 Tettnang
T: +49 7542 54656 F: +49 7542 5981.

Plastron Products Bike Lid
USA 10434 NE 17th St, Bellevue, WA 98004 T: +1 206 455 9014 F: +1 206 455 1750
Email: wrw1958@worldnet.att.com
Website: www.bikelid.com *Europe* BikeLid Europe, based in New York, contact William Williams T: +1 212 977 7234 F: +1 212 498 5461 Email: wrw1958@worldnet.att.netname. *Asia/Australia* BikeLid Asia/Pacific, based in Sydney, contact David Solomon T: +61 2 337 5022 F: +61 2 377 5022 Prospective agents please contact Plastron.

Radius Spezialräder GmbH Red Pepper
Germany Borkstr. 20, 48163 Münster
T: +49 251 780 342 F: +49 251 780 358.

Radnabel Radnabel ATL
Germany Jakobsgasse 19, 72070 Tübingen
T/F: +49 7071 238 96.

RANS Recumbents Zero-G
USA 4600 Hwy 183 Alternate, Hays, KS 67601 T: +1 913 625 6346 F: +1 913 625 2795.

Reflectalite Bicycle Bulb Service
UK 24 Orchard Road, Brentford, Middlesex TW8 0QX T: +44 181 560 2432
F: +44 181 847 2035. *Netherlands* De Poort Trading, Gedempte Oude Gracht 79, 2011 GM Haarlem T: +31 23 532 1591.

Ride-Rite Bicycles Inc. Advanta SR-1
USA 6322 114th Avenue S.E., Bellevue, Washingtom 98006 T: +1 206 228 8006
F: +1 206 271 4017 Email: Bob_Riley@msn.com
Website: http://www.BikeRoute.com/RideRite.htm *Canada* Dale Jacobs, Alberta Aircraft Overhaul, Calgary International Airport, Hanger 24, Calgary, Alberta T: +1 403-250-1177.

riese & müller Birdy
Germany Erbacher Str. 123, 64287 Darmstadt T: +49 6151 424034 F: +49 6151 424036. *Switzerland* Cortebike, Sur le Crêt 6, 2606 Corgémont T: +41 32 972 414
F: +41 32 972 428.

Robert Hoening Spezialfahrzeuge GmbH
Duet/Rollfiets, Trio, Add+bike
Germany Ulmer Str. 16/2, 71229 Leonberg T: +49 7152 979490 F: +49 7152 979499. *Denmark* H. Meyland-Smith APS, Käthe Brondum, Industrievej 27, 9830 Tars
T: +45 98 961 985 F: +45 98 961 986. *Netherlands* Freewiel Techniek BV, Sander van Dooren, Koperslager 3, NL-5521 DE Eersel T: +31 497 514757 F: +31 497515124. *Norway* MEDEMA, Peter Nelson, Sven Oftedalsvei 2-8, 0903 Oslo T: +47 22 168190 F: +47 22 168100. *Switzerland* B&M Mobility Systems GmbH, Fischermättelistr. 18, 3008 Bern
T: +47 31 376 0001 F: +47 31 376 0005. *UK & Eire* Pashley, Mason's Road, Stratford-upon-Avon, Warwickshire, CV37 9NL T: +44 1789 292 263 F: +44 1789 414 201. *USA, Canada* Frank Mobility Systems T: +1 412 695 2122
F: +1 412 695 2922.

S and S Machine Bicycle Torque Couplings
USA 9334 Viking Place, Roseville, CA 95747 T: +1 916 771 0235 F: +1 916 771 0397.
Email: steve@sandsmachine.com
Website: http://www.sandsmachine.com *UK* Griffon Cycles, 52 Caldercuilt Rd., Glasgow, G20 0AL T: +44 141 946 3739
Email: griffcycle@aol.com

Santana Cycles Inc Santana Tandems
USA Box 206, La Verne, CA 91750
T: +1 909 596 7570 F: +1 909 596 5853
Email: santanainc@aol.com
Website: http://www.santanainc.com *Austria* High Bike, Thomas Marik, Margaretenstr. 44, 1040 Wien T: +43 1 581 1165. *UK & Eire* Swallow Tandems, The Old Bakery, LLanrhaeadr Ym Mothnant, Oswestry, Shropshire SY10 OJP T: +44 1691 780050 F: +44 1691 780110. *Other European countries* Santana Europe, Weinstr. 3, 83022 Rosenheim
T: +49 8031 14573 F: +49 8031 34795.

Schauff GmbH La Luna, Wall Street Duo
Germany Postfach 1669, 53406 Remagen/Rhein T: +49 2642 93640
F: +49 2642 3358 Email: schauff@aol.com

Schubert & Schefyk KG Guylaine WL
Germany Magdeburger Str. 12, 64372 Ober-Ramstadt T: +49 6154 52466
F: +49 6154 52467.

schulz + weber TransSport
Germany Postfach 10 29 31, 66029 Saarbrücken T: +49 681 48489 F: +49 681 48496 Email: schulz_weber@t-online.de
New numbers for schulz + weber from Mid-March 1997: T: +49 681 985 0902
F: +49 681 985 0903 Sales in Germany: BICO GmbH, Strothweg 6, 33415 Verl
T: +49 5246 9201 0 F: +49 5246 9201 22.

Showme Products Christian Schumacher GmbH Emotion Three
Germany Bahnhofstr. 2, 84088 Neufahrn i. NB T: +49 8773 7399 F: +49 8773 91 02 81.

SideKids SideKids
USA 6717 Palatine N, Seattle 98103
T: +1 206 784 1190 F: +1 206 789 3202.

Sögreni of Copenhagen Aps Sögreni
Denmark Sankt Peders Straede 30A, 1453 København K T: +45 33 93 98 99
F: +45 33 12 72 71.

Sparta Rijwielen- en Motorenfabriek B.V.
Silver Bullet
Netherlands Postbus 5, 7300 AA Apeldoorn T: +31 55 355 0922 F: +31 55 355 9244.

St John Street Cycles
Voyager Childback tandem
UK 91-93 St. John Street, Bridgewater, Somerset, TA6 5HX T: +44 1278 441 502
F: +44 1278 431107
Email: sjscycles@dial.pipex.com
Website: http://www.sjscycles.com

Swallow Tandems Swallow Tandems/ Tandemania
UK The Old Bakery, LLanrhaeadr Ym Mothnant, Oswestry, Shropshire SY10 OJP
T: +44 1691 780050 F: +44 1691 780110.
Email: info@swallow-tandems.co.uk
Website: http://www.chaucer.ac.uk/swallow/sw1.htm

Tauber Bicone
Netherlands Beatrixlaan 2, 1815 JN Alkmaar T: +31 7251 12495 F: +31 7251 50246.

The Cutting Crew Ingenieurbüro GmbH
Trac-Pearls
Germany Am Mühlberg 16, 61348 Bad Homburg v.d. H T: +49 6172 928 681 or 2 F: +49 6172 23 729 *UK & Eire* Allintex, Mr. David Allen, Unit 37 Limberline Spur, Portsmouth, PO3 5DX, UK T: +44 1705 667700 F: +44 1705 667711.

The Seat of the Pants Company Burrows Windcheetah, Pickup, Velocita, Windcheetah Carbon Monocoque
UK Unit LKR4, Norman Road, Altrincham, Cheshire, WA14 4ES T: +44 161 928 5575
F: +44 161 928 5585
Email: bobdixon@seatofthepants.u-net.com
USA and Canada HP Inc., 604/1740 Esquimalt Ave., West Vancouver, BC V7V 1R8, Canada T: +1 604 925 8625 F: +1 604 925 8161. *Germany* Norbert Henkel, Radschlag, Grölking 3, 83139 Söchtenau T: +49 8053 2374 F: +49 8053 2397.

Thorpe Consulting Mako
UK PO Box 250, Ruislip, Middlesex, HA4 8UU T: +44 0976 800 682. Email: flashgd@msn.com *USA* Angle Tech Co., 318 N. Hiwy 67, Woodland Park, CO 80863 T/F: +1 719 687 7475.

Timbuk2 Designs, Inc Timbuk2 bags
USA 5327 Jacuzzi Street 3E-2, Richmond, CA 94804 T: +1 510 526 0597 F: +1 510 526 0599 Email: brennan@timbuk2.com
Website: http://www.timbuk2.com *Germany* Velo Special T: +49 721 25244 *Sweden* GBS Sports T: +46 8 23 1100 Velok T: +41 19 32 62 00. *UK* Wheelie Serious Imports T: +44 181 543 5255.

Tom Board Tom Board Frames
UK The Bicycle Workshop, 27 All Saints Road, London W11 1HE T: +44 171 229 4850
F: +44 171 221 0411.

URBICO B.V. UBiCS
Netherlands PO Box 160, 6190 AD Beek (L) F: +31 46 437 9342 Email: urbico@ilimburg.nl

Utopia Fahrradmanufaktur Roadster, Sine
Germany Eschberger Weg 1, 66121 Saarbrücken T: +49 681 816 506
F: +49 681 815 098.

Valdenaire Traffic and Mercurius
France BP 103-88204 Remiremont, Cedex T: +33 329 23 23 46 F: +33 329 62 12 33. All enquiries from Europe (except France) to Henk Schuys in the *Netherlands* Henk W. Schuys, EuroCycles, Thuvinestraat 38, 6921 BC Duiven, Netherlands T: +31 316 265 511
F: +31 316 281 427.

Vision Recumbents Vision R44/5
USA ATP Vision, 952 Republican St., Seattle, WA 98109 T: +1 206 467 0231
F: +1 206 467 0175 Email: atpvision@aol.com *Europe* FutureCycles, Friends Yard, London Road, Forest Row, E. Sussex, RH18 5EE, UK T: +44 1342 822847 F: +44 826 726.

Voss Spezial-Rad GmbH BEVO-Bike
Germany Tulpenweg 2, 25524
Itzehoe-Edendorf T: +49 4821 41409
F: +49 4821 41014.

Vredestein Fietsbanden b.v.
Monte Carlo tyres
Try your local bike shop, or as below. *Netherlands* Vredestein, Postbus 24, 7000 AA Doetinchem T: +31 314 370 555
F: +31 314 370 500. *Germany* Vredestein Fahrradreifen BV, Schulstr. 23a, 66994 Dahn T: +49 6391 5105 F: +49 6391 5207
Vredestein *Switzerland* T: +41 1954 2060.

Warwick Mills *Spinskins*
USA 301Turnpike Road, New Ipswich, NH 03071 T: +1 603 878 1565
F: +1 603 878 4306
Email: SpinSkins@aol.com
Website: http://www.SpinSkins.com

Weldite Products Ltd Trailfix Tools
UK Harrier Road, Barton-upon-Humber, North Lincs, DN18 5RP T: +44 1652 660 000 F: +44 1652 660066. *Australia* British International, 34 Bearing Road, Seven Hills, NSW 2147 T: +61 29674 4566
F: +61 29674 3854. *Denmark* Borge Kildemoes, Nr. Lyndelse, 5792, Arslev
T: +45 65 901242 F: +45 65 901 333. *Germany, Austria* Fasi Sicherheitsprodukte, Lange Lage 3, 37154 Northeim, Germany T: +49 5551 2246 F: +49 5551 65538. *Netherlands* De Poort, Gederipte Onde, Gracht 79, 2011 GN Haarlem T: +31 2353 21591 F: +31 2352 16063. *New Zealand* British International, 34 Bearing Road, Seven Hills, NSW 2147 T: +61 29674 4566
F: +61 29674 3854. *Norway* Norbike Engros, Pellygt 42, PO Box 493, 701 Sarpsborg T: +47 69 15 14 03 F: +47 69 15 72 10. *Switzerland, UK & Eire* Srasser Komponenten, Schlossgasse 8, 8466 Trullikon
T: +41 52 3194281 F: +41 52 3194281. *USA* Rainmaker Marketing Int., 210 Fell Street, San Francisco, California 94102
T: +1 415 703 0282 F: +1 415 431 5404.

Woodguards Woodguards
Germany c/o KGB, Donnerschweerstr. 45, Oldenburg 26123 T: +49 441 885 0389
F: +49 441 885 0388.

Zdenek Mesicek Mesicek High Bicycle
Czech Republic Nerudova 257, 69701 Kyjov T: +42 629 5653 F: +42 629 5653. *Denmark* Københavens Cyklebors, Gothersgade 157, 1123 Copenhagen K T: +45 33 14 07 17 F: +45 33 11 09 09. *Germany* KGB, Donnerschweerstr. 45, Oldenburg 26123 T: +49 441 885 0389
F: +49 441 885 0388. *Netherlands* Neobike Europe, Hoofstraat 6, 9712 JB Groningen T: +31 50313 4651/+31 318 1195
F: +31 50 313 8495. *Switzerland* Bob Sticha, Scheibenackerstr. 3, 9000 St. Gallen-St. Fiden T: +31 71 240 424 F: +31 71 240 426. *UK & Eire* The Seat of the Pants Company, PO Box 5, Sale, Cheshire MK33 4AP
T: +44 161 928 5575 F: +44 161 928 5585.

Zweirad und Zukunft Horizont
Germany Gauss Str. 19, 22765 Hamburg T: +49 40 395 285 F: +49 40 3902 302.

Zzip Designs Zzipper fairings
USA PO Box 14, Davenport, CA 95017
T: +1 408 425 8650 F: +1 408 425 1167
Website: http://www.diskspace.com/zzip/ *Belgium* Dirk Proost, Blue Bike, Broydenborglaan 2, 2660 Hoboken
T/F: +31 3 827 1677. *Germany* Pichler Radtechnik, Steinstr. 23, Gewerbehof, 76133 Karlsruhe T: +49 721 376 166
F: +49 721 370 722 or Voss Spezial-Rad, Tulpenweg 2, Itzehoe 25524
T: +49 4821 41409 F: +49 41014 or Henning Voss (Easy Racer Super Zipper)
T: +49 4821 78023 F: +49 4821 79693. *UK & Eire* Futurecycles, Friends Yard, London Road, Forest Row, E. Sussex, RH18 5EE, UK T: +44 1342 822 847 F: +44 1342 826 726 *USA* Angle Tech Co., 318 N. Hiwy 67, Woodland Park, CO 80863 T/F: +1 719 687 7475 or People Movers, 980 N. Main St., Orange, CA 92567 T: +1 714 633 3663
F: +1 714 633 7890.

Index